I0621622

Mao's Hijacked Generation

Edited
by
Wang Youfen and **Robin Radin**

Translated
by
Wang Youfen

Foreword
by
Michel Bonnin

NEW KNOWLEDGE PRESS

Copyright © 2024 by Robin Radin

All rights reserved

Printed in the United States of America

First Edition

Mao's Hijacked Generation

Edited by Wang Youfen and Robin Radin

Translated by Wang Youfen

Executive Editor: Wang Youfen

Designer: Peter Zamiska

Library of Congress Cataloging-in-Publication Data
LCCN   2024909539
ISBN   979-8-9905073-0-2 (paperback)
       979-8-9905073-2-6 (hardcover)
       979-8-9905073-1-9 (ebook)

Published by New Knowledge Press, Sarasota, FL
inquiries@newknowledgepress.org

No part of this book may be reproduced in any form or by any electronic or mechanical means including information storage and retrieval systems, without permission in writing from the publisher. The only exception is by a reviewer, who may quote short excerpts in review.

Dedication

To those *Zhiqing* who have never been able to return home.

Table of Contents

III. Love, Marriage, and Family

IV. The Go-Home Campaign and Afterwards

V. Confessions and Reflections

Historical Background Essay

China's Sent-Down Youth *(Zhiqing)*

Notes on the Authors and Editors

Map of China

Preface

by

Wang Youfen

July, 5th 1927 — March 2, 2018

During a span of seventeen years (1962 to 1979), close to eighteen million Chinese educated youth, about one-half of an entire generation of literate teenagers from China's cities, were sent off to remote places in the Chinese countryside, sometimes for a decade or more, to be "re-educated," "to learn from the peasants." The subjects of this massive program of social engineering are known in China as *zhiqing*, literally, "educated youth," because of their origins as literate middle school graduates from Chinese cities, but also known as "Sent-Down Youth" in English. While the Red Guard episode in China's Cultural Revolution, which lasted barely two years (1966-1968), is better known to westerners, the *zhiqing* experience shaped the lives and consciousness of an entire generation of Chinese, including China's president, Xi Jinping, among other current members of China's Politburo. The *zhiqing* program was undoubtedly the largest compulsory population shift in human history, which was carried out mainly to fulfill an ideological obsession of Mao Zedong.

This book is my effort to identify, edit, and translate a representative selection of the best first-hand accounts of the *zhiqing* experience available from literally thousands of published examples I have examined.

I was driven to undertake this project by the conviction that the world needs to know about a large-scale deportation in China which, although not as deadly as the gulags of the Soviet Union or the concentration camps of Nazi Germany, disrupted the lives of and had a lifelong impact on a whole generation of Chinese urban youth. Exiled en masse to live, potentially forever, far away from home in generally dejected rural places, they suffered all sorts of hardships and injustices in the name of receiving reeducation for the sake of "continuous revolution." Even though, after Mao's death, the regime abandoned this cruel policy, many of those who managed to return home and the minority among them who had to stay in the countryside are still struggling to survive the lost opportunity and displacement they suffered.

I have included in this collection personal accounts of *zhiqing* departure, arrival, and return, idealistic enthusiasm and abject disillusionment, tales of life, work, broken families, love and hate set in diverse rural locales, from jungle villages in China's Southeast to grassland outposts in Mongolia, from the banks of the Yellow River to the caves of Yan'an in China's Northeast. The stories narrate experiences of rape, famine, suicide, madness, true and false heroes, career derailment and career creation, ideological idealism, and ideological cynicism, among others.

One story, "Solidarity Brings Them Home," is a contemporary account of a hunger strike of *zhiqing* on a large paramilitary farm in Yunnan Province, told by its top leader, Ye Feng. Mr. Ye vividly describes the protest actions of a group of desperate young people in December and January 1978-1979 that helped influence the Chinese Communist Party Central Committee to reverse its decision to block *zhiqing* from returning to their home cities. This extraordinary success of a social group in modifying the will of the authorities was the first since 1949. It was the result of the exceptional political circumstances that followed the return to power of the old guard of leaders who had to face the failure of Mao's policies, but also of the courage and determination of the *zhiqing* left over in the countryside. About ten years later, in June 1989, the same leader who had (silently but effectively) accepted the demands of the *zhiqing*, would not hesitate to bloodily suppress a new generation of youth requesting freedom and democracy in Tiananmen Square.

This book is organized into three main parts:

First is my Preface and the Foreword by Professor Michel Bonnin, the leading historian of the *zhiqing* program and experience, which sets the stories into an historical context that is accessible to the general reader.

Second is my translations of the forty-two first-hand accounts of *zhiqing* experience I selected, which are organized under five topic headings, including "Life and Work;" "Relationships with Local People;" "Love, Marriage, and Family;" "The Go-Home Campaign and Afterwards;" and "Confessions and Reflections."

Third, at the end of the book, I provide my own historical background essay, entitled "China's Sent-Down Youth: Two Perspectives," which is a translated and edited version of a work I previously published in a journal in Hong Kong.

With great appreciation, I acknowledge the contributions to the advancement and fulfillment of this project of my co-editor and friend, Robin Radin. Special thanks are also extended to Mr. Deng Xian, who introduced me to the subject, Ms. Wenlan Peng, who assisted with crucial contacts and interviews, the highly skilled designer Peter Zamiska, and the talented illustrators Minyu Wang and Henry Li. Their expertise in book design and artwork played a pivotal role in bringing this publication to completion.

Wang Youfen, the chief editor and translator of this book, passed away on March 2, 2018, at age 90, after substantially finishing the editing and translation of the stories and related essays assembled in this book, his final major project and publication.

In a career that spanned 68 years of prolific writing and editorial leadership, Youfen spent the first 40 years employed at China's Foreign Languages Press in mostly senior leadership positions for English language publications.

Following his forced retirement in 1990, Youfen spent the last 28 years of his life, "the best of his career," he frequently told friends, as a free-lance writer, editor, translator, and publisher dedicated to promoting principles of civil society, freedom of expression, justice, and truth at home, and knowledge of China's history and culture for English readers abroad. In all his professional endeavors and relationships, he was driven by a very big heart, a prodigious intelligence and the highest professional standards.

Beginning at age 22 in 1950, as one of the first recruits of the newly established International Press Bureau of the new PRC government communications apparatus, Wang Youfen was a true pioneer and soon a towering figure in English language journalism in revolutionary China.

Though suffering lengthy episodes of career course derailment and physical exile, particularly in the late 1950s as a victim of Mao's Anti-Rightist campaign and again in the late 1960s in the Cultural Revolution period, Youfen enjoyed elevation to increasingly senior leadership roles at China's Foreign Languages Press. In the 1970s he became its vice-chair and in 1988 the publisher and editor-in-chief of its internationally distributed English language news weekly, the *Bei-*

jing Review. In the spring of 1989, under his leadership, the *Beijing Review* published two editorials favoring the reform views of the then Chinese Communist Party General Secretary, Zhao Ziyang, who supported the Tiananmen Square student pro-democracy protests. In the aftermath of the bloody crackdown on those protests that June, Youfen was stripped of all his official positions, purged from party membership, and soon forced to retire from government service.

Freed from the constraints of government employment and party membership, for the next 28 years, Youfen pursued an ambitious agenda of writing, editing, translating, and publishing, until his death at age 90. These publications included his translation into English of a six-part interview by a famous Chinese dissident playwright, in *Harper's Magazine*, his translations into Chinese of Jim Moore's biography of Bill Clinton and of Mark Perry's history of the CIA, among other popular non-fiction works.

In 2008, Youfen was honored as chief editor and translator of the book, *Chinese Calligraphy*, published by Yale University Press, which was awarded the prize by the Association of American Publishers as the best book of the year in both its Humanities and Art and Art History categories.

At age 84, in 2011, he helped launch a new publishing company in Beijing which translated and published in Chinese ten notable books by U.S. authors. One of those translated books, Pete Earley's best seller, *Crazy*, about the problematic role of prisons in the administration of mental healthcare in the U.S. influenced the drafting of new mental health legislation in China.

At age 87, Youfen took up as his final project the creation of this book of *zhiqing* memoirs. His motivation to spend so many of his late years on this subject matter evidences his conviction that no understanding of China and the consciousness of its people and leadership today is coherent without an understanding of the lasting impact of the *zhiqing* experience.

All of the stories in this collection were originally written and published in Chinese in the PRC, most in the early 1990s, and most in government-controlled publications that have not existed for many years.

Foreword

by

Michel Bonnin

The collective experience described in this book is unique in human history. Whereas migration from countryside to city is a regular feature of modernization throughout the world, large-scale and organized migrations from city to countryside are extremely rare, especially when the people concerned are young middle or high school students who are supposed to become peasants for life. This is precisely what happened in the People's Republic of China--on a small scale in the 1950s, on a significant scale from 1962 to 1966, and on a large scale between 1968 and 1980. In my book called *The Lost Genera-tion–The Rustication of China's Educated Youth (1968-1980)*[1], I give a global presentation of the motives of Mao Zedong and of the Chinese authorities for launching this program, of the methods they used, and of the effects that the movement had on Chinese politics, economy and society--particularly on the fate and mentality of a whole generation of urban youth. I call it a "Lost Generation" because most of its members lost the naive conceptions they had before going through this ex-perience and also because most of them lost the chance to get a good education and to fulfill their dreams and aspirations for the future. I shall not enter into more detail on the histo-ry of this Rustication (or Sent-down) Movement (in Chinese: *shangshan xiaxiang yundong*) since this is very well done in Wang Youfen's Historical Background Essay found following the Voices stories.

Wang Youfen, the editor and translator of this book, was a member of the preceding generation, as can be learned from the included biography, but he was interested in the memory

1. Michel Bonnin, *The Lost Generation: The Rustication of China's Educated Youth (1968-1980)*, Hong Kong, The Chinese University of Hong Kong, 2013, 515 p. The book was originally published in French in 2004 and then in Chinese in Hong Kong (2009) and in Beijing (2010) .

15

of the exceptional experience depicted here and had many friends among members of the generation of educated youth (in Chinese: *zhiqing*). One of these *zhiqing*, a man named Ye Feng (see his story about the petitioning movement he led in 1978-1979, "Solidarity Brings Us Home") introduced Wang Youfen to me and we had long conversations on the phone about his publication project. Unfortunately, Wang suddenly passed away before I was able to travel to meet him in Chengdu. This sad event gives a special meaning to the publication of the present book.

Wang devoted his life to bringing information about China to an English-speaking audience. For decades, he did this in an official capacity, which was not always a pleasant thing for an independent-minded person, but after retirement he was able to engage in totally unofficial activities, and I know he particularly enjoyed this last project of his.

We should be grateful to Wang Youfen for having undertaken the challenging task of selecting and translating 42 stories from among the thousands written by former educated youth after their return from the countryside. Once they were back in their hometowns, especially from the 1990s until the present day, they published their personal accounts in books, in magazines, and on dedicated websites. The sheer number of memoirs shows how deeply the experience left its mark on an entire generation. The desire to remember came from the complexity and richness of this period in the life of these urban young people. It was not a black-and-white experience, not totally disheartening as life in a prison or a labor camp. It was more varied, mixing hardship with more positive feelings engendered by a rustic or exotic environment and by the comradeship linking young people confronting the same difficulties. Nor was it like the Red Guards experience--a brief maelstrom during which people were swept up in uncontrollable events and unable to understand what was happening to them. It was a long period of more than ten years during which the whole society was influenced--not only the approximately eighteen million *zhiqing* themselves but also their parents and siblings, as well as the peasants who were ordered to host them.

What is remarkable about the selection presented here is its authenticity, the accuracy of expressed feelings, the complete absence of official set language and political correctness. It provides a broad and truthful presentation of the fate of the *zhiqing* generation[2]. Many aspects of this exceptional experience are described here, without pathos and sensationalism but with sincerity and intelligence. We are far from the rosy picture encouraged by the authorities. Put together, these stories constitute a denunciation of the absurdity of that period and of the cruelty of the society during the Maoist era, presented through the simple description of facts without rhetorical embellishment. We see here only the ordinary life of an extraordinary time, when people were treated as laboratory animals, ordered to transform themselves fundamentally so as to become "New Men", ready to sacrifice their entire lives wholeheartedly when the Party and its "Great Leader" requested it.

This was of course impossible, and when the *zhiqing* be-

2. To my knowledge, two other interesting collections of *zhiqing* memoirs have already appeared in English, but their focus is more limited: educated youth sent to the countryside before the Cultural Revolution (Deng Peng, ed. and transl., *Exiled Pilgrims, Memoirs of the Pre-Cultural Revolution Zhiqing*, Brill, 2015) and educated youth sent to Hainan Island (Ou Nianzhong and Liang Yongkang, eds., *Mao's Lost Children: Stories of the Rusticated Youth of China's Cultural Revolution*, translated from the Chinese by Laura Maynard, Merwin Asia, 2015).

gan finding themselves as the victims of terrible work-related accidents, of unjust political accusations, of sexual harassment or rape, they quickly began thinking of ways to leave the countryside. This was the case even for the minority who were real volunteers at the beginning. They had to face up to the sudden and possibly permanent social and economic demotion they had suffered. They were exiles now, defenseless, at the mercy of local cadres for their life conditions in the countryside and dependent on the relationships (and financial capabilities) of their parents for any possibility they might have to get back to their cities. As shown in some of the testimonies in this collection, illusions concerning the absence of corruption under Mao's regime cannot resist real knowledge of the period. Many local cadres and even some doctors (who could provide medical certificates) were able to obtain money, gifts and other advantages by exploiting the strong desire of the *zhiqing* to return to their homes.

The reader of this book will discover many dramatic aspects of the situation in which the *zhiqing* found themselves, but also the warmth they discovered in friendship and love even in the worst environment, as well as the humor and fun that could grow out of absurdity when experienced collectively. A song written by Ren Yi, a *zhiqing* from Nanjing, contains these lines:

**Rising with the sun and coming back with the moon,
I undertake the heavy job of repairing the globe.**

Throughout the country, *zhiqing* used this witty expression ("repairing the globe") to describe what they were asked to do: plow the land. Educated youth singing this nostalgic song found solace in sharing their common homesickness, but the absurd reality was that the author of the song was tracked down by the police and condemned to death (his sentence later commuted to 10 years in prison). The story relating Ren Yi's ordeal, "Song of *Zhiqing*: Death to the Composer," testifies to the atmosphere of political terror of the time, when normal human feelings were considered crimes and hypocritical lies were needed to survive.

Zhiqing faced serious threats to their physical well-being. They encountered frequent accidents because they were often made to do dangerous jobs for which they had not been properly trained and because official propaganda endlessly encouraged them to take heroic risks. Some *zhiqing* learned the useful art of "fake heroism" (as in "A Model Worker, the Bear and Me"), but more idealistic young people risked losing their lives or living with permanent handicaps. A moving example of the fate of accident victims is given in "Misery of a Blind *Zhiqing*." Illnesses were also a greater danger than in the cities because some areas had unique diseases or because medical help was difficult to find or simply nonexistent.

Why, then, was there such a prolonged and large-scale policy of transferring urban graduates to the countryside when it caused so many problems and aroused so much dissatisfaction? My thesis is that the post-1968 rustication movement had multiple motivations but was mainly a political and ideological movement, an important element in Mao's strategy of "training revolutionary successors" and preventing a return to "capitalism" after his death. Some have argued that the need to alleviate the youth unemployment problem contributed to the size and longevity of the program, but this would have been true--or partially true--only before the Cultural Revolution and in the short period between 1968 and

1970 when the authorities didn't know what to do with the Red Guards. In the long run, the urban economy had a continuing need for new labor as demonstrated by the number of peasants employed in the cities during the same period. The rustication movement cannot be justified, either, by its contribution to the development of the countryside, because *zhiqing* were mainly employed as agricultural laborers whereas in most places there was already an oversupply of such laborers. It is true that, after some time, a minority of *zhiqing* were able to secure non-agricultural jobs. Those *zhiqing* who were able to become "barefoot doctors," for example, could have the feeling of doing something useful. Their training was rudimentary and their equipment inadequate, and they were often confronted with medical cases that made them feel totally helpless, but they learned on the job and some of them later became full-fledged doctors after they returned to their hometowns (see "When I Was a Barefoot Doctor"). *Zhiqing* who worked as teachers in local schools could also make use of their knowledge. But neither barefoot doctors nor local teachers could get enough satisfaction from their jobs to forget their families and hometowns. It would have been more rational to train local youth to fill these jobs. At the time, local youth who had the chance to go to primary and middle schools in neighboring towns were also obliged to go back to their villages after graduation. They were called "returned educated youth" (*huixiang zhiqing*). Their experience is often forgotten, but "Perspective of a Returned *Zhiqing*," written by a famous writer who had been one of them, presents their point of view. We learn that they were jealous of the urban *zhiqing*, especially concerning their prestige among the local girls and the priority given to them in the distribution of interesting jobs.

We see from such memoirs that, although the urban youth were supposedly sent to the countryside to be reeducated by the "poor and lower-middle peasants", there was no real doubt in people's minds regarding the superiority of the city to the countryside. Nor could sending some urban youth to live there help the villages to overcome their terrible backwardness, when the main problem was Mao's agricultural policy itself. It was the Maoist obsession with "cutting the queues of capitalism" that prevented the peasants from living a better life and kept them in a state of quasi-serfdom, unable to decide for themselves what to plant and how to plant it. They were not allowed to raise poultry or pigs and could not sell anything they produced in order to buy daily necessities. All they could do was toil from sunrise to sunset for mere survival rations. Many *zhiqing* became aware of the problem and understood that they could only add to the collective poverty by sharing the produced grain when it was distributed after the harvest. As soon as the Maoist policies were abandoned at the beginning of the 1980s, agricultural production jumped and in many places the peasants' living conditions improved. By that time, however, most of the *zhiqing* had already left. With or without them in the villages, there had always been a kind of limited underground resistance, even from the local authorities, to the excesses of the official agricultural policies, as is shown in the story "Chasing Away the 'Black Households.'"

Speaking of the "Black Households," several stories deal with the sinister effects of another important feature of the Maoist regime: the system of class labels that created a category of pariahs in the New China. This was an ever-growing group since the children of the people labeled as enemies when the regime was established sadly inherited their parents' label and because new groups were created, most notably the ones called "Rightists." In 1957, many intellectuals were encouraged by Mao to tell what they thought of the regime, and when their criticism exceeded what he considered to be acceptable, this triggered his ire and he declared them to be Rightists. As with other offspring of the "Black categories," the children of the Rightists were always discriminated against. Black categories were treated as if they had a contagious disease, which meant it was dangerous to be close to them. Thus, in the countryside, the *zhiqing* were prevented from having relations with local black categories members. If they did, they were accused of colluding with them, of accepting the "sugar-coated bullets" of the "enemy" (another expression invented by Mao). This happened to the famous writer Zhang Kangkang, who was lucky not to be more severely punished than we see in her story, "A Criticism Session Aimed at Me."

People were often accused of totally fabricated crimes, and the whole family would suffer injustice day after day. Honest and simple people (like the Mongol woman in "A Flurry of Snowflakes") had their lives ruined because the regime needed to create "enemies" in order to maintain an atmosphere of terror and obedience. Sometimes the enemies were rehabilitated, but often too late. Being a member of the "black categories" was all the more damning in that it meant you would be considered a favorite target for the next political movement launched by Mao--and there was always a new one brewing before the previous one ended. In some places, former landlords and rich peasants had to sew labels on their clothing showing their status, exactly like the Jews under Hitler. This practice was not as pervasive as in Nazi Germany, but we have other testimonies confirming it.

As shown in section II, "Relationships with Local People," interactions between *zhiqing* and the people of the country-side were diverse. In some cases, as in "My Country Mother," individual relations could be quite good. But generally, they were neither very good nor very bad, each side understanding that the decision to send the urban youth to the villages had come from above and could only be modified eventually by the authorities. In the meantime, everyone had to avoid making things worse. There was always, however, a gap, and this collection shows that the official rationale of the movement as a way to reduce the difference between the country-side and the city was nothing but a lie. In fact, the huge gap existing between city and countryside had been exacerbated by the regime's establishment of the system of residence permits (*hukou*) and could not be reduced by sending those urban youngsters to "repair the globe" in the countryside. Even love, for example, might emerge between a *zhiqing* and a peasant girl, but it could not bear fruit because the *zhiqing* would normally reject it for fear of becoming a peasant for life. The *zhiqing* might regret this, but he could do nothing to save the young peasant woman from the sad fate await-ing her--marriage arranged by her parents for a dowry with a man they had generally never seen. There were a number of Romeos and Juliets engendered by the Sent-down move-ment, but very few had happy endings. Sympathy from the female *zhiqing* could not help the young peasant girls either, as shown in "Ah, Guifang."

As for those few female *zhiqing* who married peasants,

they rarely did so voluntarily. They were forced by economic circumstances or because they had been raped. For unmarried male peasants, those fair-skinned and delicate city girls who would not ask for a dowry (because the practice had disappeared in urban areas) were like a gift from heaven. Girls exiled to the country without family protection thus faced overwhelming pressures, both social and sexual, especially if they came from a disadvantageous class background (see "The Death of Mei"). As married cadres were also tempted by the presence of those young city girls, sexual harassment was frequent (as in "The Price of Dignity"). Rapes by officers in paramilitary farms were also a major problem, which was acknowledged officially in 1973.

This situation was all the more ironic in that the Cultural Revolution was a period of extreme official puritanism. Normal feelings between male and female *zhiqing* were considered to be bourgeois crimes. A love letter given to a fellow *zhiqing* could lead to severe political consequences and acute psychological problems. But, after a few years, the authorities realized that if they wanted the *zhiqing* to "take root" for life in the countryside, the best way was to encourage them to get married there, either with peasants or with other *zhiqing*. Then, it became easier to date, but as contraceptives were unavailable or reserved for married people, unwanted pregnancies caused a new headache. Still, in the dull and uncertain situation in which they found themselves, romance could provide some color and excitement for the *zhiqing*, but only if they were able to avoid pregnancy and if they were not confronted with the terrible situation of only one member of the couple having an opportunity to leave. A lighter aspect of life in the countryside is wittily presented in "A Tryst at the

Floodgate," describing the transformation of a floodgate hut in the Mongol steppe into a much coveted "maison de rendez-vous," as we say in French.

For *zhiqing* couples, the biggest headache was planning for the education and future of their children. They could not accept the thought that their offspring would receive as little education as the peasant children, in which case their children would have no way to live in an urban area later. The authorities then authorized their children to take their schooling in their parents' original city if a relative still living there were willing to take care of them. This was not always possible, and the system could pose many problems when the relatives resented the extra burden. Those children, then, were raised without their parents' love and care. The result could be dramatic, as shown in "Life Trajectory of a Shanghai *Zhiqing*."

Mao Zedong died in 1976 and his successor, Hua Guofeng, tried for two years to maintain the Great Leader's outmoded ideology of "training revolutionary successors" and "preventing revisionism" through the *zhiqing* movement, after which the authorities seemed increasingly uncertain as to how they should deal with the educated urban youth. They decided, however, not to put an abrupt end to the movement and not to allow all *zhiqing* to come back home: there was too great a risk of unemployment and a shortage of housing if all *zhiqing* were suddenly to return to their hometowns. The *zhiqing* saw this discouraging decision as a turning point and possibly their last chance to fight for their right of return. An especially interesting feature of this book is the description of the petitioning movement, which finally convinced the authorities to abandon their costly and unpopular policy. Only the petitioning movement in Mengding Farm (Yunnan) is presented here, but its great significance is evident in the stories "Solidarity Brings Us Home" and "Love Cemented by Hunger Strike." We see here that those *zhiqing* who had suddenly lost hope of leaving the countryside were fully prepared to risk their lives to fight for the right to "go back home," and we can understand the real despair that this movement had engendered among all those who feared being trapped in the countryside forever. The success of this spontaneous movement was an exceptional event in the history of the People's Republic.

When most of the *zhiqing* had gone back to their hometowns, they faced new challenges which would probably justify compiling another book, but some of the difficulties they had to confront can be glimpsed in the stories "Love Cemented by Hunger Strike," "Misery of a Blind *Zhiqing*," and "Life Trajectory of a Shanghai *Zhiqing*."

Lastly, it is particularly meaningful to have a section dedicated to "Confessions and Reflections" of the *zhiqing*. Reflecting on the crimes and other evil deeds that many people were encouraged to commit in Mao's time is discouraged by today's Chinese authorities, although some of the concepts which justified those crimes (such as "class struggle under socialism" or "fight against revisionism") were officially abandoned at the end of the 1970s. The Chinese Communist Party has never liked acknowledging its previous mistakes, and this silence has permitted ordinary people to rationalize their past bad behavior as merely obeying orders or following the mainstream. Others, however, recognize that they did things they should not have done under any circumstances. They acknowledge their misdeeds and beg for their victims' forgiveness. In recent years, some former Red Guards have publicly expressed remorse. Sent-down youth (who at the beginning were mostly former Red Guards) had less opportunity in the countryside to harm other people, but still quite a number of them did, especially in the turbulent years of 1968-1971. "An Eternal Regret," "Participating in Class Struggle" and "My Wish for Redemption" are excellent descriptions of the context which led to unconscionable behavior. They show how Party leaders encouraged brutality and sadism and contain thoughtful reflections about the personal motives which made a number of *zhiqing* take part in collective injustice and violence. Here is an example drawn from "My Wish for Redemption":

"At the time, I could hardly explain why I did it. In retrospect, it was clear that I had my own axe to grind: I wanted to demonstrate that I had drawn a line of demarcation between myself and the "bad elements" and their misdeeds. I was motivated by a desire for self-advancement, including membership in the CCYL (Chinese Communist Youth League). These selfish aims were concealed in political wrappings such as "sense of justice" and "devotion to a lofty cause."

Finally, in "Dialogue Between Two *Zhiqing* Brothers," two former *zhiqing* brothers reflect upon the place of the movement in history. I am not fully convinced by the comparison with the Children's Crusade of 1212 in Europe, because that crusade was actually spontaneous whereas the Sent-down Movement was entirely organized by the authorities and because this specific "crusade" of the French and German Middle Ages was mainly a kind of migration of poor people to more favored regions like the South of France and Italy. However, I totally agree with the idea developed in this dialogue that the *zhiqing* generation was the one that made a decisive break with the aspiration to "revolution," which had been the obsession of all generations of Chinese Youth since the beginning of the 20th century. The irony is that it is precisely because Mao Zedong at the end of his life had tried to use the young people born under the new regime to pursue his vision of a "continuous," violent and utopian revolution that this generation was in a way vaccinated against revolution and ready to support the pragmatic leaders who brought it to an end and promoted a reform which was more "revisionist" than any communist regime had previously dared to promote. Clearly, the Red Guards and the *zhiqing* had learned from their experience, but the lessons they had drawn were radically at odds with Mao's expectations. This book will greatly help its readers to understand why.

I. Life and Work

Song of *Zhiqing*:
Death to the Composer

by Zhang Danxiang

34

Ren Yi, a *zhiqing* from Nanjing No. 5 High School, had just spent a week combating a flood that threatened a major railway north of the city. On returning to his village in nearby Jiangpu County, Jiangsu Province, a neighbor handed him a letter that stunned him.

It was sent by Zheng, one of his school friends who had stayed behind in Nanjing because he was handicapped. Zheng said that he had heard a song composed by Ren, entitled Song of *Zhiqing*, being repeatedly broadcast by Radio Moscow. Owing to ideological differences, the Sino-Soviet relationship had deteriorated to such an extent that just four months before, in March 1969, an armed conflict had broken out on the Sino-Soviet border at Zhenbao Island. Zheng thought the broadcast was bad news for Ren, and he warned in his letter that Ren might be in danger.

Though handicapped, Zheng was good at assembling transistor radios. He had given Ren a shortwave transistor set before his departure so that Ren could keep himself better informed by listening to foreign broadcasts. But many of the radio stations, such as Voice of America and Radio Moscow, were officially banned. Listening to "hostile radio broadcasts" was susceptible to a criminal charge.

Ren shut himself up in his room and tuned in to Radio Moscow. A little past four o'clock in the afternoon, he heard the song he remembered so well being broadcast on the radio. The Russians had changed the title to Song of Chinese *Zhiqing*. It was sung by a male chorus, accompanied by a band.

White clouds soaring in the blue sky,
The lovely ancient city of Nanjing nestles

By the side of the beautiful Yangtze,
There I was born and brought up.

Oh, the great rainbow-like bridge thrusts at the clouds
To reach the other side of the Yangtze River
Mount Zhong, magnificent and mighty,
Lies near my hometown like a crouching tiger.

I said goodbye to Mom,
Bidding farewell to my hometown.
The golden times of my school days are all gone,
Leaving only a paper album from my youth.

Ah, the road that lies ahead
Is so rugged and so long;
I leave my footprints, both deep and shallow,
On remote alien lands.

Rising with the sun and coming back with the moon,
I undertake the heavy job of repairing the globe.
Fulfilling this glorious, sacred duty,
Now turns out to be my fate.

Ren could hardly remember having listened to the broadcast to the end. He was seized with fear. His head seemed to have exploded and his clothes were soaked with sweat.

The seriousness of the matter could be easily understood in light of the famous saying by Mao Zedong: "Whatever the enemy opposes, we support: whatever the enemy supports, we oppose." Now that Radio Moscow was broadcasting Ren's song, there must be something terribly wrong with it. The

Chinese authorities must now consider it to be politically harmful to China.

Mindful of the Party's policy toward all wrongdoers--"Leniency to those who confess, severity to those who resist"-- Ren decided to give himself up to the police. He stuffed some of his clothing and daily necessities into a bag and hurried back to Nanjing. Instead of going home, he went straight to the Nanjing House of Detention. The man who received him was a veteran policeman. After hearing his case, the policeman pondered for quite some time and then said to him: "You just wrote a song, didn't you? Don't be afraid. Nothing will happen to you." He even accompanied Ren to the bus station and encouraged him not to worry before waving him goodbye.

Upon returning to the village, Ren found things were going on as usual. At a meeting of young activists studying Mao's works, the Party secretary of the people's commune asked Ren to conduct the participants in singing Song of *Zhiqing* as if nothing had happened. Probably the Party secretary was unaware of the Moscow broadcast.

Ren had been a music lover from childhood. While still a primary school pupil, he became a member of the city ensemble of small children and received training in singing. Later, he joined a municipal art troupe of middle school students, devoting himself to guitar and playing the *erhu*, the Chinese two-stringed fiddle.

By the time Ren graduated from high school, all colleges had ceased to enroll new students. He had no alternative but to go to the countryside with his schoolmates. He felt that they were not welcome there, because the village had little cultivable land and too many people. For Ren, hardships in rural life were no great challenge. What really tormented him was the barrenness of spiritual life.

One evening in late May of 1969, Ren and some of his companions gathered in his room. They sang old songs to kill time. When their resources were exhausted, one of boys turned to Ren, saying: "Since workers and peasants all have their own songs, why not write a song for *zhiqing*?"

Ren composed his song that night by the light of a kerosene burner. He quickly finished both the music and the lyrics, which seemed to flow from his heart. His instructions for singers read: "Somber, slow and nostalgic." He sang The Song of *Zhiqing* for his companions the following evening, accompanying himself on the guitar.

The song soon took wing. It was copied by hand, mimeographed, printed as sheet music and, most importantly, passed on from singer to singer. Before long it had spread to all parts of the country. Ren heard from a *zhiqing* who was assigned to work in the remote province of Heilongjiang in Northeast China. When he arrived there in early 1970, the *zhiqing* said, many people in his production team were already singing it. One of his companions there, a good harmonica player, would play the melody with tears flowing down his cheeks.

Ren continued to live in fear, though he never imagined that the disaster awaiting him would come from Shanghai. Just before the Spring Festival in 1970, many Shanghai *zhiqing* returned from all over the country for family reunions. Many of them assigned to the Putuo District liked to sing the song, and it soon spread to several middle schools throughout the city. Some people with an unusual political instinct reported this to the district and municipal governments, describing it as "an abnormal phenomenon in the class struggle". The

Shanghai municipal authorities then sent a report to Beijing, where it finally landed in the hands of the Gang of Four, all of them members of the powerful Party Center's Leading Group of the Cultural Revolution. Jiang Qing wrote an instruction on the report saying: "Grasp class struggle in the ideological field". Two other members, Zhang Chunqiao and Yao Wenyuan, gave Shanghai specific orders on promptly setting up a judicial investigation group to deal with Ren's case and undertake criticism and denunciation of the "black song".

On February 19, 1970, Ren was arrested. He was sent to the same Nanjing House of Detention to which he had attempted to deliver himself seven months before. The next day, he was sent to a "struggle session" held at Nanjing No. 5 High School, his Alma Mater, to be exposed and denounced as a hostile element. The bulletin boards along some of the streets in the city were full of posts accusing Ren of various crimes. These included "challenging the Chairman's brilliant instruction on sending *zhiqing* to the countryside" by evoking homesickness, and "embellishing the revisionist educational system" by describing his old school days as golden times. One post said Ren's "reactionary black song" represented an attempt by the enemy at "utilizing literature and art to attack the proletariat and poison the minds of the young generation".

On May 24, 1970, Ren was given a death sentence by the Nanjing Municipal Military Control Commission. But when General Xu Shiyou, a Long Marcher and Chairman of the Jiangsu Provincial Military Commission, saw the death penalty for Ren, he decided to commute the sentence to 10-year imprisonment, saying "how can we execute a young student without any criminal record just for composing a song?" In those years, a ten-year imprisonment was the minimum penalty for the so-called counterrevolutionaries. In Ren's own words, "it was like the starting fare for hiring a taxi".

The downfall of the Gang of Four in October 1976 gave Ren new hope. He started writing appeals to the Jiangsu Provincial High Court and other organizations. His mother, who was teaching at a school in another county in Jiangsu province, tried to assist him by sending letters of complaint to relevant departments. She was encouraged by many *zhiqing* who worked around the area. Knowing that she was Ren's mother, they would sing Song of *Zhiqing* when they passed her living quarters.

On January 4, 1979, a district court in Nanjing acquitted Ren of all charges and released him. By now, Ren had served almost nine years of his ten-year sentence. He was thirty years old.

He soon found a job at a textile company, and later married a woman worker whose brother had been his high school classmate and fellow *zhiqing*. At the time of his release, news about his case of injustice and rehabilitation was widely covered in the press. But with the passage of time, few people of the new generation knew anything about it. He felt that his painful life experience was not only his own cup of tears but represented the sorrows of the country and the nation. He decided to tell his story by writing a book entitled Pathetic Song Triggers Life-and-Death Crisis, which was published by China Social Sciences Press in Beijing in 1998.

A Criticism Session
Aimed At Me

by Zhang Kangkang

44

In our work team at the vegetable garden, there was an *er-laogai* (literally meaning persons undergoing a second round of labor reform) named Su Gong, a former Kuomintang official. Aged about fifty, he was small in stature and had kind eyes. Unlike most others, he was always neatly dressed and had the air of an elegant, self-possessed scholar.

In our brief, work-related conversations with him, I identified him from his strong accent as a Cantonese, which made me feel close to him since my family had come from the same province. Sometimes I even felt that he bore some resemblance to my father. I once passed by him when he was working alone in the cucumber field. Out of curiosity, I asked him which part of the province he came from. He raised his head to glance at me but did not answer. Feeling embarrassed, I said that my hometown was Xinhui. Only then did he tell me the name of his hometown, his eyes narrowing to reveal a faint smile. After a while, he asked me whether I could speak Cantonese. I said no, because I had been born in Hangzhou. Somewhat disappointed, he looked up at a group of *zhiqing* working nearby and again fell into silence. I smiled at him and walked off.

After that, I found myself nodding to him whenever we met in the farm field or along the path, but he would look away from me, his face expressionless. Whenever I went to the well to fetch water by myself, however, or carried a heavy load of vegetables, he would come over and give me a hand.

Once when my female companions and I were pulling radishes out of a vegetable plot, we broke nearly all of them because the earth was too dry and hard. Seeing our heads covered with sweat, Su Gong came over with two pails of water, which he poured into the plot. The earth soon became soft, enabling the radishes to come out easily and intact. None of us thanked him.

That autumn, I found myself in desperate need of money, a minimum of ten yuan besides my own daily savings. I approached a few of my *zhiqing* companions, but to no avail. With a monthly salary of 32 yuan, every one of us had a tight budget. Discouraged, I stopped seeking help.

One day after work, a girl companion and I sat on the edge of the well platform in our vegetable garden, whispering about my financial trouble. When we couldn't find a solution, I started sobbing.

I forgot that behind the well platform some *erlaogai* were still at work. They were mending baskets which we had used to carry earth. Later, we were startled by someone coughing behind us. It was Su Gong, a pail in hand, his head lowered. Keeping his eyes away from me, he said, "Don't cry. If you don't mind, I can lend you ten yuan". His Cantonese accent was understandable only to me. In response to this unexpected offer, I stared at him blankly without giving an answer. When I understood what he meant, which took me a while, I nodded my agreement. I was so desperate for money that I forgot all about the position of *erlaogai* and the need for class struggle awareness.

After work the following day, I slowed my pace on our return trip in order to stay behind. When I was left alone, I went to the well platform. Some moments later, Su Gong came over and handed me a tiny roll of paper. I found two 5-yuan banknotes in it.

"I will return the money to you," I said, my head lowered,

"Never mind. Return it whenever you can," he replied.

That ten yuan was indeed a great help to me.

Whenever I met Su Gong in the field or along the road after that, I looked away from him in shame. I didn't know why he had helped me or how I was going to reward him for his favor.

In the months after my trouble was over, I began to worry about Su Gong's political status. I wondered if he had lent me the money with the aim of corrupting a *zhiqing*. Perhaps he hoped that I might become an accomplice in some evil plan he was hatching. Such thoughts filled me with fear and confusion.

Meanwhile, Su Gong went quietly about his business, never mentioning the money I owed him, as if nothing had happened.

Several months had passed and it was already winter when I returned the money to him. On that day, most of the female *zhiqing* in our group were storing vegetables in the cellars. I waited and waited, hoping to return the money to Su Gong when no one was around. Perhaps my anxiety and the secrecy of my behavior in recent days had aroused the suspicion of certain politically sensitive people. Someone might have been watching me when I hand-delivered the money to Su Gong. He didn't say anything as I mumbled my thanks.

What happened later remained a puzzle to me. Even today, I cannot understand how our squad leader, who was the vegetable garden supervisor, could have known that Su Gong had lent me money. The female companion whom I consulted at the well platform could never have betrayed me. Neither could Su Gong have done so because he himself was involved. Who else could it have been?

Was it true that "watchtowers" were installed everywhere to keep us always under surveillance, and that every move I made would not escape the "brilliant eyes of the masses"?

The following day, upon my return from work, I was informed that a criticism session would be held in the evening, and that I should prepare a speech -- a profound self-criticism on my dubious stand in class line-ups, and my failure to make a distinction between ourselves and the enemy.

I was stunned, thinking that I must have committed a heinous crime. Anxiety and fear tormented me. I didn't know what I should say to get out of trouble.

It was already quite dark that evening when members of our women's squad working in the vegetable garden gathered in our dormitory. Due to an electricity shortage, we all sat on the kang bed under candlelight. Our squad leader, a girl from Hegang, Liaoning Province, opened the meeting with a short speech. A hard worker unskilled at public speaking, she criticized me for borrowing money from a "re-employed person". My action represented a serious loss of revolutionary purity and denigrated the image of all *zhiqing*. When she was through with her few remarks, a second girl promptly jumped from the kang bed and fired a barrage of indignant questions at me:

"Have you let all your revolutionary comrades go to hell? You didn't seek help from us, but stretched out your hands to the enemy. Where were your class feelings and class consciousness? I was very upset by your action. Why would an *erlaogai* lend you money? Have you ever thought about that?"

She didn't wait for my response but continued her barrage.

"Our enemies are still present and have never resigned themselves to defeat. They place their hope on China's third and fourth generations. You are an example of their success in carrying out the strategy of peaceful evolution . . ."

The fierce fire of her barrage hardly allowed me to raise my head. After a while, I realized that the vehement speaker in the faint candlelight was Little A, a female *zhiqing* who had been appointed deputy head of another team in our squad only a few days before.

A *zhiqing* friend whispered in my ear, "Don't listen to her blathering. Her mother has just divorced to marry one of the leaders at the regimental headquarters of our farm. See how contented she is!"

Under the low ceiling, Little A's high-pitched voice sounded like the clash of sharp swords with sparks flying.

"If I were you," she continued, "I would rather starve to death than borrow money from an *erlaogai*. What are you really after? Do you want to join hands with the enemy? Your example shows a new trend in class struggle. Don't think that you can hoodwink us revolutionary *zhiqing* with a few words of fake self-criticism. You must make a revolution in the depths of your soul and expose the ulterior motive of the *erlaogai*..."

To me, her words sounded like nuclear blasts in verbal warfare. They made me shake in my shoes. I felt I was being dismembered and trampled upon. Under the pressure of all these false charges, with so many political derogatory labels stuck on me, my fear gradually turned into bitterness. My original plan was to make some kind of self-criticism. But at this moment, my head seemed to explode, and I couldn't recall the words I had prepared. Looking at Little A's shadows shaking violently on the wall, my bitterness turned into rage. I became so furious that I lost all reason. I interrupted her by shouting agitatedly at her:

"How dare you stand there lecturing me without the slightest self-doubt? Why didn't you stretch out your hand to me? Where were you when I needed help? And besides, what's wrong with the 're-employees'? Aren't they human beings? Are they wrong to help a *zhiqing*? I want to tell you, *erlaogai* are not convicts; they are farm employees. Do you understand that?"

Suddenly, I found myself an eloquent, confident speaker. At that moment, I didn't want to do any self-criticism. I wanted to defend myself because no others spoke in my defense. The dormitory room quieted down. All those present stared at me. Feeling I was fighting a lonely battle, I decided to burn my boats and score a quick victory. To overwhelm my opponent, I blurted out the following remark when I could no longer restrain myself:

"You are having a good time, aren't you? Your family doesn't need to borrow money. If I wanted to be like you. I'd ask my mom to find an official to be my dad!"

No sooner had I made this remark than I was filled with regret. I never thought that I could utter such venomous words. Little A's eyes reddened. She broke into a loud cry and ran out, hands covering her face.

I assumed I had made a mess of things and was bound to pay a terrible price. I sat there dazed and felt the blood draining from my face.

Yet things turned out much better than I had expected. After pondering for some moments, the squad leader yawned. She said that I still fell short of political understanding, that I should make more effort in my studies. Then she dismissed the meeting. The following day, several female companions said quietly to me that Little A had been arrogant and had got what she deserved for her overblown criticism. They also said they had not expected a person of few words like me to be so sharp-tongued. I appreciated their sympathy.

Little A ignored me after that, and I did the same to her. At the bottom of my heart, I felt somewhat sorry for what I had said.

After some time, no one talked about the event anymore, and that was the end of it. When meeting me on the road, Su Gong pretended not to know me at all. We passed each other in silence. His melancholy eyes seemed to convey a sense of regret. Perhaps he thought that he had implicated me by lending me money.

I wanted to say a few words to him. But I never did. Later I was transferred to a tile and brick making factory. On a severe winter morning, from a far distance, I saw him walking slowly on the snowy ground. I haven't seen him since.

Who Was to Blame?

by Lin Pingzhen

One early spring night in 1972, I was chatting, joking and singing with three female *zhiqing* companions under the faint light of a vegetable oil lamp in our dormitory. This was how we killed time during the long nights in the countryside. Soon after Guihua went to her separate room at the western end of the dorm, the rest of us went to bed.

At midnight, however, I was suddenly awakened by a frightful scream. When I came to my senses, I started crying "Thief!" and woke my two roommates, Heng Zhi and Xu Gui, telling them that Guihua was being robbed. I jumped from my bed, got dressed, and tried without success to open the door. My two companions could not budge it either. Heng Zhi then said, "It must be locked from the outside." The three of us shouted at the top of our voices, calling our production leader Gao and other villagers for help. Our shouts spread into the quiet night.

Several minutes later, peasants in the neighborhood arrived. Flashlights in hand, they carried hoes and shoulder poles as weapons. We were joined by our production team leader, the Party secretary of our production brigade, some elderly women, and several others. Uncle Li was the first to come to our aid. He discovered that our door had been tightly latched with a bamboo slip between two tiny door rings. Outside our door stood a barefoot Guihua, wearing nothing but her undergarments. On seeing me, she rushed into my arms, shivering. I quickly brought her to our room, put her in my bed and wrapped her in my quilt. In the meantime, Changchun, a demobilized soldier in our village, dispatched three detachments of young peasants in search of the offender.

It took some time for Guifang to tell us in bits and pieces about her horrible experience. She had been fast asleep when she was awakened by a faint sound like a rat gnawing at something. Then her door was opened and the bright light from a flashlight dazzled her vision. She promptly sat up, turned on her flashlight, and started crying "Thief!" But with the intense light directed at her, she could see nothing. When she tried to leave her bed, a pair of strong arms held her down and a kitchen knife was pressed against her throat. A deep voice said, "Keep quiet, or I'll kill you!" She kept crying out and fought back by kicking and striking at the assailant. After a fierce struggle, she managed to escape from her room. The man fled and soon disappeared into the darkness.

When people came to Guihua's room, they saw the kitchen knife and the flashlight on the earthen floor. The lamp had been knocked over, and vegetable oil was flowing down from a brick table, soaking a notebook on which Guihua had copied many foreign folksongs.

By this time, all the young men on the search mission had returned. They had not found anything. On inquiry, Guihua only replied that the assailant was a strong man, but she could not tell anything about his specific features.

People were exhausted after working several hours that night. The Party secretary asked everyone to go home, saying that he would report the matter to the commune leadership in the morning. The village then regained its usual quietness. Guihua kept quivering in my arms. We stayed awake for the rest of the night and greeted daybreak with sleepy eyes.

Early that morning, the Party secretary left for the commune headquarters. For some reason, he took with him Guihua's oil-soaked notebook of foreign folksongs. We waited anxiously for him until he returned at noon, looking unusually somber. Guihua's notebook had been retained by commune officials, supposedly for investigation and analysis. In the afternoon, two of the male *zhiqing* in the neighboring village were detained by the commune's military department, who said, with mind-boggling illogic, that none of the male peasants in our village could have done such a thing because all of them had come from families of "good" class status. The only possible culprit should therefore have come from among the *zhiqing*. After being held in custody for a couple of days, the two male *zhiqing* were released because there was no evidence whatever against them.

As time passed by, the matter simply faded away with no conclusion, but it was not long before a rumor spread through the village. While working in the field, a female villager said, "Look at Guihua. She looks terrible in those tight pants. Her eyes sparkle like a wild, seductive woman's." Another added to the slander by saying, "A few days ago, she said in the field that she had dreamed of a man pressing hard against her body. I think it was not a thief going after her. She must be dreaming about men, because she is so crazy about them." The wife of the Party secretary added to the talk with apparent inside information by saying, "There is something you don't know. Her notebook was filled with words about love and passion…. The commune has confiscated her notebook, saying it was something that belonged to the capitalist class…"

Anyone would have found such mud-slinging intolerable, especially a teenage girl. In the eyes of certain people, Guihua didn't suffer an assault that night; the episode was purely a product of her own imagination. The whole thing was attributed to her fondness for foreign folksongs, and to the profound influence of "bourgeois ideology".

A Model Worker, the Bear and Me

by Liu Yuanshu

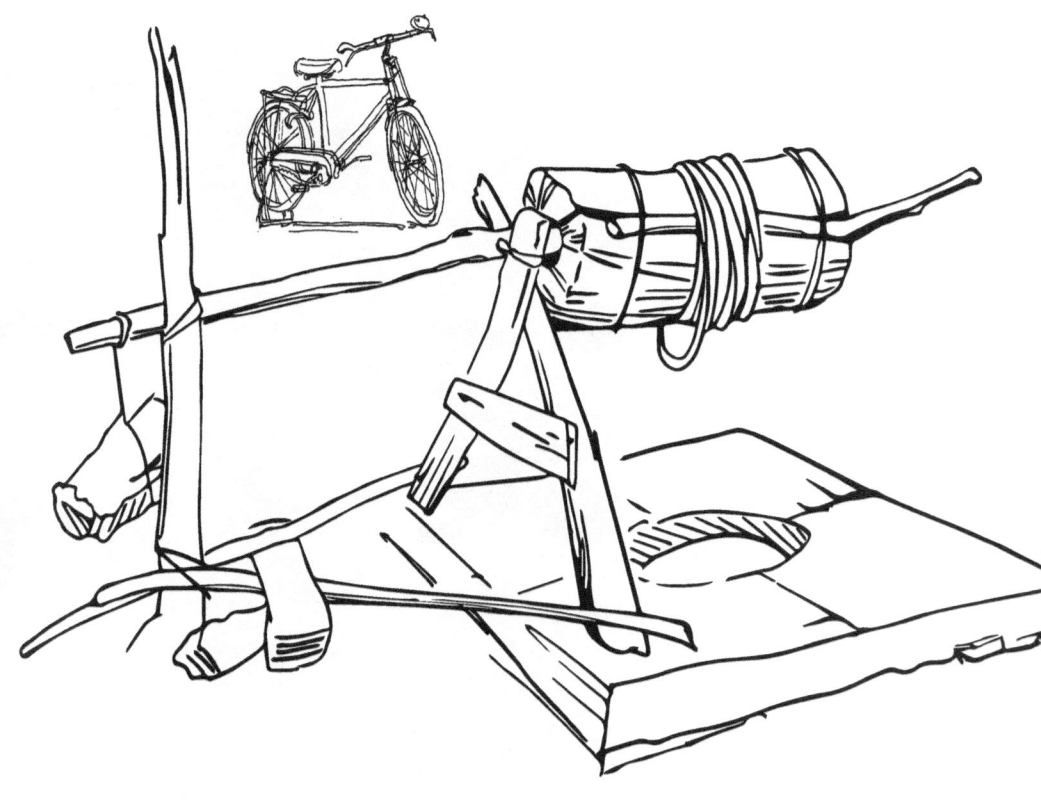

That year, I was serving as a clerk in a company on one of the paramilitary farms administered by Heilongjiang Construction and Production Corps in Northeast China. My job was to receive telephone calls, draft speeches for company leaders, and do news reports and other propaganda work for the farm. The task that bothered me most was to write stories about praiseworthy deeds and people.

One day, the political department of our regiment gave us a phone call instructing us to select and train someone to become a model worker.

Consulting our instructor, I said: "Let's refrain from appointing a general from among the dwarfs. If we don't have a model worker, we just say so."

"Even a simpleton wouldn't say that!" The instructor cast me a slighting glance. "You have a hero sitting by your side!"

"Who is it?" I asked.

"Zhen Xiangdong, the deputy head of the first squad of the second platoon."

"Zhen?" I shook my head fiercely in disapproval.

Zhen's Performance at School

Zhen Xiangdong was a classmate of mine in middle school. His original surname was Jia (贾), which was a homophone of the Chinese character 假 meaning "false". His personal name Xiangdong (向东) literally meant "oriented toward the east"; it could also be interpreted as "oriented toward Mao Zedong".

To avoid being misunderstood as "falsely oriented toward Mao," he decided to change his surname. One day, he put up a poster beside the gate of our school announcing that he had changed his surname to Zhen (甄), which was a homophone of 真 meaning "true". From that day on, his new name became well known on our campus and beyond.

He was well known, too, for making innovative, revolutionary proposals. Once he proposed to the military officers who were then managing our school that the portrait of Chairman Mao should be hung on the eastern wall instead of the western wall because the East, represented by Mao, symbolized socialism while the West stood for capitalism. From the day his proposal was adopted, all of us sat in the classroom with Chairman Mao's portrait behind our backs.

Later he made a series of proposals to the workers' propaganda team who shared responsibilities with the military officers in managing our school. During physical education class, he suggested that in lining up, we dress to the left instead of to the right, because left represented revolution and progress, while right symbolized reaction and backwardness. Afterwards, he developed this idea further by advocating using the left hand in a handshake, salute, writing, and holding chopsticks at meals. He got all his ideas accepted except that of changing the habit of cleaning one's body at the toilet, where most people found the use of the left hand difficult.

He later wrote to the traffic control department in Beijing, saying the traffic signal system should be changed to "red light signals 'go', whereas the green light signifies 'stop'". His logic was that "red" meant revolution, which should never stop, while green signified decadent capitalism, which should be put to a stop. The traffic control department saw some sense in his argument and adopted his proposal. It was said that only after several head-on car crashes had occurred did they revert to the old practice.

In the Eyes of His Companions

Not long after we arrived at the farm, a fire broke out in our *zhiqing* dormitory. Fortunately, we discovered it in time and succeeded in moving out all our belongings. Even so, Zhen persisted in rushing into the flames. I grasped his arm and said: "Old friend, there are no more things to save from the fire. Aren't you risking death?"

"The portrait of the Chairman is still on the wall. I'd defend him to the death. I beg you to allow me to go in and take it off the wall," he shouted, sobbing.

This was incredible. Chairman Mao's portrait had not been hung on the wall with a frame; it had been pasted there and could not be taken off.

Strangely, the more I tried to hold him back, the more forcefully he tried to rush into the fire. But once I relaxed my grip on him, his impulse weakened. I then realized he was just going through the motions to impress us. Damn it, I thought to myself, I'll let you realize your dream of becoming a hero! Instead of holding him back, I gave him a push toward the fire. This was something he had not expected. Crouching down with his buttocks toward us, he didn't dare to take a single step forward. His antics caused us to roar with laughter.

At a company meeting, the instructor spoke about his "praiseworthy spirit" and promoted him to be the deputy head of the first squad.

That winter, most members of our company went logging in the mountains. I accompanied them as a propagandist. After putting up a big blackboard against a tree trunk, I started chalking an essay I had composed the previous night to spur them on. Suddenly, an orderly of our company ran in my direction shouting: "Bad news! Something terrible just happened up there!"

I rushed with the orderly to the scene of the accident, where we found Zhen Xiangdong lying motionless on the ground, eyes closed, pinned beneath a good-sized tree.

We moved the tree away and cut off two thick branches. Then we took off our leg wrappings and used them to improvise a stretcher. We were some ten kilometers away from our regimental hospital and there were no vehicles of any kind. We eight young men took turns carrying him on a brisk march.

We were all out of breath when we saw Zhen stir slightly on the stretcher. He slowly opened his eyes and asked us, "Comrades, what has happened to me?"

"You were hit by a falling tree while logging," one of us replied.

"Comrades, ...Logging is much more important. Just leave me alone..."

A *zhiqing* from Shanghai, the youngest among us, said to me, "Comrade clerk, please hurry up and note down his heroic words."

Hardly had the young Shanghainese finished his remark than Zhen started to murmur the Chairman's quotations: "Determined.... not afraid of sacrifice.... push aside all obstacles.... to fight for victory."

He stammered a few more of Mao's quotations, and then with a turn of his head, he closed his eyes and fell silent. Apparently, he was wounded so badly that he again lost consciousness.

We eventually succeeded in reaching the regimental hospital, thank goodness. As doctors and nurses took over the stretcher, the eight of us collapsed and sat on the ground gasping for breath.

About half an hour later, the chief surgeon with grayish temples came out of the emergency room. We all got up from the ground and asked him about Zhen's condition.

The doctor shrugged his shoulders and asked us: "Who is the leader of your group?"

"I am," I said, stepping forward.

He didn't say a word but handed me a sheet of paper with a red ink seal stamped on it. I was afraid it might be a death certificate.

The other members of our group gathered around me, all anxious to look at the paper. On it were written the words: "Overall checkup showed nothing wrong with the patient. Clinical impression: problems with his thinking. Recommendation: more ideological education."

We all concluded that he must have put the tree on top of himself to feign injury. We would have given him a violent beating if the doctors and nurses had not intervened.

A Political Task Assigned Me

I was recollecting these past events when the instructor interrupted my thoughts by saying, "Comrade Liu, you must hurry and complete writing the story about Deputy Squad Leader Zhen's outstanding deeds. A report must be submitted to our regimental headquarters in three days.

"Instructor, I've reported to you many times about Zhen's dirty tricks. If such a person is set up as a model worker, the result....."

"What will be the result? I know all the things you talked

about. Selecting him is required by our current situation, by our work and struggle, by the need for propaganda. You mustn't demand perfection from a heroic figure."

After a while, he added, "You must do this job. You must fulfill it as a political task, regardless whether you understand its significance or not."

A Chinese saying goes that a military order is as weighty as a mountain. So, I had to obey the instructor's order though it went against my own will. I worked overnight writing out a long report entitled "The Outstanding Deeds of Comrade Zhen Xiangdong". It became an official document for circulation in the entire regiment.

Another ridiculous document that I wrote was entitled "Advanced Experience Gained by Our Company Leadership in Discovering and Training a Model Worker". Our instructor made a stirring speech based on this document at a mass rally organized by our regiment, winning long applause from the audience. He was promoted to be a battalion instructor soon afterward. On the third day after his promotion, I was appointed a clerk of his new battalion.

Black Bear Visiting Beehives

In the spring of 1972, the fourth year since my arrival at the farm, I was sent deep into the mountains as a bee-keeper with another *zhiqing* nicknamed Big Nose. Hailing from Ningbo, an ancient seaport city in eastern China, Big Nose was my leader as well as my only co-worker.

Bee-keeping was too little challenge for the capable and too much for the incompetent. Aside from dealing with bees, our only routine was to cook for ourselves. Life in the mountains was hard and monotonous. All year around, you could barely see a single soul of the opposite sex. It was so boring!

Water had to be brought up from a shallow pit we had dug on the grassy land below the mountain. It had to be carried in a pail by the two of us on a shoulder pole. The water in the pit was just enough to fill our pail once every day. Since the water was turbid, we had to use alum power to settle the dirt.

Big Nose would often leave the mountain to visit his girlfriend. He went whenever he liked and could easily find excuses to go. Besides being my leader, he was two years my senior and an experienced bee-keeper. So, what could I say?

The good thing about him was that he always came back at night. During the day, I had a yellow dog to keep me company. I had no problem except that I had no one to speak to.

Once, however, he didn't come back before sunset. I was really scared. The faint light from my kerosene lamp flickered like a devil's eye blinking at me in the night. It seemed to be an extension of the ghostly glow in the graveyard on the opposite mountain slope. Strangely shaped rocks around the small hut and the dark shadows of the nearby forests all looked like monsters glaring at me. Roe deer and red deer bellowed and bleated like old folks coughing in their sickbeds. Owls hooted, and wolves howled, sounding like the moaning wind at one time or a screaming child at another....

I let the yellow dog outside to keep watch for me. Then I sang a few Peking opera arias in a loud voice to embolden myself.

Taking a double-barreled shotgun down from the wall, I inserted a few scatter shots in one of the barrels and a single big shot in another. After putting a kitchen knife under my pillow, I went to bed and soon fell asleep.

I was awakened by the desperate barking of the dog and the sound of its clawing at the front door. Soon the barking switched to a long wail. I got off my bed, took the shotgun with me, and opened the door a crack to take a look. The dog squeezed itself inside and hid behind my back with its tail between its legs.

I instantly latched the door and looked out through the window to see what danger might be lurking outside. I saw a big, black shadow moving about among the beehives, sometimes standing, sometimes squatting on the ground. The shadow seemed to stop at each of the dozens of hives.

At first, I thought it might be a foreign spy or a hostile element coming to commit some act of sabotage. But a closer look revealed it was a big black bear weighing perhaps four or five hundred pounds.

Missing a Chance to Become a Hero

Obviously, the bear was after the honey, not me, but just in case, I moved a table against the door and put a big wooden board over the window, leaving only a narrow opening for me to look out and aim my shotgun.

After a tour of the apiary, the bear began clawing open the hives. Having smashed close to a dozen of them, he began throwing them on the ground one after another. He then used the broken hives to crush more hives, destroying another dozen or so.

Then swarms of bees rose up in the air and circled the animal's head with a deafening noise. The bear just ignored them and enjoyed his delicacies, repeatedly filling his big mouth with honey taken from the honeycombs.

Again and again I asked myself if I should shoot the bear. If I could kill him with my shotgun, I would become the man of the hour on our farm the following morning. I would be praised as a hero for protecting state property. Women would admire me, and I might even win the heart of a female *zhiqing* more beautiful than Big Nose's girlfriend.

On second thought, however, if with my two shots I missed hitting the white-haired patch below the bear's neck, where the heart was, what would happen then? The bear would rush at my hut, which he could easily destroy since it was made of bark shingles plastered with earth and straw. He was only some twenty meters away and could reach me in seconds before I was able to reload my shotgun. I found myself wishing for a machine gun.

I decided to play it safe. Good fortune was always possible as long as I remained alive, I told myself. The honor of being a hero was not for everyone. I would rather be a nobody than risk my life.

I never imagined that a miracle would happen.

The bees were obviously infuriated by the invasion and started their counter-attacks in a well-organized manner. Swarms of them took turns attacking the bear, persevering in their struggle to defend their harvests.

The bear who had exulted over his booty a short while ago now found himself in deep trouble. He waved his paws violently in a futile attempt to drive the bees away. Then he rolled on the ground, trying to get rid of them by crushing them. But new swarms of the insects continued to surround and assail him.

No longer able to stand the attack, the bear growled and tried to run away, with swarms of bees chasing after him. It was not long before the bear collided with a big tree. Then he turned around and ran in the opposite direction, only to fall down after crashing against a huge boulder. Lying flat on the ground, he tried a few times to get up, but fell again.

It dawned on me that the bear might have been blinded by the venom of the stings. He finally managed to get up and ran around aimlessly for a while, with swarms of bees still pursuing and attacking him. Then he fell down and never got up again, lying there motionless.

I then heard the roaring of a tractor engine. It was Big Nose with a team of loggers who had worked at transportation and were on their way back to their dormitory. All of them were astounded by the sight of the dead bear. After listening to my account, Big Nose punched me in the shoulder. He dragged me aside and whispered to me: "You blockhead! The bear was already dead, why didn't you shoot him in his white-haired chest? It would have shown that you were the one who killed him!"

Glancing at the people on the tractor, I slapped my own face and said to myself: How stupid of me! Too late now to regret having missed such a great chance to become a hero.

By the Side of the Yellow River — Random Notes on My Rustic Life

by Liu Dexi

máozhǔ xí wànsuì
毛主席万岁

November 13, 1965

(Seeing the Yellow River the first night after my arrival)

Last night marked the beginning of our lives as *zhiqing*. Excited by our new environment, we tossed about in makeshift beds and could not fall asleep. We talked about exemplary *zhiqing* like Chen Guoji, Yu Shanling and Xing Yanzi, whom we regarded as our icons. Could we ever match them?

Then we heard the first crows of cockerels. We didn't feel like sleeping at all. Suddenly, I had an inspiration and proposed that, "Since we are staying awake anyway and are so close to the Yellow River, why not go take a look?" The Yellow River, China's mother river and one of the largest in the world, had always been a source of wonderment to us all.

Everyone was overjoyed by the idea. After walking through fields full of rice stumps, we arrived on the bank of the river. The sky soon became so pitch-dark that we couldn't discern our own fingers in front of our faces. Liu, the eldest and most worldly in our group, explained to us that this was the darkness before daybreak.

In a few moments, a patch of faint light appeared far away downstream. Then golden rays shot up, followed by the rise of the big, round sun. It resembled a huge freshly washed apple that appeared above a horizon made of a long stretch of shimmering yellow water. It was the first time in my life that I saw so clearly the magnificent Yellow River, a river that would accompany us day and night over many years. The torrential waters ran eastward like a golden silk ribbon that fluttered in the river bed. Water birds hovered over the river and white sails of fishing boats dotted the vast watery expanse -- the fishermen had weighed anchor and had started a new day by chanting their work songs.

With a blue sky decorated by white clouds, the river scene was as picturesque as a Chinese ink painting. Surrounded by such wonderful scenery, we could not refrain from singing a popular song starting with the line: "There is a big river with broad waves...." Then, behind our backs came the familiar giggles of girls, which we male *zhiqing* would describe as the tinkling of silver bells. Aha! The female *zhiqing* had followed on our heels. They soon joined our chorus. We sang The East Is Red, The Yellow River Cantata and other songs. We were all very excited, and some of the girls wept.

On our way back, someone said, "The Yellow River is really beautiful. But how beautiful will our future lives be?" For some time, there was silence. No one responded to the question, since the answer would be anybody's guess.

November 20, 1965
(Zhang Mei resisting "sugar-coated shells")

Yesterday, a current of cold air arrived from Siberia, and a northeastern wind blew hard. The temperature dropped down to twelve degrees below zero Centigrade. Having dug ditches for the whole day, we all felt exhausted and retired soon after supper.

Before the construction of a *zhiqing* dormitory, the female *zhiqing* stayed temporarily in a wing of the house of Dr. Zhang, a Chinese traditional physician who lived at the western end of the village. Having just gone to bed, the girls heard knocking at the door. It turned out to be Auntie Zhang, the doctor's wife. She arrived with a big earthen basin, saying: "Girls, the weather has worsened. Don't go out to the toilet at night. You can use this basin for urination."

Moved and grateful, the girls thanked Auntie Zhang for

her kindness. No longer needing to brave the severe cold outside, they slept soundly that night.

The following morning, while working in the fields, our group leader Zhang Mei learned from villagers that Auntie Zhang, who had become the wife of the widowed Dr. Zhang, had been a concubine of a landlord in an adjacent village before liberation. Zhang Mei, to prove her worth as a Communist Youth League member, immediately ran back to her living quarters and opened Mao Zedong's Selected Works. She focused on reading Chairman Mao's article on the classification of the rural classes.

Feeling enlightened, she began to see Auntie Zhang's seemingly kind provision of the chamber pot as a "sugarcoated shell", an expression Mao had used to warn his comrades against corruption by the exploiting classes after the victory of the revolution. Was their hostess's show of kindness, Zhang Mei reasoned, a "sugarcoated shell" aimed at our female *zhiqing*? Was it an attempt by the unrepentant landlord class to win away China's younger generation from the poor and lower-middle peasantry? She decided to remove this poisonous influence from her *zhiqing* companions and report the matter to the commune's Party committee.

I and several other *zhiqing* disagreed with her judgment. We felt Auntie Zhang's deed had reflected normal human feelings and was an expression of the concern of the old generation toward us young people. At least, it was an act of humanitarian concern.

Zhang Mei's words soon got to Auntie Zhang, who came to the female *zhiqing*'s room that night and took back the basin, apparently to avoid the suspicion that she was firing sugarcoated shells at the younger generation. Without the basin, all the girls had to go outside at night to the toilet, shivering in the wind. This suffering caused much complaint against Zhang Mei.

Zhang Mei was confused, wondering why the Chairman's wise judgment on the issue of class struggle had failed to work in her case. Seeing that Zhang Mei had tasted the bitter fruits of her own rigid thinking, we male *zhiqing* gloated in secret.

December 11, 1965

(Rehearsing an operetta to celebrate the New Year)

In line with the campaign of the so-called socialist education launched by the Party in the rural areas, the commune and brigade leadership instructed our *zhiqing* group to prepare a revolutionary operetta in celebration of the New Year with the peasants. With the holiday barely three weeks away, even great playwrights like Cao Yu and Lao She would have considered this an impossible task, not to mention us *zhiqing* who knew nothing about opera or drama.

Liu Zhongchang, the eldest member of our group, quietly asked me to solve our dilemma, but I said there was nothing I could do. Upon learning of our conversation, Zhang Mei jeered at me and said, "To compose a revolutionary operetta, you have to become a revolutionary first. Lacking the sense of class struggle, how could he compose a revolutionary operetta?"

Pleased with her dismissal of me, I could now enjoy watching Zhang Mei's struggle from the sidelines. As our group leader, she was kept busy running around, trying to make a success of the operetta project, but, short of literary talent, she was unable to produce a script even after five days had passed.

Liu Zhongchang came to her aid at this crucial moment. He proposed to transform the finale of the popular opera The White-Haired Girl into a single operatic piece. He would do this by making Xi'er, the unfortunate white-haired girl of the title, join the Communist-led army. He would transform her father, Yang Bailao, from an oppressed peasant into a rebel. And he would end the operetta with a scene of the peasant masses rising up against the despotic landlord Huang Shiren. Although the operetta would be neither the old White-Haired Girl nor an entirely new work, it would reflect class struggle nevertheless. To Zhang Mei, Liu's proposal was the answer. She lost no time in organizing a group of *zhiqing* and making arrangements for a rehearsal. She herself would play the white-haired girl, the female protagonist.

January 12, 1966
(Presentation of the operetta)

On New Year's Eve, we premiered our operetta. The warm applause it won was beyond our expectations. The peasants were so deeply moved that some of them wept while others uttered deep sighs. The slogan "Down with Huang Shiren!" was repeatedly shouted.

All the players were overwhelmed by their success. Zhang Mei in particular could barely conceal her smug self-satisfaction. It was obvious that she considered herself an outstanding organizer as well as a talented opera singer who had performed her role with great artistic charm. I had my doubts.

In the afternoon, when I raised the subject with Dr. Zhang, he smiled and observed: "Our production brigade consists of two villages: the Shi Bridge Village and the Zhang Bridge Village. We are sandwiched on a stretch of beach land between two rivers, the Yellow River to the north and the Jialu River to the south. We live in seclusion due to the lack of transport, and culturally, we are very backward. Take our village for example. We have 26 households with a population of 150 people. Only three of us -- the production team leader, the accountant and I – have had even a few years of schooling. All the rest are illiterate. You don't need a dramatic presentation to attract a crowd here: even a visit by a fortune-teller or a rat-poison peddler would do it." He was right, of course.

September 15, 1966
(With the advent of the Cultural Revolution, who will become the next target of attack?)

Ever since Chairman Mao gave an audience to Red Guards at Tiananmen Square on August 18, the revolutionary movement in the countryside had been accelerating. It started with the campaign to put an end to the Four Olds (old customs, old culture, old habits and old ideas -- ed.) and then switched to searching the homes of former landlords and rich peasants. With the deepening of the movement, the people were going to struggle against the capitalist roaders. But who were the capitalist offenders? The Party secretary of our production brigade? The battalion commander of the militia? Our production team leader? They were the ones who held the power, and so they would never turn themselves into targets. But still the movement had to go forward. It was much later that I realized how these power brokers decided to run the show.

The rural cadres are shrewd in their own ways. After repeated discussions among themselves, they decided to make *zhiqing* their scapegoat. At a meeting, Li Qing, the production brigade accountant, argued eloquently that *zhiqing* were the only cultured group in the village. "In the Cultural Revolution, who should be the target of revolution other than them?"

But to struggle against *zhiqing*, an approval was required from Han Dafu, a cadre who had come with us and served as our supervisor. A short man about forty with big but listless eyes, Han had been working as an assistant in a neighborhood committee in Zhengzhou, capital of Henan Province. It was said that initially he had been reluctant to go along with the proposed struggle against us. But since his family background was not one of working people, village cadres had threatened that if he didn't change his lenient attitude toward us, they would charge him with the crime of boycotting the movement and mobilize the masses to attack him as a die-hard capitalist roader.

Han backed down and decided to sacrifice *zhiqing* to save his own skin.

The village cadres were pleased and appointed him vice-chair of the Brigade Cultural Revolution Committee, with the accountant Li Qing as the chair.

September 25, 1966
(Zhiqing became the so-called "three-anti elements")

One evening during harvest time, when I was on duty as a watchman guarding the cotton that was ripening on the southern beach land, our team leader Hu came to inform me to attend a meeting that evening.

The meeting took place on the ground in front of the office buildings of our production brigade. Two bright vapor lamps hung over a dense crowd. Zhang Mei was directing *zhiqing* in singing revolutionary songs, chanting verses such as: "Heaven and earth are immense; but they are not as immense as the kindness of the Party" and "Father and Mother are dear to us, but they are not as dear as Chairman Mao".

It was Li Qing the accountant who presided over the meeting alongside Han Dafu the supervisor. After Han announced the opening of the meeting, Li ordered that an ex-landlord surnamed Tian be brought before the gathering. A short, wizened old man with few teeth, Tian was ordered to make a clean breast of his evil deeds. He said slowly in reply: "My father was a landlord. After he died, you put the landlord label on me. You denounced me in the cooperative movement. You struggled against me during the Great Leap Forward. After I have died, how will you be able to find my replacement, someone you can target to struggle against?"

This unexpected reply from Tian, whom villagers nicknamed Tian huoya (man with few teeth), amused the audience and triggered laughter. Li and Han, the two men on the podium, tried to bring the session back on the right track by shouting: "Down with Tian huoya!" "If Tian does not surrender, we will destroy him!" Tian showed no sign of fear, probably because he had been tempered in so many political movements. To the peasants, there seemed little novelty in struggling against such a "veteran" class enemy as Tian. He was soon led off the rostrum by two militiamen.

It was now Han's turn to speak. He glared at the audience with wide open eyes, and then read out a list of *zhiqing* names. The list included me, Luo and two others who were all close to me. I was wondering what he was going to do with us when Han declared with a stern face: "These people are anti-Party, anti-socialist and anti-Mao Zedong Thought. They are the so-called three-anti elements among the *zhiqing*!"

Good heavens! I hadn't expected such an iron hat to be falling on my head. I was completely nonplussed.

Zhang Mei, who had long stood by, roared like a wolf, shouting: "Down with the three-anti elements!" She gave a cue for us to be led to the rostrum to face the audience.

Upon hearing Zhang Mei's accusations, I now understood that, because Luo, Yang and I had come from the same school and had been very close, we were accused of forming a cabal, with me as the chief culprit. The principal charge against me was a remark I had made about Chairman Mao when discussing current events with other *zhiqing*. One of them had said: "Liu Shaoqi (then chairman of the People's Republic of China) has visited Indonesia, Burma and Cambodia in a single trip. Why didn't Chairman Mao go and visit foreign countries?" I had replied off the cuff, "Probably because he is a bit too old. It would be inconvenient for him to go abroad."

When the meeting was dismissed, it was already one o'clock in the morning. We no longer felt as relaxed as when we had arrived at the meeting. Both the accused and other members of our group were heavy-hearted. Some of the female *zhiqing* wept.

October 5, 1966
(Writing self-criticism)

For days around the National Day, I was writing my self-criticism under the custody of Zhang Mei. With her help, my self-criticism was approved by the brigade leadership. Zhang Mei had asked me to put the following words into my self-critical paper: "'Long live Chairman Mao!' is the outcry of people over all China and the entire world. It was terribly wrong for me to say that he is a bit too old. (Translated as 'long live', the Chinese original word *wansui* means ten thousand years - ed.) Compared with ten thousand years, the Chairman is still in his prime. He surely can lead us to bury imperialism, revisionism and all reactionaries and carry the world revolution to the end."

Because of my good attitude and "profound self-criticism", I was "liberated" to return to the fields for work. I was really glad.

A Winning Game and a Brush with Death

by Fu Xiaofan

When young students from my school in Chengdu were sent down to work at an army-run farm in remote Yunnan in 1971, one of my schoolmates took a go game set with him. This board game is said to have been invented in China more than five thousand years ago. Despite my poor skill, playing go formed an indispensable part of my life in those years.

Soon after our arrival at the Mengding Farm, we became disappointed and depressed because of the harsh natural environment, the heavy physical work and the poor living conditions. It did not take us long, however, to reconcile ourselves to our fate. We silently endured all sorts of hardships in labor and daily life, but the worst part was the monotony. There was no entertainment, no cultural life. Exhausted after a day's work, we found playing go a relaxing game and a good way to kill time during holidays.

An increasing number of us developed an interest in the game. Whenever there was a contest, a small crowd would gather around the two opponents. The spectators watched quietly for the most part, but sometimes they would offer advice and comments, occasionally erupting in hoots and cheers.

One day, in the thick of a contest held in one of our bedrooms, the manager of the farm came in. Due to the paramilitary nature of the farm, people addressed him by his army title of "Company Commander." His unexpected visit surprised us and so we all faced him in silence. He picked up a playing piece, which was usually called a "stone," though ours were made of glass. He examined it carefully in the sunlight, frowned, and then asked: "What is this?"

"A playing piece in go," one of us replied cautiously.

"Go?" His face stiffened, "I have never heard of it. It must be something that belongs to the capitalist class. I declare it be confiscated."

Having said this, he picked up the whole game set and was about to leave. At the entrance, he turned around and said; "I will throw the whole thing into the manure pit. You all have to submit a written self-criticism." We looked at one another, not knowing what to do.

After a while, we came to our senses and realized the seriousness of the matter. Confiscating the go set would deprive us of a major means to spend our off-hours. We decided to send two representatives to reason with the company commander.

The two youngsters summoned up the nerve to enter his office. One started by saying, "Company Commander, Sir, go has existed since ancient times. It was not something invented by the capitalist class."

"Impossible!" he retorted, "I have seen Chinese chess, but never heard that we Chinese people play go. It must be a foreign invention, a gadget enjoyed by the capitalists in their decadent, luxurious life."

Hit by a brainwave, the other representative said, "What's wrong even if it was a foreign invention? Weren't playing cards invented abroad, with portraits of foreigners on them? Playing cards is allowed in China, so why not go? Please return the set to us."

Angry now, the company commander snapped, "Stop your lame arguments. No one is allowed to play go. I am determined to throw the set away. There are so many pieces, black and white. They only serve to make people's thinking too complicated."

Frightened, the one who had spoken first said, "Oh, please don't do that! Chairman Mao and other Party leaders play go too. In his writings, he drew a parallel between playing go and working out strategies and tactics in warfare." Checkmated by this remark, our company commander fell into a long silence. Eventually, he waved his hand, a signal that it was time for us to leave. He then gave us an opening by saying, "You go back. I will consult with the political instructor of our company."

We were on pins and needles for the next several days. One of my companions went to the manure pit with a stick, but he could find no sign that the go set had been thrown in.

Eventually, a messenger came from the company commander's office with a smile on his face and the game set in his hands. He said that after consultation between the two leaders, they decided to return the go set to us, but they wouldn't allow us to play the game during study time or at meetings. We greeted the news with a big hurrah.

While we had won a victory over our company commander, quite a few of us, including myself, were defeated by a small but dangerous insect in Yunnan's subtropical rain-forests -- the mosquito. In June 1972, I became seriously ill with encephalic malaria. For a couple of weeks, I lingered at death's door.

At the start of the illness, I felt not too well one morning and asked someone to deliver my written request for a sick leave to the company commander. I was pleased for the chance to skip work on a wretched, rainy day. Lying in bed, I recalled how I had enjoyed three "long vacations" since coming to the farm over a year before. I had been stung in the head by a bumble bee that became tangled in my hair while I was working in the forest. My head soon became swollen like a watermelon. That earned me a ten-day sick leave. On another occasion, I was carrying a shoulder pole with two full pails of boiled water for our work group up in the hills when one pail spilled on me. Later, a blister as big as a small bowl appeared on my leg. During the recovery period, I got a fly to crawl over the blister I had torn open, hoping it would help prolong my leave by making the wound fester. But to my wonder, no contamination happened. Fifteen days later my leg healed. I had to pick up my hoe and go back to work again in low spirits. On another day, while hoeing in the fields, I accidentally cut my entire toenail off. This gave me a 30-day-long "work-related injury leave." Though the sharp pain caused me to break out in a drenching sweat, I hated our work so much that the leave made me ecstatic. Not only was the heavy toil too much for many of us, but we could hardly see the results of our work. Take rubber tree planting for example. It took at least eight years to tap latex. Work in other fields was also not very rewarding, sometimes even counterproductive. This was due to the lack of feasibility studies and good management.

While I lay there in my sickbed reflecting on these matters, my illness grew worse. I got a high fever. The practitioner at our clinic thought I was suffering from a bad cold. He gave me many penicillin injections, but to no avail. My high fever persisted. The company commander then arranged for me to be transferred to a small hospital at our battalion headquarters. Four of my companions carried me on a stretcher for miles through a driving rain until they reached the Nanding river. There they hired a small boat and risked crossing the roaring stream. The hospital at the battalion headquarters made the same diagnosis as our clinic. Their treatment did nothing except to delay an effective cure. For days I didn't eat anything, but vomited all the fluids in my stomach. On the seventh day, I was transported by tractor to a bigger hospital at our regiment headquarters. There I was finally diagnosed with encephalic malaria.

Until much later, I was unaware of the havoc caused by this terrible disease in the area. It had killed five *zhiqing* on our farm and eliminated the entire populations in two villages inhabited by minority peoples. The later tragedy had taken place despite efforts made by medical teams dispatched from big cities such as Beijing and Shanghai.

Twenty minutes after I arrived at the regimental hospital, the farm authorities were informed that I was dying and therefore prepared a coffin for me. Yet miraculously, I managed to survive, thanks to the efforts of the medical staff at the hospital. Thereafter, I became known as "the *zhiqing* who had climbed out of a coffin". The same kind of disease claimed the life of a female *zhiqing* on our farm the following year. The coffin prepared for me was re-allocated for her use, though its size was a bit too large. I didn't feel lucky for my narrow escape. Nor did I feel very sorry for her death. I only carried on my struggle to continue living in that wilderness with silent tenacity. That year I was nineteen.

Stories about Three Old Snapshots

by Wang Xiaoying

1. Waving Good-bye

Did I display a vigorous, carefree spirit in this snapshot? On the back of it was my inscription: "Daddy and Mommy, I am leaving. For the sake of communism, we have no reluctance to go to all the corners of the earth."

The photo was taken in the summer of 1968 when I was going off to work on a tea farm near Mount Huangshan in Anhui Province. Fearing my parents would be saddened by my departure, I had this flamboyant photo taken by a schoolmate. I knew that as long as I appeared in high spirits, they would feel better.

My parents had asked for a leave from the May Seventh Cadres School, where they were supposed to be reforming themselves through labor. I pretended to be very relaxed and casually put the photo into my mother's pocket. She took it out and looked at it again and again before passing it to my father. He then looked at the front and back of the photo, examining it carefully, never raising his head to look me in the eye.

My school was very near to our home. Actually, we were close neighbors. Xiang Ming Middle school numbered 151 on the street, whereas our home numbered 157. The rebels in my parents' work units had put up many big-character posters at our door. Almost all my schoolmates came over to read the posters, which were full of accusations against my parents. During that period, I often received anonymous phone calls abusing my parents. I felt deeply insulted but could do nothing but remain silent.

Once work assignments for us graduates were made public, many of my fellow students started pestering our teachers with complaints about their difficulties in leaving Shanghai and requested to stay behind. I, however, did not hesitate.

An additional factor that prompted my decision to leave was that my younger sister was a graduate of the junior middle school attached to Shanghai Foreign Languages Institute. Like me, she was awaiting a work assignment. If I went to the countryside, she would have a reason to stay in Shanghai. I did not know, however, that she had already applied to go to an army farm in Heilongjiang Province in China's Northeast. The application was rejected despite the fact that she had written it in blood – by biting her own finger -- in order to show her resolution. Heilongjiang was a crucial border region for national defense, and she had failed to pass the vetting of her political background since she belonged to a "black" category – a daughter of a "Capitalist Roader". The tea plantation at Mount Huangshan had been a farm for reforming criminals which was later transformed into a *zhiqing* farm. Since no political vetting was required, my application was soon approved. The ultimate result was that I went to the tea farm in Anhui Province while my younger sister became a tender in a Shanghai textile mill. For our family, this seemed to be the best possible outcome.

Because the rebels in my father's work unit had sealed all the bookcases, cupboards, wardrobes and suitcases of all sizes in our house while our parents were away at the cadres school, I had to obtain a letter from our school to show them that I needed a suitcase for carrying my things to the countryside. A rebel there came over to unseal a suitcase for me. He spent much time in selecting one and finally picked up a small, worn suitcase. Seething with anger, I protested that it was too small, saying that I would settle down in the country and needed a much bigger one for carrying all my articles. With a cynical smile, he scolded me, saying, "You are going there to reform your ideology, not to enjoy life. Why do you need so many things?" Not wanting to court more trouble, I swallowed his humiliating words in silence. Later, I took the old suitcase with me and put some of my things in the luggage of my schoolmates.

The evening prior to my departure, my parents hurried back home from the cadres school. This was the first time for their eldest daughter to leave home. Many of my schoolmates came to bid me farewell. Our house became so crowded that some of them had to sit on the staircases. That night, none of us had a wink of sleep.

At three o'clock in the morning, I left home for the long-distance bus that would start our journey at five. Considering their own status as "Capitalist Roaders," my parents did not go to the bus station for fear of complicating my situation. They said good-bye to me at the door of our house. My father said aloud, obviously for our schoolmates to hear distinctly, "Xiaoying, you will be farther away from your daddy and mom, but closer to Chairman Mao!"

With a forced smile, I waved my hand at them in the same manner as I had done for the snapshot.

My schoolmates saw me to the bus station. As the bus horn sounded, tears began to stream down my cheeks and soon I burst into a heartfelt cry. Fortunately, my parents did not see the embarrassing scene of me breaking down. I wanted them to think that their daughter was tough and resolute, able to cross thousands of mountains and rivers, smilingly, and with a wave of the hand. ⸺·

2. To Remain Young After Treading on All Mountains

This photo was taken in the autumn of 1968, more than two months after I arrived at the tea farm.

In it I'm wearing a somewhat gloomy look. My depressed mood was not due to hardships, but to my worries about my parents, who were a thousand li away. Had my mother's wounds healed where rebels had kicked her in the waist? Would my father's hypertension recur due to repeated meetings of criticism against him? Could my elderly grandmother and my younger sisters manage to live on a mere monthly stipend of twelve yuan each? With clenched teeth, I could endure hardship and fatigue, but mental distress was harder to endure.

The tea farm at Mount Huangshan, despite its picturesque beauty, was by no means a Shangri-La. The smoke of "class struggle" rose and fell in an endless cycle. People remained jittery. Keeping aloof from each other, they were as guarded and isolated as if they were in their own little blockhouses.

The photo was taken by my younger cousin. A high school graduate in 1967, he had applied to go to Yunnan Construction Corps, which managed many army farms. At my mother's request, he made a detour to visit me. My mother used to seek his help whenever I or my siblings (we were all girls) had troubles. At the beginning of the Cultural Revolution, a group of rebels had their eyes on the house we lived in. They wanted to make it their headquarters. We were ordered to evacuate within three days. My cousin came to help us. Wearing an armband of the Red Guards, he gave a lecture to the rebels on policies and tactics that were the Party's lifeline, and he recited Chairman Mao's quotations without faltering. Seeing that they were no rivals to him in debate, the rebels went off, disappointed and crestfallen.

My cousin took a photo of me deep in the mountains, where he directed me to assume a heroic pose. He planned to send the photo to my mother, hoping that it would help set her mind at ease. The design of my pose was all his: A machete in hand, one foot set on a rock, I was supposed to be looking forward to the future with confidence and passion. He gave the photo a rather poetic inscription: "To remain young after treading on mountains". He had borrowed these words from the title of a Chinese novel about the epic Long March. Unfortunately, I was in a bad mood, and my facial expression was far from heroic.

My cousin had come on a day when we were assigned to collect kindling in the mountains in preparation for the severe winter. At that time, coal was still unavailable in this mountainous region. Our mess hall needed kindling for making meals and boiling water. Once winter set in, no transportation would be possible because of the heavy snow. So, immediately after harvesting tea in autumn, we spent much of our time collecting firewood in the mountains for the entire winter. This posed no problem for the strong *zhiqing* boys, especially those who had come earlier and knew the surroundings well. They often completed their quotas in half a day. After taking their meals at noon, they no longer needed to go back to the mountains. The *zhiqing* girls were physically weaker. To them, especially to new arrivals like me who were unfamiliar with the territory, gathering firewood was a difficult task. We didn't know which of the mountains had many groves of trees, nor did we know the easiest mountain paths leading to rich firewood sources. We often went into the mountains in the early morning, but still failed to complete our quotas when the sun was going down. First of all, we didn't know where to look for dense thickets. We could only cut a few small trees here and there. Gathering them together took much of our time and effort. Secondly, we didn't have the know-how for the job. After cutting down some small trees, we chopped off all their branches and tied the trunks into bundles. Then we used shoulder poles to carry them. The result was that our shoulders soon became sore and swollen, but when we turned in the firewood at our base, each of us was credited with only a couple dozen kilos.

In the days that followed, some *zhiqing* veterans showed us how to do the job. They told us we shouldn't chop off the branches, which could also be used as fuel. We only needed to tie the trunks of the cut-down trees into a bundle at the bottom end and leave the top end loose with all the branches. When we came down from the mountain, we just put the bottom end of the bundle on our shoulder while leaving the top end trailing on the ground. The weight on our shoulders was thus reduced by half. By making use of the resistance caused by the trailing part of the bundle, we could safely rush down the mountain with little danger of falling. With the extra weight of all branches, we could easily meet our production quotas. Gradually, we got the knack. The only secret the veteran *zhiqing* held back from us was the locations of the dense thickets, which were essential to their livelihood. As we became more acquainted with the mountains, we too had our own secret locations that were rich in firewood.

I had experienced several adventures in fulfilling my job. One day, when I was tying a bundle of firewood, I rolled down from a steep mountain slope along with the bundle. Fortunately, I had only a superficial injury. On another occasion, when I was cutting a branch off a tree, a swarm of hornets attacked me, leaving my face swollen for more than two weeks.

I was too eager to do my job well. Once I carried a bundle of firewood that was so big I had to alternate between walking and resting during my trip back from the mountains. As the mountain path dimmed after sunset, the dark forests around me produced a rustling sound in the wind. Scared and tired out, I sat on a stone slab and started crying. Members of my work team who passed by could not help me because they had their own loads on their shoulders. My boyfriend, who had stayed behind because he had stepped on a sharp bamboo stump, was recovering from his wound. On hearing about my problem, he took a flashlight and stumbled up the mountain. The two of us hauled the big bundle down together.

When my cousin visited, he accompanied me into the mountains. We gathered a huge amount of firewood. Dividing it into two bundles, each of us carried one back home. My quota was easily met. I asked my cousin why he had not come to Mount Huangshan, since the Shanghai authorities allowed his school to send some of its students here. Exhibiting his share of heroism, he said: "Huangshan is too close. I wanted to go to the frontier regions. The mysterious Xishuangbana (in Yunnan) is the place where I can bring my talents into full play." My cousin was more naive than I was. He later had many ups and downs in the Yunnan Construction Corps, and went through a number of ordeals. He now serves as a reporter at the Yangtze Evening News. When we get together, we often talk about our youthful days. More than once, when I asked him how he fared in Xishuangbana, he would answer me with a bland smile: "Let's look forward, not back." —

3. Flowers Bloom and Fall on Time

To begin with, I have to make it clear that this is not my wedding photo.

During the spring festival of 1971, my would-be husband and I took a leave from our farm to visit our families in Shanghai. By that time, we had just confirmed our relationship as lovers. To keep a souvenir, we went into a photo shop on Fuxing Middle Road and had this picture taken. We became quite nervous because we were too shy to let others know. We kept the picture to ourselves until we got married four years later. This was probably the most romantic episode in my love affair.

As far as I can remember, the education given me at school and by the society at large in my early teens encouraged me to ignore sexual distinctions. Equality between the two sexes was interpreted in those days simply as :

"Men and women are the same. What men can do women can do as well." We refrained from doing many things women usually did, such as having our hair curled, wearing make-up, or putting on fashionable, colorful clothes. This self-denial arose from fear of charges such as "behaving in the style of the capitalist class" or "echoing the sentiments of the petty-bourgeoisie". The beautiful word "love" had been distorted and become a dishonorable term. A boy in our high school had served as a cadre in the Communist Youth League. Living up to the image of a young progressive, he had helped many "backward" fellow students. Once, incidentally, he was found to be the secret admirer of a girl in his class. His reputation plunged in the blink of an eye. Denounced as a "stinking man" by girl students, he was soon removed from his post as a League cadre.

I went to the tea farm when I was already twenty years old, but I remained an ignoramus. Several close friends went there with me. During the Mass Exchange of Revolutionary Experience (*geming da chuanlian*), when young people enjoyed free train rides and went to all parts of the country to spark revolutions, my friends and I had made acquaintance of several very talented college boys. One of them secretly adored a friend of mine. On learning that we had come to the tea farm, he made a long trip to visit us. Once we became aware of his intentions, we began to regard him as a "criminal." Every one of us put on a stern face, refused to talk with him, and even rejected his request to borrow mess hall coupons from us. Our behavior embarrassed him badly. He was forced to leave, obviously with much pain in his heart. We never heard from him again. As a matter of fact, my friend actually had a fondness for him but dared not reveal her true feelings. Otherwise, she feared, we might laugh at or look down upon her. So she feigned to dislike him more than we did. With the passage of time, we began to realize how stupid, cruel and pitiful our behavior was!

After all, we were born women. Consciousness of femininity, long suppressed and benumbed, had been nurtured back to life by the creeping influence of literature. Books that were popular among us included Song of Youth, Tracks in the Snowy Forest, Builder of New Life, Sow Thistle Flowers, How the Steel Was Tempered and The Gadfly. I had shed tears over the failure of Lin Daojing's love for Lu Jiachuan, and heaved long sighs over the separation of Liang Shengbao and Mei Xia because of their different objectives in life. When Tracks in the Snowy Forest was circulated and read with great enthusiasm among my classmates, one of them was so obsessed by it that she kept holding the book until the next girl on the waiting list demanded its release several times. The second girl grumbled to others that the classmate who held back the book was a "nasty girl" who was interested only in the love affair of the protagonists. She took the folded page as evidence for her accusation. Consequently, all the girls in our class despised the book-holding classmate and considered her thinking "unhealthy". In actual fact, all of us loved to read the romantic episode starting from the folded page of the book, and the fold was never flattened.

I used to go with my mother to watch Shaoxing opera, a musical drama sung in a southern local dialect in which all roles are played by women. My mind was full of ancient tragic female characters in love stories, such as

Lin Daiyu, Zhu Yingtai and Cui Yingying. Far back in my junior middle school days, the teacher in charge of my class was so distressed to find this drift in me that he warned: "Wang Xiaoying, you are treading a dangerous path!" More than once the Communist Youth League tried to help me extricate myself from the quagmire replete with seductive "talented scholars and beautiful ladies". I repeatedly made sincere self-criticisms, but still could not resist the temptation. Behind the backs of my teachers and schoolmates, I stealthily took from my father's bookshelves works by famous dramatists of the Yuan and Ming dynasties, such as Wang Shifu, Tang Xianzu and Guan Hanqing, and read them voraciously.

Anyhow, in the face of repression, hindrances and travails, our emotions and passions gradually ripened until they reached full maturity. Flowers bloomed and fell on time. Suddenly one day, I awakened to find a bud of love in my heart. After going through rain and windstorms, I was finally able to reap the fruits of love despite the twists and turns of the road. ——

Buying A Swiss Watch
Across the Border

by Yang Luyong

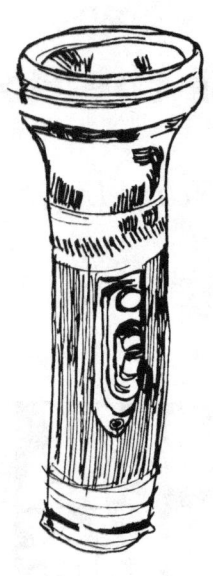

Soon after the autumn harvest in 1975, I was eager to go back to Chengdu on home leave, which was allowed only once in two years. The time for my departure was drawing near when Deming, a close friend who worked with me on a paramilitary farm in Longchuan County, Yunnan Province, came to see me, looking nervous. He told me that his family had sent him several catties of *tu-chung*, the bark of a small tree native to China that was highly valued as a traditional medicine. They wanted him to sell the stuff at a country fair across the Sino-Burmese border and use the money to buy a sophisticated Swiss calendar watch which he was to send back to Chengdu. The watch was intended as a "gift" to grease the palm of a key official in charge of transferring *zhiqing* back to urban posts.

Deming and I both knew that quite a few *zhiqing* had sold *tu-chung* across the border, but so far we hadn't become involved with such dealings. After some discussion, we decided to go to Wenbian, an acquaintance at the Dai minority village who was well-informed about trade across the border and had often visited the country fair on the Burmese side. He generously promised to take us along, but he said that we must go by way of mountain paths at night since *tu-chung* would be confiscated by plain-clothes Customs officials we were likely to encounter in the daytime.

One windy, moonless night, Wenbian led us toward the edge of the Longchuan Plateau and onto a mountainous caravan path through a dense forest. He held a flashlight, and Deming and I followed closely behind him. The path was barely visible in the dim light, and it grew increasingly steep and rugged. Wenbian had to use a sword to hack the undergrowth on both sides of the path. Deming and I kept tripping and falling as we scaled one peak after another. At about five o'clock in the morning, we reached the No. 71 Border Stone, which marked the boundary between the PRC and Burma.

We walked along a small path that extended into Burmese territory. When I crossed the international border for the first time in my life, my heartbeat quickened and my breathing became heavy. Nervous and excited, we felt dizzy, and our footsteps were unsteady.

In the fields far and near, numerous flashlights blinked in the bamboo groves as people came from all directions for the country fair. Along a street about a third of a mile long, bamboo booths had been set up and business had already started under hurricane lanterns amid the din of a large crowd. There was a wide range of commodities, mostly forest and native products and articles of daily use.

Wenbian gave us a few instructions before going about his own business. In front of a booth, a Burmese used fluent Mandarin to negotiate a deal with us. Eventually, we bartered five catties of *tu-chung* in exchange for a Swiss calendar watch and two pieces of Dacron. By now, it was already broad daylight. Business was reaching its peak, with more and more people arriving at the fair.

We were feeling happy and ready to leave after putting our exchanged goods into a bag when something unexpected happened. Several *zhiqing* from Kunming, the provincial capital, who had settled in villages in the border areas, were caught stealing goods from a street shop. A fistfight started between them and the local people. Knowing that they themselves were in the wrong, the Kunming *zhiqing* took to their heels. Deming, fearing that the two of us might be mistaken for members of the Kunming group, decided to run off with them toward the Chinese border.

Some Kachins and Jingpos, both of them ethnic groups of the border areas, took up the chase, armed with swords, shoulder poles and old-fashioned black-powder shotguns. When we were close to the border stone, a deafening sputter of shotguns erupted and Deming shouted in pain. He squatted down to cover his leg with his hands, blood streaming down his pants onto the ground. I hastened to help him get up and pulled him toward the Chinese side of the border.

Standing miserably by the side of a highway, we took a lift on an ox-cart that was carrying sacks of fertilizer to a paramilitary farm in Ruili County. The cart driver was a *zhiqing* from Chengdu like us. He transported us to a clinic on his farm. The medical orderly cleaned Deming's wound and wrapped it up.

My pale-faced companion was obviously too weak to travel with me for the rest of the arduous journey back to our own farm. He would have to stay behind until he had recovered. Because my home leave was already scheduled, I could not stay to keep him company. Before we separated, Deming delivered the watch to me, asking me to take it safely back to Chengdu and stressing that it was crucial to his transfer to an urban job.

I embarked by myself on the mountainous path that connected Ruili with Longchuan, believing that my memory would lead me back to our farm. However, I never anticipated that this narrow, rugged and tricky trail could have disappeared miraculously from sight after I had passed through the dense forest. Dusk was falling and I was afraid to go any farther. I decided to go back in the direction where I had gone for the country fair. But the farther I went, the denser the forest appeared, and the steeper the mountain slopes became. When the curtain of night shrouded the whole forest, I had completely lost my way.

Nighttime in the forest was like being in a den full of devils who used all their magical powers to frighten me. A howling gale arose from the mountains, wild beasts roared, dark animals scuttled by my feet, drops of something cold fell onto my neck. Seized by intense fear, I squatted under a tree, making myself as small as possible. With wide-open eyes, I waited anxiously for daybreak.

When morning came, I tried my best to orient myself and looked for the indistinct path that would lead me out of the forest. Instead, I either stumbled into a more convoluted labyrinth or returned to my original point of departure. Nightfall drove me to despair, and fear was replaced by loneliness, misery and grief. I broke into a loud cry. More strongly than ever, I missed my family, my companions at our farm and even the thatched shanty home I had so loathed. I made an oath then that if I could be lucky enough to get out of the forest, I would stay at the farm for the rest of my life rather than undertake stupid adventures like this one.

On the third day, I again spent long hours in hunger, exhaustion and despair. I knew I had taken another step toward death's door.

Awakened by the roar of wild animals at midnight, I instinctively climbed up to the top of a big tree. Only then and there did I discover a fire flickering in the distance. It had to be a bonfire lighted by the members of a caravan.

When I stumbled toward the bonfire, two Jingpo men jumped up and drew their swords, suspecting that I was a horse thief. After hearing my story, they offered me some pickles and rice wrapped in plantain leaves. This was the most delicious supper I had ever tasted in my life. After day-break, I followed the caravan out of the forest on foot and returned to my thatched hut by the side of the Nanwan River. As for the Swiss watch, it was confiscated by Customs offi-cials at a checkpoint on my way back to Chengdu.

I seemed to have awakened from a nightmare. The Swiss watch, which had cost my friend Deming's blood and almost my own life, now turned into a sheet of paper -- a certificate of confiscated smuggled goods. This painful experience helped me to see the true value and potential richness of life. To do labor was hard, but the effort was made on solid ground. Only by abandoning the pursuit of illusory things could we reap the fruits we hoped for. Perhaps this insight was the reward I received for working in the countryside as a *zhiqing*.

When I Was a Barefoot Doctor

by Zheng Tianxin

In 1969, I was sent down to work in a secluded village in Wuping County, Fujian Province. Though it was only a few hundred miles from my hometown of Xiamen, a major seaport city in southeastern China, in my mind it seemed farther away than the United States. The time I spent and hardships I went through to reach the village, and the difficulties in contacting my family after arriving there, were much more than those when I traveled to the United States many years later. The village was very poor. A strong farm laborer used to earn ten work-points per day, which were worth a mere 27 fen. When the peasants were to be remunerated at the end of the year, even if one had some surplus after deducting payment for grain, he or she would receive barely any cash. As *zhiqing*, we tried our best to do our work, with our skin sunburnt and our limbs bruised in many places. Yet without support from our families, we could not have avoided hunger and would have lacked clothing in winter. The limited amount of staple food provided us was actually taken from the rice-bowls of the local peasantry.

Our complete lack of independence tormented many of us. I was then twenty-two. I and several others belonged to a category called *laosanjie*, meaning junior or senior middle school graduates in the years 1966-68. We were older than many of our companions.

My father had been "put in a cowshed," a euphemism for compulsory confinement of people subject to criticism and investigation. My mother was a housewife. Driven by a sense of shame and helplessness, I wet my pillow with tears every night.

Our sufferings, though, helped us to mature. Besides learning from the peasants, the majority of us *zhiqing* were considering how to make the best use of our limited knowledge. Some strove to become good farm hands or village cadres. Some practiced singing and dancing in their spare time, hoping to join the so-called Mao Zedong Thought Propaganda Teams. Others tried to become village teachers or shop assistants at rural retail stores. As a daughter of a "bourgeois Rightist", I knew I would have no chance for such positions. When at school, I had loved mathematics and physics. But in the countryside there was not even electricity, let alone equipment for scientific experiments. After much reflection, I thought the only alternative for me was to become a barefoot doctor.

The countryside had an acute shortage of doctors and medical facilities. Women delivered babies on the bare earth in cowsheds. People had to cross steep hills and walk several miles to see a doctor at the commune clinic. Many diseases went untreated owing to poverty, inaccessibility or lack of medical knowledge.

I had studied acupuncture for three months at Xiamen Hospital of Traditional Medicine before going to the countryside and was a little more knowledgeable about health problems.

I shared my thoughts with my companions, all of whom supported me in my quest to become a barefoot doctor. They allowed me to try acupuncture or other traditional Chinese medicine on them. At the same time, they reminded me that if I became a barefoot doctor, there might be little chance for me to leave this poor village in the future.

On hearing my plans, my mother began to suffer from insomnia. By contrast, my father was very excited. He hand-copied some essays for me from ancient Chinese medical books borrowed from friends, such as "Rhapsody on the Nature of Medicine" and "One Hundred Verses on Concocting Chinese Medicinal Soups". My elder brother, who was in a far-away province, mailed me a copy of Handbook for Barefoot Doctors. This was one of the few books published in those days when it was widely accepted that the more knowledge a person had the more reactionary he or she would become.

My brother–in-law, who was a doctor, gave me a series of lectures through correspondence over a long time. During my home leaves, he taught me anatomy by using the bodies of rabbits and chickens.

The Party secretary of our production brigade was greatly concerned about how to run cooperative medicine. On hearing my idea, he immediately encourage me by saying: "So long as you work hard at it, the people of Luozu Village will never treat you badly."

He led me to a hut near a brook and told me that this was the site for the medical unit. The single-room hut was about 20 square meters, with earthen walls and floor. There were three old pieces of furniture: a table, a long bench and a cupboard. He handed me fifty yuan and said: "Keep this as the starting fund. Guard the money as a dead man would guard his coffin. I don't want to see cooperative medicine fail again."

I was careful about spending every fen. I made a wooden sickbed and a medicine chest all by myself. My companions helped me gather medicinal herbs on the hills. Stethoscope, acupuncture needles and other paraphernalia were all items I brought from home. I read again and again the Handbook for Barefoot Doctors and compiled a list of the basic medicines necessary for both medical and surgical uses and purchased them in small quantities. For each acupuncture treatment, I charged a fee of 2 fen. For prescription medicines, I charged an extra fee of 5 fen plus the cost of the medicine itself. The peasants were extremely poor in those days. They relied on work-points they had earned for their grain rations. They would sell one or two pigs they had raised during the year in order to meet expenses and buy new clothes for the Chinese New Year. They raised chickens with a one-chick-per person policy to earn money for salt, vegetable oil and other small household items. Some peasants could not even afford to pay the small fees charged at the clinic. They had to pay with eggs, which I then had to sell for cash in order to buy medicine.

A Chinese saying goes that new-born calves are not afraid of tigers. Displaying the same fearless spirit, I and a local barefoot doctor who worked with me shouldered the responsibility for dealing with all the health problems of our village. I took the Handbook with me wherever I went, making it the topmost item in my medicine bag. I placed myself at the beck and call of my patients and always went to see them without delay. After examining a patient, I would compare his or her symptoms with what was described in my books and then proceed to deliver treatment. I often stayed behind to observe my patient's reactions and to look up more instructions in my medical books. I departed only when I felt that nothing would go wrong with the patient. Probably because of the uncomplicated bacterial spectrum in the hills, the fresh air, the simple diet, and the type of labor-intensive farming using physical labor and primitive tools, the diseases prevailing in our area were not that varied. To my own surprise, I was successful in curing a great number of patients.

Gradually, folks outside of our village also sent for me. It often happened at midnight that someone would knock at my door. I would take my medicine chest, follow the visitor, and walk a few miles with a flashlight along rugged paths to see the patient. Some of my *zhiqing* companions, worried for my safety, would volunteer to accompany me in making the trip.

I also suffered many setbacks and failures. A country woman died painfully of a stroke in my embrace while I was looking on, completely at a loss for what to do. The first baby I helped to bring into the world was dead upon delivery.

I was then completely ignorant of issues related to childbirth. I only knew that instead of bearing children in a cowshed, women should deliver on clean beds. Publicity on hygiene was the best I could do when confronted for the first time with delivery problems.

One early morning, when I was combing my hair, a small boy in the village came hurriedly to my abode, saying that his mother was having labor pains, with the umbilical cord already coming out. I ran into their house and discovered that the lower parts of the baby were out while its neck and head still remained inside the vagina. I grabbed its body and tried to pull it out with all my strength, but to no avail. Panic-stricken, the woman's husband seized me by the waist and pulled me with great force. With a thumping sound, the bed on which the woman was lying collapsed. Once I came to my senses, I discovered that the woman had fallen to the ground while I was holding the dead baby high in the air. I felt such a deep sense of grief that I couldn't eat or sleep. To alleviate my fear and regret, the unfortunate woman sent me eggs boiled in rice wine for three days in a row.

People in the hills were grateful for my successes and tolerant of my failures. Instead of blaming me, they would console me. They showed great concern for me when I fell ill or was injured while working in the fields.

I tried to improve my professional skill as best I could. Whenever I had problems, I would go to the commune clinic to consult with doctors there. Doctors and nurses who had been sent down to the countryside from cities were also my good teachers. I made full use of my spare time to do more reading, especially during the slack season in winter. Besides medical books, I tried to read foreign novels with the help of dictionaries in order to improve my English. I began to feel life was rich and meaningful. My function and role as a barefoot doctor gave me courage and consolation. I no longer regarded myself as a burden to society.

In subsequent years, I had many opportunities to choose a new profession. But I never changed my mind: I wanted to be a doctor all my life. At the age of thirty, when I already had a young son, I went to study medicine at a medical college. At the age of forty, I traveled by myself to the United States to do advanced studies in obstetrics. My experience as a barefoot doctor in that remote village was the beginning of my life-long pursuit of a medical career.

Writing Chinese Characters

by Zhao Lihong

On a rainy day, when I was sitting in the office before a meeting of our production team, a wrinkled old woman staggered up and asked me in a low voice: "Can you write Chinese characters?"

I was confused by such a queer question. She should know that as a *zhiqing*, I must have received enough education to be able to read and write. She looked very serious, though, so I nodded to her.

"Then, can you write letters?"

Again, I nodded.

Her dull eyes sparkled. She then asked me hesitantly: "Can you write a letter for me?" While awaiting my response, she took out from her inner breast pocket two badly crumpled letters and said: "My son sent me these. I would like to send him a reply. Please help me. Will you?"

I readily agreed to help her. Her son was working away from home. He had sent the two letters at an interval of six months. In these brief letters, he reported only that he was healthy and had enough to eat, and he asked about his mother's health. This was what a barely literate peasant could have written to express his thoughts and feelings. Although his handwriting was rather poor and contained a few wrongly written characters, I was moved by the unadorned simplicity and sincerity of the letter writer. If he could receive a letter in reply from his mother, I thought, it would be a great consolation to him.

I took out my pen, found a sheet of paper, and improvised a table by turning a large, empty bamboo basket upside down. Now I was ready for her dictation.

"Tell him that I have no ailments or mishaps. I go out every day to work in the fields. At the end of each year, I will get some cash. Ask him to set his mind at ease, concentrate on his work, and not miss home." She stood behind me droning on for some moments.

I felt it was a bit absurd for her to ask her son not to miss home. I myself missed home every night. I couldn't help it.

"Do you miss your son?" I asked her

She replied with a wry smile, saying: "Of course I do. But I want him to work longer outside the village to earn more money. Otherwise, how can he find a wife?"

I finished her letter in no time, having tried to be concise in expressing her thoughts in her own tone. I read the letter to her. While she was listening, big tears flowed from her small, wrinkled eyes. After I handed the letter to her, she thanked me again and again as if I had rendered her a great service.

News about my letter writing soon spread among the peasants. Making a mountain out of a molehill, she had described me as a warm-hearted man of rare talent. Many more illiterate peasants came to visit, asking me to "write Chinese characters" (xiezi) for them. This was a broad term they used to cover everything that could be done with a pen or a Chinese writing brush. Things I wrote for them included letters, receipts and due bills, as well as couplets written on long strips of red paper that hung at both sides of a door on festive occasions.

My fame as a man capable of "writing Chinese characters" soon reached the ears of our production brigade leaders. They now regarded me as a talent whose potential could be tapped. They summoned me to their office and gave me my first assignment: the task of slogan writing.

During the Cultural Revolution, all cities had turned into "red seas", with walls of all public places covered with portraits of Chairman Mao, his quotations, and all sorts of revolutionary slogans, all done in red.

The same practice had come into vogue in the countryside. Take our own production brigade for example. Its office buildings, the threshing ground of our production team, and any other public place with white walls, were all covered with similar paintings, quotations and revolutionary slogans. But compared with the "red seas" of the cities, the countryside still lagged far behind. There were many blank spots not yet reached by the "red broom".

It was said officials from the commune were coming to our brigade on an inspection tour focusing on "revolutionizing the environment". A shock force was formed to eliminate blank spots before their arrival. I became a member of the team along with three others: a primary school teacher, an elderly gentleman who was good at Chinese calligraphy, and another *zhiqing*.

Riding on bicycles laden with paint pails and brushes, we went from door to door of the rural households looking for white walls. The most common slogans we wrote on them were quotations from Chairman Mao such as: "Never forget class struggle!" "Grasp revolution to promote production!" "Repudiate self and criticize revisionism." When we had finished writing on all white walls, we were instructed to "revolutionize" the roofs of all houses. Since this could not be done with roofs of the thatched huts, the black tiled roofs became the targets of revolution. Instead of red paint, we had to use whitewash so that our writing could stand out against the black background. Because of the enormous space we were to write on, we had to replace the painting brush with a sweeping broom, dip it in thick whitewash and attach it to a long pole. To reach the roofs, we had to stand at some distance and apply the broom from there. The slogans we wrote on the roofs were immense in size. Each character could be as large as two square meters. They were discernible more than a mile away.

However, there were many more blank spots beyond the walls and roofs. The "red broom" must now reach inside each and every household in search of them. The wall over the kitchen range was the most crucial place in any household. Peasants had been accustomed to putting a statue of the Kitchen God on the top of their range, or an image of that god on the wall above. The wall was usually painted with images of cranes in clouds, bats, ska deer and other Chinese symbols of good fortune and blessings. Soon after the outbreak of the Cultural Revolution, the kitchen god statues had been removed but the paintings remained. Since they belonged to the "old culture", peasants were now ordered by village cadres to whitewash them and replace them with Chairman Mao's quotations and revolutionary slogans.

Peasants had no aversion to our writing on their outside walls and roofs, since it added a bit of color to their houses and did no harm to their everyday life. It was a different matter when revolution penetrated inside their homes. Although the paintings on their kitchen walls had been done by local folk artists and were not very artistic, the peasants liked them because of the warm atmosphere they helped to create and the good omens of fortune, peace and blessings they represented. Now, they were to be replaced by cold-blooded slogans painted in red. People could not bring themselves to love such a change. I could detect their aversion in their unsmiling faces and their silence.

Standing on the clean top of a kitchen range and writing slogans on the wall, I felt guilty for my intrusion into other people's hearths, destroying objects they had loved. I reprimanded myself for playing such an abominable role.

Then I suggested to the brigade leadership that while writing slogans on their kitchen walls, we might try to embellish them with some painted designs. They accepted my suggestion, presumably because they themselves also liked paintings. When I was a boy, I had seen local craftsmen hand-printing bed sheets. Inspired by this experience, I started to work on a small invention. In addition to slogans, I cut flower and other designs on a pasteboard sheet to use as a stencil. Then I tacked the pasteboard sheet on the wall and sprayed different colors through the stencil openings. The result was a colorful painting of my own design alongside the slogans.

For peasants displeased by my previous work, I tried to compensate by adding a few pleasant paintings to their kitchen walls: a pine tree or a couple of wintersweets, a few cauliflowers, cucumbers or red peppers. My other favorites included a fish laid out on a plate, a flying crane or eagle in the sky, a sailing boat on a river or a lake. When applied to a freshly painted white wall, the colorful inks would gradually spread and fade. The result was very similar to a Chinese ink painting on a sheet of rice paper. My paintings looked so attractive that they were a pleasant surprise even to me.

I became a most welcome visitor to people's homes. Peasants began to treat me with sugared tea and cakes. Some brigade leaders who had new housing invited me to decorate their walls. To each of my paintings, I would attach my signature alongside a painted seal in the style of a professional artist. When I revisited these villages ten years later, I found that many peasants still kept my paintings on their kitchen walls. Children who had had to look up at my work back then had become adults.

After completing our rush job of painting slogans, I was assigned a new task, again one of "writing Chinese characters".

Our commune was going to convene a meeting of activists on the study and application of Chairman Mao's works in their everyday life. The head of a production team in our brigade was selected as one of the speakers at the meeting. He was a tall man about the age of fifty. Since his name was Gao (meaning tall), people called him Gao *duizhang*, the "tall team leader". He had attended primary school, and was able to read and write. But he had never drafted a speech. So the brigade Party branch decided to give this important job to me, thinking that a man able to "write Chinese characters" should be capable of writing anything.

I used to write many things down in my diaries -- my impressions of people, my feelings about the natural surroundings, my observations on life, etc. But I had never written anything on my studies of Chairman Mao's works, let alone others' experiences in studying them. I didn't know Gao, the tall team leader, nor did I know how he had studied Mao's works and applied them. But I could not refuse such an assignment.

I went to talk with Gao several times. I found him to be an honest man. He had played an exemplary role in working hard despite various illnesses. I asked him how he had studied Chairman Mao's works, but he wasn't able to say much. He only told me that he had read Chairman Mao's essays entitled "The Foolish Old Man Who Removed Mountains" and "Serve the People". I asked him to say more, but he simply responded by smiling at me with an honest, sincere expression in his eyes. When I pressed him further, he merely said, "Do what you think fit. Write whatever you deem proper."

This was truly challenging. I sat there a whole day without writing a single word. Then instruction came from the brigade leadership saying that I must hand in the draft speech the following morning. I had no alternative but to resort to my own imagination. That night, to keep myself awake, I washed my face with cold water several times as I wielded my pen under a flickering vegetable oil lamp. After writing several pages, I designed a climax for Gao's speech: After he had fallen ill during a busy season, Gao studied Chairman Mao's "The Foolish Old Man" on his sickbed. It was this essay that inspired him to overcome his illness and forget his ailments. At daybreak, feeling reinvigorated, he jumped from his bed, pushed the window wide open, and saw "the sunrise against the glowing rosy clouds in the east." I used many adjectives to describe the glorious scene at dawn in order to express Gao's excitement at the enlightenment triggered in him by reading Chairman Mao.

Early the following morning, I handed my draft speech to the brigade leadership. They praised it highly, far beyond my expectations. When it was passed to Gao, he raised no objections.

Gao went to the commune meeting in a new Chinese tunic suit. When he was bicycling past our brigade, I felt a bit jittery because I knew that he was carrying the speech text with him. I thought to myself, I had ghostwritten the speech for him out of my own imagination. Now he was going to deliver it at the meeting. Was this the proper way to do the job? I doubted it.

The meeting on the application of Chairman Mao's works in everyday life was a major event in the commune, and so a live broadcast of the event was arranged. While working in the fields, I listened to Gao delivering his speech with awkward pauses. He raised his voice when he came to the paragraph describing the great inspiration Chairman Mao's essay had given him that night and the excitement he had felt at dawn when he pushed open the window to watch the sunrise. It was funny to hear the many adjectives so often used by middle school students being read out by an aged voice.

I stood in the fields in silence and listened to his speech, my face reddening and my heart thumping. I felt I was playing a dirty trick on the good-natured team leader. The more he raised his voice, the more embarrassed I felt. Fortunately, none of the people around me noticed my expression.

Strangely, no one criticized me afterwards for having ghostwritten a bad speech. On the contrary, I began enjoying a modest reputation in the commune as someone good at "writing Chinese characters".

During my spare time, I also wrote a few news reports for the commune broadcast station. Sometimes I was even allowed to write during work hours, which was a good break from the physical effort.

At that time, broadcasts from the commune speaker system were the main source of information about the outside world for the villagers. When peasants around me heard my news reports being broadcast, they would speak highly of me. As for the old lady for whom I had written a letter, she would praise me before her fellow villagers whenever she had a chance, saying: "A scholar has come to stay in our village!"

The Feeling of Hunger

by Zhao Lihong

142

When my head began to swim, my vision blurred, my limbs felt powerless, and my stomach rumbled, I knew I was suffering from hunger.

I remember a folk tale I read when I was a small boy. It tells about two wealthy young fops who, fed up with all the enjoyments of life, wanted to know what the most painful thing in the world would be. One said it must be a knife cutting deep into the body. The other argued that to be burned by a fire would be more painful. Their conversation was overheard by a girl from a poor family who happened to pass by. Both of them were wrong, she said, and she claimed to know the correct answer. The two young fops asked for her answer but she refused to share it with them. They pleaded with her and swore that they would do anything for her if she would tell them the answer. With a smile, the girl said to them, "Stop taking food for three days. Then come back and I'll tell you the answer". After three days, the two young men came and prostrated themselves before her. Already knowing the answer, they described to her the terrible feelings they had after three days of fasting. The girl told them with a smile: "Now you know the meaning of hunger."

This folk tale kept recurring to me when I worked as a *zhiqing* in rural Yixing, an ancient town not far from Shanghai. I wondered why the feeling of hunger haunted me so.

The people of the village where I worked always had porridge for breakfast and supper, eating rice only at lunch. Probably because our toil from morning to night was too exhausting, or because I was growing, or because our diet had little meat, fat or oil, I seemed to have an insatiable appetite and felt hungry almost all the time. While working as an apprentice to Master Wei, a carpenter in the village, I felt hunger haunting me like a ghost. It started by rumbling in my stomach and then crept over my whole body -- penetrating into the skin, seeping through the spine, and gnawing at every nerve. My feet began to quiver and my hands trembled. My vision became blurred. I could not keep my hands steady while sharpening a knife or an axe on the grindstone. In sawing a plank, I would stray away from the chalk-line. I often struck my hand with the back of an axe when trying to make a hole in a plank by hitting the top end of a chisel. I could only stumble like a drunkard after a day's work when walking toward Wei's home, where I was given room and board. Along the way, all thoughts and images disappeared from my consciousness except a big bowl of steaming porridge.

Running Master Wei's household was Jin Xiuxiu, wife of his elder son. She was a rather pretty woman, but she was in fact a nasty person. Neighbors used to avoid her when she picked a quarrel and started cursing people in public. It was her job to make porridge for the family's supper.

Before the meal, she would untie her apron and throw it on the kitchen counter, then cast a patronizing glance at me and say with a snort, "Lucky for you someone else does the cooking!" I could only ignore her sarcasm and take a bowlful of porridge. I would sit outside on the stone slab beside the door and start wolfing down my supper, hoping to drive the demon of hunger away.

My stomach seemed to be a bottomless pit. Several bowlfuls of porridge still fell short of satisfying my appetite. I knew that my stomach was already completely full, but, strangely enough, I wanted to eat more.

One evening, I was sitting on the stone slab outside the door, enjoying the sunset glow and the view of distant hills, when a loud scream behind my back startled me from my reveries. It was Jin Xiuxiu, shrieking and clanging a ladle against an empty porridge pot. "Damn it!" She cried, "We've got a starving devil here! I put in three catties of rice to make the porridge, and now, it's all gone! Aren't you afraid of bursting your stomach open? You starving devil!" Her loud cries echoed throughout the village.

My head pounded, and I felt as if someone had pushed me into a fire. Hot tears welled up in my eyes. I felt like throwing up all the porridge I had eaten.

Someone behind my back patted me gently on the shoulder. I turned around to find that it was Master Wei's wife. She had an ugly, triangular face, so thin and full of wrinkles it looked like a withered leaf. Her small sunken eyes and two protruding teeth made the look of pity she gave me a bit terrifying. But she was an old woman with a golden heart. She said to me, her eyes radiating warmth, "Let her do all her shouting. Just ignore her. Eat your fill when you feel hungry." Her faint, slurred voice soothed and calmed me like a cool breeze from the lake.

Deep into the night, I couldn't fall asleep. Outside the window, there was a soft rustling sound in the wind. Was it a long sigh from the small trees by the lakeside, or the murmur of gentle waves on the lake? Behind a thin cloud, a crescent moon was peeping wearily at me with sleepy eyes but still I couldn't sleep......

How wonderful it would be, I mused, if people could stay alive without eating! Perhaps this would help them to do away with much suffering and trouble. What was the point of learning carpentry? Even if all the wood in the world were made into furniture, joy and contentment would never befall a hungry carpenter. If it were possible to invent a medication -- a single pill that would eradicate hunger and enable a man to do whatever he wanted to do with full energy -- I would give up everything and do my utmost to turn such a dream into reality.

But the demon of hunger never ceased to haunt me. Every morning, I got up from bed with an empty stomach. On seeing the steaming porridge in the cooking pot, fear and loathing arose in me. The utterance of "a starving demon" began to resound in my ears, shaming and tormenting me. One morning, Master Wei's wife approached me, her face wearing a mysterious smile. Usually, I helped myself to the porridge, but she seized the ladle from me. Her way of ladling seemed strange. She repeatedly stirred the porridge at the bottom of the pot as if trying to scoop something up.

"Here you are," she said, handing the filled bowl to me, that mysterious smile still lingering on her face. "Take your time. Don't burn your mouth." I took the bowl from her and stirred the porridge with my chopsticks. I felt something solid in the bottom of the bowl. There I found five white sticky rice balls. This had never happened before. I was in a daze when the old woman came over to me again. She gently stroked my shoulder with her skinny hand and said quietly to me, "Eat them up. They'll keep you feeling full longer."

My vision became blurry with tears, which soon dropped into my bowl. I couldn't taste the sticky rice balls. I only felt some warm, soft lumps of food going slowly and smoothly down to my empty stomach.....

From that day on, I always had some sticky rice balls in my porridge for breakfast.

I will never forget them. I have never eaten anything that

evokes such pleasant memories as those sticky rice balls, not even the most delicious delicacies. Regardless of whether I am hungry or full, I often think of them -- warm and soft -- with a thin, wizened face in the background that resembled a shriveled leaf

Collecting Kindling Barefoot

by Ma Zhong

艱苦樸素

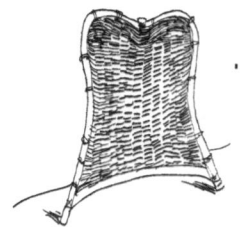

The place I was assigned to work was known as the Xie Family Slope, a village in Huanglong County, three hours' drive south of Yan'an. It was a sparsely-populated hilly area with many gullies and ravines. When I was there, a production team consisted of anywhere from a few to a few dozen households. Our village was a production team of twelve families with about 70 people.

My own family was based in Beijing. My father was the only job-holder, but he had many mouths to feed. I worried constantly about their livelihood from my place in the countryside, but I didn't hear from them for long stretches. My parents were illiterate and my siblings were too young to write.

One night, when drying my shoes beside a charcoal stove, I was summoned to a team production meeting. I thought it would be brief and left my shoes by the stove. When I returned, the room was full of thick smoke. My shoes were baked out of shape beyond usability. Since I had no money to buy a new pair of shoes and didn't want to ask my parents for help, I decided to live without shoes. My companions and villagers were shocked to see me going to work barefoot.

Plowing the fields or transporting manure was no problem. But going up and down the hills to do other jobs was difficult. Walking barefoot on gravel paths, though painful at first, was tolerable. The real trouble came from caltrop and other spiky or thorny plants growing profusely along the way. Once, when I went up the hills to gather kindling, I slipped down a rain-soaked slope and got a bad cut in my leg, shedding much blood. Worse, a spike from a broken tree branch sank deep into my bare foot. Unable to dislodge it, I stumbled home, carrying a bundle of kindling on my back. I then borrowed a pair of pincers from a villager and, with clenched teeth, managed to pull the spike out of my foot, which remained swollen for several days. Even during my recovery, I never missed a single workday, hoping that by the end of the year I would have some money to send home.

The first letter I received from home was penned by one of my former schoolmates. The letter itself contained only chitchat, but the envelope contained a separate note that said my father had fallen ill and had been absent from work for two weeks. My mother, it said, was extremely worried. She had begun to show signs of lunacy and become half-blind. My friend urged me to send them some money as soon as possible.

I became obsessed with the need to raise money for my family. I soon learned that the brick kiln run by our production brigade used to purchase kindling--sixty fen for 100 catties (equivalent to 50 kilos) of wet kindling or 80 fen for the same amount of dry kindling. I immediately found a grindstone to sharpen my axe. Next morning I went into the hills before daybreak. It was so quiet, I could only hear the occasional cries of owls, which were quite frightening, but thoughts of my parents' sickness emboldened me. I started working until I had collected two big bundles of kindling. Leaving one aside, I headed toward the brick kiln with the other on my back. My clothes were soaked with sweat when I arrived. The kindling weighed more than I had expected -- some 65 kilos!

I hurried back to the village just in time to join my companions and villagers going out to work in the fields. After doing my stint and taking breakfast, I went up the hills and carried the remaining bundle of kindling to the brick kiln. Again I hurried back to the village and, taking a bun with me, followed the others to the fields to continue our work. When lunchtime came, I went into the hills for the third time and returned with one more bundle of kindling. After taking a bite of food in the village, I again ran to the work fields. Such a maddening schedule, which meant walking barefoot some fifteen miles in addition to kindling collection and regular work, became my daily routine. Now much thinner, I added more calluses to my feet and more bleeding cuts to my legs, with a few wounds starting to fester. Despite my physical pains, love for my ill parents and hungry siblings prompted me to persevere.

Several months had passed when I fell sick. I never imagined that during my sickness a more severe blow would befall me. Somehow, the brigade leader was informed that I was selling kindling to the brick kiln. He severely criticized both our team leader and the brick kiln manager, saying that they had ignored the reeducation of sent-down youths to such an extent that "a capitalist tendency" had appeared among us. He asked our team leader to guide us youths to "fight against selfishness and repudiate revisionism" so that we would "cut off the tail of capitalism" with great determination.

Our team leader told me this news with a heavy heart. He said I could no longer go to the hills for my own collection of kindling. The kindling I had sent to the brick kiln, which amounted to approximately 5,000 kilos, would be confiscated. In addition, I would have to do a thorough soul-searching at the next meeting.

The collected kindling, the fruit of my sweat and blood, did not bring me a single copper in return. Instead, I was denounced as "an example of selfishness" and "a typical person refusing to cut off the tail of capitalism". I went through several criticism sessions. For quite a long time, I couldn't raise my head to face people. But inside, I felt greatly injured by such injustices.

Fun in Inner Mongolia

by Yang Li

During the Cultural Revolution, I spent four years as a *zhiqing* working on the grasslands of Inner Mongolia. I experienced hardships and distress as well as joys and happiness. In writing my reminiscences, I would rather recall the fun than the woeful experiences.

The Mobile Toilet

The first day we arrived at a pastureland in Xilinguole League, where we were assigned to live and work, the production brigade to which we belonged held a struggle session against the so-called "hostile elements of four kinds". Seven or eight such "hostile" people stood in a line against the front wall of the brigade office. The two women among them were said to be wives of former herd-owning exploiters. Besides commune and brigade officials, present at the meeting were a few dozen herdsmen and about 50 *zhiqing*. We all sat on the ground facing the "hostile elements". Representatives from the people's side, including one from the *zhiqing*, spoke in turn. None of the *zhiqing* there had learned the basics of the Mongolian language, so we could hardly understand a thing. Nevertheless, we sat still as if we were listening attentively, to show our enthusiasm and our firm stand in the class struggle.

As the vehemence of the speakers came to a climax, one woman standing against a wall suddenly squatted on the ground with her long robe hanging down around her. We wondered what she was going to do. After a while, she stood up. Only then did we realize that she had just urinated right there before the audience. We were stunned. I looked around. Excepting us *zhiqing*, everyone present sat still as if nothing

157

had happened. We began to exchange whispers. A few female *zhiqing* among us bent down their heads, as if they themselves had done something wrong.

It was not long before we learned the rationale behind this Mongolian habit. Unlike most regions of China, Inner Mongolia had large open territory and was sparsely populated. People there traveled on horseback and lived in yurts. There was no necessity to set up toilets on the vast grasslands. A Mongolian robe was useful in many ways, which included protection against cold and serving as a mobile toilet. However, it took some time for us *zhiqing* girls to get used to such a convenience.

Riding on a Ram's Back

Soon after our arrival, two other *zhiqing* and I were assigned to work at a sheep breeding station. To improve the local species of sheep, five Australian rams had been imported to breed with the ewes. The rams cost more than ¥1,000 per head, which was more expensive than a good horse. Enjoying first-class treatment, the rams were fed with corn and carrots. We had never once seen any such vegetables at our meals. The carrots looked so alluring that probably more than half of them went into our bellies.

We would take the rams for walks every day and graze them on the pasturelands until they were needed for insemination. One day, I was put in charge. Since this was my first time alone on the grassland with the animals, I found the experience exciting at the start. But after some time, I began to feel bored. There was no one to talk with. It was so quiet around me, I wondered whether I had gone deaf. I uttered a few shouts to make sure that I had not lost my hearing. Then I sang a couple of songs. At this moment, a ram came over and raised his head, looking at me curiously. I caressed his head and found him very docile. Then I grasped his horns and straddled his back. I never imagined that a ram could be so strong. He walked around with me on top for a while, and when he stopped walking I got on another ram. I found it so amusing that I did the same with the rest of the animals.

At noontime a herdsman came over for me to take the rams to the breeding station. After delivering them, I went away to drink tea. I soon heard people at the station arguing heatedly over something. I went to investigate and found all the rams standing there still. They seemed confused or sick. Showing no interest in the ewes, they were obviously not ready for mating. A herdsman asked me in Mandarin: "What's wrong with the rams?" My heartbeat quickened. I didn't dare to tell them what I had done to the rams, fearing that I might be charged with the crime of sabotaging production. "I don't know. They were all right a while ago," I murmured. People at the breeding station could do nothing but give up.

As a 17-year-old girl, I did not understand why this had happened. Not until much later did I realize that they all failed to rut because I had tired them out.

Getting Water from a Well

On the grasslands, drinking water had to be drawn from a well. One day during our first winter there, a *zhiqing* girl went with me to a well to fetch water. It was a freezing cold day. Since each of us wore a new, long, fur-lined robe and thick felt boots, we didn't feel cold. I was responsible for drawing water from the well with a canvas pail and delivering it to my companion. She would pour the water into a big vat placed on an ox cart. Owing to lack of experience, we spilled some of the water over our boots and forgot to hitch the ox to a post. Probably losing patience with us greenhorns, the ox pulled the cart off. We wanted to chase him and bring him back but discovered that we couldn't move -- the spilled water had frozen our boot soles firmly to the platform around the well! We tried stepping out of one boot at a time and yanking it from the platform, but to no avail. Neither could we go back without our boots on in such cold weather. Frightened, we shouted desperately for help, but there was not a soul to be seen in the wilderness. We were ready to burst into tears when, half an hour later, a herdsman on horseback passed by. Finding us in such a ridiculously awkward situation, he rode back to his home to fetch a shovel. Laughing heartily, he cut loose the ice under our boots with the shovel and soon released us from the platform.

Adventure on a Camel-Drawn Wagon

We *zhiqing* lived to the west of a long stretch of lowland that separated us from the office of our production brigade in the east. One evening, a small group of us *zhiqing* girls got into a camel-drawn wagon taking us to the office to see a film. The wagon driver was a herdsman who sat on the humped back of the camel. After the film show, we learned that the herdsman had some errand to do the following day and needed to stay there overnight. I plucked up my courage and volunteered to drive the wagon home. The herdsman agreed to this because, he said, the camel was good-tempered and knew its way back.

The night was pitch dark. I climbed onto the camel and turned around to look at my four companions. They were almost invisible in the darkness. The first leg of our journey went quite smoothly. Soon after we entered the lowland, however, the ground became rugged and I soon lost my sense of direction. The camel stumbled along, growling all the way. I couldn't sit steady, shifting to the left and then to the right, always in danger of slipping off. I was terrified. A person could be severely injured falling off a camel! I held fast to the hump, sweating profusely. Thank heaven, the wagon eventually came out of the lowland and approached our yurt. Greatly relieved, I got down from the camel's back, only to find that not one of my companions was on the wagon. All four had been jolted off. I ran to the edge of the lowland and shone my flashlight. After some time, all four girls came up. Some of them had gotten a lot of dirt on their garments. One had a sprained ankle. I was a bad wagon driver, they said, complaining that I had not only jolted them off the wagon, but had ignored their shouts for me to stop. I begged their pardon and explained that I had not heard anything. Most likely it was because I had been scared out of my wits. In the meantime, the camel sagged its thick eyelids as if it were laughing at me in secret: If you weren't up to it, why did you volunteer to be my guide?

My Narrow Escape from Disaster

by Wu Xiaoge

The place I was sent to work was a secluded, backward mountain village in Xinhua County, Hunan Province, Central China. During my stay there, the most unforgettable event was an assignment given me on a dam construction site where disasters befell many youngsters like me.

In the early winter of 1972, I was instructed by our production brigade leader to go to a working site on Chetianjiang, a small tributary in the Yangtze River system not too far from our village. Along with me were sent many young males from other villages in our commune. I was full of expectations because, as a corvée laborer, I could eat my fill. I was then nineteen.

Chetianjiang was a small river only a few dozen meters wide. It slithered down slowly like a silver ribbon through gorges with high, steep mountains on both sides. The local authorities had designed a reservoir by building a big dam for generating hydro-power and irrigation. The basic idea was not a bad one. The problem was that the building material had to be blasted out of the mountains on both sides of river. After each blast, some of the rocks would become loose. They might roll down at any time from the heights, posing a great danger to the laborers who were transporting the rocks from the ravines to the dam building sites.

Leaders of the construction headquarters were well aware of the danger. But at that time, only politics and class struggle were given prominence. Human lives were as worthless as dirt. The principle of "people foremost" was put forward only many years later. So, the only thing the leaders did in dealing with that danger was to prepare a batch of coffins in a nearby warehouse. The coffins were a ghastly sight, lying there quietly awaiting their masters.

Thousands of young people about my age had come to the riverside which, though picturesquely beautiful, posed this potentially fatal threat. There were more than a hundred from our commune. We lived in peasant homes, a few dozen of us sleeping on the floor of each room. We were awakened before daybreak. Rubbing our sleepy eyes and carrying our tools on our shoulders, we went to work on the construction sites and did not come back until dusk. Instead of eating my fill as I had expected, I found out that food was rationed on the construction site. At mealtime, our cook would pour a ladle full of rice into the earthen bowl held by each of us, adding a few pieces of pepper and other vegetables, which we would finish in no time.

Once, a member of our young work crew had stomach trouble and didn't want to eat, while several of us still felt hungry after taking our meal. He pointed at the highway ahead of us and asked us if we would like to enter a race, with the winner to take his share of food. No sooner had he said this than several of us started running like mad. I emerged the winner despite my small stature. But because I had over-exerted myself, I fell at the last moment. Blood dripped from my arm and my legs. Holding that bowl of rice, I felt tears streaming down my cheeks.

At first my job at the construction site was earthwork. Though very tough and exhausting, it was safe. Later I was transferred to a transportation team. It was the most danger-ous of all the jobs. With a pair of us in the front and another pair in the rear, the four of us used to carry a big rock tied up with thick iron cables. Our destination was the worksite where the dam was to be built. Although there was always a respite between one rock blasting and the next, no one could tell when the loose rocks would fall off the steep mountain face. I myself witnessed many times scenes of human bodies being smashed apart and strewn in all directions by huge falling rocks. There were even instances of bodies squeezed between two fallen rocks so that a new dynamite blast was needed to take out whatever was left of the bodies. There were casualties almost every day. During that period, I saw more than ten deaths with my own eyes. The whole worksite was filled with terror. I lived in constant fear, never knowing when a disaster might befall me.

Surely enough, it happened one afternoon. As usual, the four of us were trudging through a ravine with a heavy load--a rock weighing about six hundred pounds suspended from thick shoulder poles. Suddenly we heard a loud voice shouting "Run for your lives!" Raising our heads, we saw that a big rock had just slid off the mountaintop and was rolling down toward us. We threw down our poles and hid ourselves behind the rock, not daring to move an inch. After making a loud thumping sound, the big rock flew over our heads and then we felt a strong quiver of the earth at our feet. It took us quite a while to stand up, only to find that just close by, the rolling rock had made a deep depression in the ground where it had landed. The rock we had been carrying had broken into several pieces. We would have been killed if we had not put the rock down and used it as a shield. No longer able to stand such horrors, I said to my companions: "We've narrowly escaped death. It's about time to quit working. Let's leave early."

I never expected that this initiative of mine would land me in trouble. Soon after supper, we were notified that there would be a meeting that night and that I above all must be there. I sensed that something bad would happen to me.

When I entered the conference room, I saw Party Secretary Liu of our commune standing with arms akimbo under a hurricane lamp. He glared at me with great hostility. When the more than one hundred laborers from our commune had all arrived, he opened his speech by saying, "Do you know what this meeting is for? Tonight, we'll teach a good lesson to that son-of-a-bitch, a lesson that will touch his very soul. He was so audacious as to have incited our class brothers to a strike. His father is a notorious bourgeois Rightist....."

His speech was followed by a lot of slogan shouting and abuse. I was pushed to stand in front of the crowd. Someone slapped me in the face. Confronting denunciation and criticism, I remained silent throughout the session.

I was recently told that Secretary Liu had died the previous year at the age of seventy-five. I no longer bear him any grudge, but I cannot help wondering whether, before he died, he ever thought about Chetianjiang River, whether he ever thought about a young man whom he had denounced and humiliated, whether he ever thought about the young lives that had been destroyed by the flying rocks?

The day following the denunciation meeting against me, as I came back from the construction site, I cast a glance at the small convenience shop near our dormitory. The young woman shop assistant was looking at me. Seeing no other people around, she asked me in a low voice, "Did they hold a denunciation meeting against you last night?"

I answered with a nod.

"It isn't a big deal," she said, "I know you're a nice guy. Heaven will bless you."

Suddenly, I felt a strong warm flow surging in my heart.

I couldn't believe my ears. Since my arriving here, I had taken notice of this girl. She was very pretty. Though her job was much sought after, I could tell from her sad eyes and pale face that she was not happy.

Spring came around after six months. During this period, I went through many ordeals. Because I was good at transplanting rice seedlings, our production leader called me back to our village. I managed to leave that terrible place at last. My grandmother, who had been expecting me all the time, cried when she saw me walk into the house. She looked me over, touching me from head to foot. She sobbed, "At long last, you're back. Every day, I prayed for god to protect you. Heaven surely has a clear vision." I couldn't hold back my tears.

Several decades have passed since then. I often dream of those mountains with their strangely shaped rocks. Were the coffins in the warehouse all used up: Has Chetianjiang River retained its original beauty? More importantly, do our countrymen in the People's Republic of China know the full story of what happened up there?

II. Relationships with Local People

A Flurry of Snowflakes

by Ye Tan

I woke early to find the streets covered with snow. A few flakes were whirling in the air. The whole of New York City was still asleep. The lights in the nearby skyscrapers had probably been on all night. At this moment, my thoughts flew across the Pacific, paused over Beijing, and then settled on the rugged grasslands of Inner Mongolia.

In the autumn of 1968 I got to know Dagula, a Mongolian woman with whom I and several other *zhiqing* were assigned to work herding a flock of sheep. Before we met her, a leader of the production brigade warned us that her husband was a member of an allegedly separatist organization called Inner Mongolian People's Revolutionary Party. He had been put into custody and was undergoing reform through labor. The leader instructed us to keep a line drawn between her and us.

Our journey started with an ox-cart caravan going toward her yurt. She came from afar to greet us, saying "*Sai-nu, sai-nu!*" (Wish you well!), but no one responded to her greetings. She was about thirty, wearing a pink Mongolian robe that fit her well, with a purplish girdle tightened around her waist. Her black Mongolian boots were also decorated with purplish lining. Slightly taller than average, she had typical Mongolian features: high cheekbones, a straight nose, chin protruding a bit forward. Her tanned, reddish face suggested good health and her big, brown eyes with long lashes seemed always to be smiling.

Quite strange, I said to myself, Her husband was arrested only a few months ago, yet she shows no hostility toward us outsiders.

Dagula seemed to sense rejection from us and stood aside for a while, but when we started setting up our yurt, she came to our aid. We didn't spurn her offer because we didn't know

175

how to pitch a yurt, and had no more experience with construction than small children with building blocks. Pleased, she shouted to her children to come out of the yurt to help us. There were four of them, two boys and two girls. The eldest was a boy about thirteen or fourteen. The youngest, the other boy, was only two years old. His name was Ailibu. I liked him best – he was such a cute child. He toddled along like a teddy bear. Not yet sure of his steps, he helped by tidying up after us.

When the yurt was completed, we were all very excited. I raised Ailibu in the air. He struggled to get away from me and ran toward his mother. A smiling Dagula picked him up and, pointing at me, said something to him. Since my Mongolian language was very poor at the time, I could only understand a single word that she spoke: "Sai-hun", which meant "good guy".

We had just awakened when we heard someone knocking at the door the following morning. It was Dagula. Smiling, she held out a fragrant plate of cheese with a thin layer of sugar on top. We were astounded by her gesture of goodwill because we had been warned about "sugar-coated bullets," a well-known term used by Mao Zedong to signify the danger of being corrupted by unarmed class enemies after the victory of the revolution. We waved our hands to express our refusal. Obviously, she knew what we meant, but she seemed incapable of understanding why these teenage students from Beijing refused to eat her cheese. Was it because we thought the cheese was dirty or tasted bad? She used various gestures and facial expressions to explain that the cheese was fresh, tasty and wholesome. We got what she meant but missed the fact that her goodwill was real -- it came from the bottom of her heart. After our rejection of her offer, we asked her to leave. She went back, and, standing in front of her yurt, shook her head.

After learning about the event, one of our leaders gave us a long lecture, saying that our action was correct. The intention of Dagula, he warned us, was to bribe us, and we should avoid falling into her trap. He also assured us that if we persisted in this admirable behavior, we would be absolved of the evils caused by reading too many books, and would overcome the bad influence of our parents, who were all bourgeois intellectuals.

Not long after that, we noticed that there was a flagpole in front of Dagula's yurt. In this border region of China, each household with a trustworthy family background (i.e., herdsmen, not the exploitative herd owners – Ed.) had a national flag fluttering in front of their yurt. Obviously, people like Dagula were disqualified from flying a national flag. But no one could prevent her from putting up a flagpole. What she hoped for, I presumed, was to create the impression that their family members were "good guys" who possessed a national flag but were not displaying it at the moment for some reason (say, because their flag needed to be washed).

An old saying goes: "Beyond the Great Wall, autumn begins with a cool September when grass starts to wither." The same is true with winter, which comes to Inner Mongolia much earlier than it does in Beijing. When people in the national capital go to the Western Hills to enjoy the sea of red maple leaves, Inner Mongolian grasslands are already covered with thick layers of snow. But our local leaders, who were preoccupied with class struggle issues, failed to remind us in autumn to collect dried ox dung, which would be our essential fuel for the long winter. One day, after herding our sheep, we came back to our yurt, only to find that we had no more fuel to cook our meal, let alone to heat our home. We looked at one another, wondering how we could pass the severe winter without any fuel. It was precisely then that Dagula came to knock at our door. None of us responded, since we were all in a bad mood. She knocked again. I was the one who finally opened the door. An aroma of cooked beef assailed my nostrils. This time, we could no longer resist her "sugar-coated bullets". Dagula sat and watched us devouring our meal. She began talking and gestured to us to fetch fuel from her big pile of dried ox dung. We readily did so, consoling ourselves by saying that we would return the same amount of fuel to her afterward.

A subsequent event made me feel close to Dagula. It happened on a day shortly after we had moved to a new pasture. I was herding the sheep on my return trip when a snowstorm arose. With the wind blowing hard, our sheep moved rapidly leeward, making it hard for me to guide them. It was already dark when the storm stopped, and I had lost my way. I took the saddle from my horse and was ready to stay overnight in the wilderness with the sheep. Before long I spotted a light in the distance. I initially mistook it for starlight, but when I saw it flickering, I realized that it was a flashlight. I rode my horse in that direction, only to find it was Dagula, who had walked several miles to look for me. She had to travel on foot because as a member of a "counter-revolutionary" family, she was not entitled to ride a horse.

I slipped off my horse and literally jumped for joy. Dagula smiled, her eyes narrowing. She then turned around to shout in different directions: "I've got it! I've got it!"

Puzzled, I asked her: "What have you got?"

She flashed her light at me and said with a smile, "I've got you!"

Before long, several of my *zhiqing* companions came on horseback from different directions.

They asked Dagula to go ahead with me on horseback while they would take care of the sheep and herd them home. They had not had time to cook, they said, and asked me to take supper with Dagula.

When we arrived at Dagula's yurt, her elder son, who was also out looking for me, had not yet returned. The three younger children stood in a row in front of their yurt to welcome us, holding flashlights. On entering the yurt, Dagula discovered that the beef had been overcooked and partially scorched. She raised her hand to beat the children, but I stopped her, assuring her that the beef was still edible. Dagula said apologetically to me: "I beg your tolerance."

Her words tormented me deeply. In fact, it was Dagula who had shown great tolerance to us despite all the troubles we had caused her.

The region where we worked and lived shares several hundred miles of border with Mongolia. If local inhabitants wanted to cross the border in order to live in Mongolia, there was no way for the Chinese border forces to stop them. One day, I asked Dagula in secret: "Since they treat you so badly, why don't you leave this country to join your uncle on the other side of the border?"

"What?" She seemed stunned.

I repeated my query to her.

She appeared to have lost her usual composure. Looking at the sheep in the distance, she said slowly: "Leave here?

Where could I go? This is my home!"

On hearing her words, I could not but cast another glance at the bare flagpole.

I always refrained from sharing my views about Dagula with outsiders, thinking this would be safer for her as well as for me. I never anticipated that Dagula would talk gladly to others about her good relationships with us. One that she spoke to was a Mongolian man with a single eye. His vision may have been impaired, but he was keen-sighted in detecting current trends in class struggle. He reported Dagula's words to the leadership. An enraged leader immediately gave orders that we move our yurt away from Dagula's and work with another family of pure class origin.

The night before to our departure, without speaking a word, Dagula milked our cow and helped us to pack up and load some of our belongings on our ox-cart. She knew that she was to blame for our unhappy separation. Before she left, she gave us several horsehair nooses for keeping lambs in place. She had made them the previous night. She also presented us with her big shepherd dog, which used to keep night watch for her family. I expressed our thanks to her, to which she responded with a forced smile. Then she turned around and whispered something to her youngest child, Ailibu, and pushed him toward us. The small boy toddled to me and asked in the Mongolian language, "Tell me what you think about us: good guys or bad guys?"

I raised my head only to see Dagula standing about a dozen paces away and looking at me. Since I had just been reproached by our leaders and still bore some resentment toward Dagula, I merely picked the child up and played with him, ignoring the question. After a while, Dagula came over to me. She pointed at Ailibu and the three other children in the distance, put her hand on her chest, and then asked me in awkward Chinese: "Us.... good guys or bad guys?" I don't remember exactly what I mumbled, but I definitely didn't say: "You are good guys." I was afraid that she would again pass my words on to others.

The following day, it began to snow. Dagula rose very early. She helped us to dismantle the yurt, load the pieces onto the ox-cart and harness the animal. Everything was ready in a short time. The big shepherd dog was wailing at Dagula from the rear of our cart. Dagula and I looked at each other in silence. Snowflakes were falling on her hair, cheeks and eyelashes. Only then did I realize that within the past year or more, she had become so much older. Her eyes had once shone with vigor and hope, but now they appeared listless and weary, full of anxiety and doubt.

We passed over one slope, then another, and I could no longer see her yurt. Only the bare flagpole out front was still visible, standing lonely in the wind and snow. I felt an impulse to jump off the cart, run back to Dagula's yurt and tell her: "You're good guys!" But finally, I didn't budge, allowing the cart to carry me to a remote place.

Soon after our separation, I was already planning my visit to Dagula during next year's Spring Festival, an occasion when local folks traveled on horseback to visit their old neighbors and enjoy each other's company.

The Inner Mongolian grasslands were really immense. Almost nine months had passed without my seeing Dagula, and during the interval, I heard news about her only occasionally. Nothing seemed to have changed much about her family.

At long last, the Spring Festival arrived. I mounted a horse to travel to Dagula's yurt. When passing our production brigade headquarters, I spotted Dagula's husband, who had just been released from custody. The "treasonous organization" he was alleged to be a member of proved to be non-existent. The official statement on his case said that "his arrest was justified; his release is also justified." I didn't care about the logic or illogic of the statement. I just wondered why he had not gone home. While other people were playing a guessing game during a drinking bout, he stood aloof, looking dazed, holding a bowl of liquor, his eyes streaming with tears. I inquired among the others and was stunned to hear that Dagula had died of illness the week before.

It was incredible, but there was no doubt about it: Dagula was dead. She had left this world. The god of death had relieved her of all the hardships, humiliation and worries that had tormented her in life.

A few decades have passed since then. Whenever I recall the events of those years, they appear in my mind's eye like a dream. But they are not a dream. Whenever I see snowflakes, I will think of Dagula's inquiring eyes at the time of our separation. Deep in my mind, I have repeated numerous times the words that I should have uttered but never did.

....  ....

The Issue of Survival

by Liang Limei

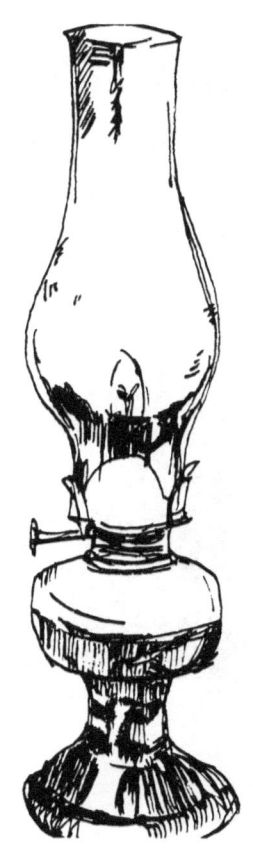

When we *zhiqing* received grain from the local production team, we might as well have been snatching food from the mouths of the peasants. We were an extra burden that aggravated their food shortage. Grain was so vital to their survival, many peasants could not understand why we had been sent there. No wonder some of them were hostile to us. The problem became especially acute during the spring when some peasants had consumed all their grain before harvest time and had no cash to buy food. To keep from starving, they had to eat pumpkins, sweet potato vines and wild vegetables.

One day, at the entrance of the village, I met a peasant woman whom villagers called Third Sister. I greeted her and asked her where she was going.

"Out begging," she answered with a forced smile.

"You must be joking." I said, astounded.

"No, it's true," she said to me with a serious look, "I need to go out begging. My mother-in-law is getting old and deaf. She has trouble with her legs and can't walk far. My children are still young. I don't want them to lose face. That's why I don't bring them along. We have only a small amount of grain left. I need to give it to them, or they won't survive until the new harvest comes in."

She wept, and I could see from her typical beggar's outfit that she was perfectly serious about the begging: She carried a large, crudely-made porcelain bowl in her basket, and a stick in her other hand – the kind that beggars used to fight off attacking dogs.

I was suddenly overcome by guilt. Only a few days before, she had given me two pieces of bread made from wild vegetables, rice husks and rice flour. I had praised their good taste, without knowing that her family was facing the threat of starvation.

I immediately ran back to our dorm and returned to her home with four packs of dried noodles I had brought back from my hometown, Xiamen. After a couple of days, when I went to the supply and marketing co-op to buy kerosene, I saw four packs of dried noodles on the counter. Out of curiosity I asked Li the shop manager, "Do you sell these Xiamen dried noodles?"

Li told me that Shengzai, husband of Third Sister, had come to barter these noodles for salt.

"What did he get for them?" I asked Li, wanting to know why Shengzai had bartered noodles for salt instead of eating them,

"Shengzai wanted to barter four packs of dried noodles for ten catties of salt. I agreed to give him only eight catties," Li said.

"A pack of dried noodles is four times the value of one catty of salt. You only gave him eight catties of salt for four packs of dried noodles. You cheated him!" I shouted.

"Huh, his family can hardly afford regular meals, let alone eating noodles," Li responded with a sardonic smile. "You rich people don't know the hardships of poor folk. We mountain folk can do without noodles, but we cannot do without salt. You may think I cheated him, but I'd like to see you behave more like a philanthropist. Let me tell you: Shengzai is sick. He has no money to see a doctor, not even the cash to buy salt. You come from a family of returned overseas Chinese and must certainly have a lot of money. Why don't you give them some of your money to spend?"

Meeting with such a rebuff, I felt both ashamed and annoyed.

I felt ashamed because of my complete lack of understanding with regard to the hardships of the peasants. For example, only several days earlier, Spring Fragrance, the daughter of a villager named Lin, had come to me with five eggs. She wanted me to buy them at eight cents each. It was also my wish to buy them. But thinking this might lead to gossip about me among the peasants, I told her that I had no money.

The gossip had centered on what was meant by "returned overseas Chinese". Spring Fragrance's mother ventured to explain that any returned overseas Chinese must be a capitalist. When people said they didn't understand what a capitalist was, she answered, "A capitalist is a landlord with a lot of money."

To have villagers commenting on my family background was what I feared most. Belonging to a family of returned overseas Chinese had brought me many more troubles than the average *zhiqing*. Since I could not explain things clearly to people around me, I just said to them repeatedly, "I'll prove by my actions that I am a daughter of the laboring people."

That was why I lied to Spring Fragrance about having no money. But she was reluctant to leave. When she saw some small change on my windowsill some moments later, she was thrilled and shouted, "Little Liang, you've got some money here!"

The coins added up to only thirty cents. Cruelly, I said to her, "This is all I have. If you insist on selling your eggs to me, I can only pay you six cents each." Not daring to make the decision herself, she ran back to ask her mother. Because they had run out of salt, her mother agreed to my offer. After the event, I often felt sorry about what I had done. Three decades have passed since then, yet I still feel guilty about my unkindness toward that small girl.

What annoyed me most was the harassment I suffered from the village accountant. A crafty man, he would show "concern" for me each time I returned to the village from a visit with my family in Xiamen. He once said that I had violated the Party's policy on the re-education of urban youths by overstaying my home leave. Then he went on to lecture me on the official policy toward children of the capitalist class. I cut him off by insisting that my father was a worker and not a capitalist. "Anyhow, he was an overseas Chinese," he responded.

He then announced that my share of rice should be reduced because of the extra days I had spent on home leave, but that he had decided not to cut my allotment. He asked me what nice things I had brought back from Xiamen. I just ignored him: I was in a bad mood so soon after leaving home. Eventually, he produced a big, dirty bowl and said he wanted to borrow a bowlful of peanut oil from me.

He had never returned anything he "borrowed" from me. To get rid of him, I took my oil can outdoors and filled his bowl half full, saying, "You don't need to return this." But he was still not satisfied. He wanted me to fill it the rest of the way. I said I had to give the rest of the oil to families who had helped me by heating my meals or giving me pickles and vegetables. I took the can, closed my door and went off to visit other villagers. Only then did the accountant leave, taking his half-filled bowl with him.

Frequent extortionary tactics like this really upset me, though I could do nothing to avoid them. On another occasion, the same village accountant came to "borrow" money from me. I said I had no cash, but he replied, "You're from an overseas Chinese family. How could you be short of money?" Totally shameless, he seemed determined not to leave without getting some cash. A strong cold wind chilled me to the bone as I stood in my north-facing front door. The deadlock continued until I could no longer stand the icy wind. I gave in and handed him a one-yuan banknote.

I complained to Biao Zhengchang, leader of our production team, about this unbearable treatment, but he said with a laugh, "Why did you come here to share our grain? Even if I had to beg, I would never go to your hometown Xiamen!"

His insults brought me to tears. "Do you mean we *zhiqing* are beggars coming here to take your food?"

"It's the truth, isn't it?" he retorted. "Our production team has too little land and too many people. Our quotas are low. Each year we have to allocate three thousand catties of grain to you five *zhiqing*. But the amount we must deliver to the government remains the same, not one catty less. We used to have surplus grain in our storeroom. We could lend some to team members if they were starving. Now, our storeroom is empty. Unable to get grain loans, the production team members shout abuse at me."

Although I knew he had spoken the truth, I still felt terribly wronged. I kept on crying and said, "We came to the countryside at the call of Chairman Mao. He also taught that all comrades in rural areas should welcome us. If you weren't going to welcome us, why did you accept us?"

Not yielding an inch, he rejoined, "How could I refuse to accept you? A group of leaders from the commune and the production brigade came to put pressure on me. They wouldn't leave until I promised to accept you. As long as they stayed at my home, I had to provide them with food. How could I afford that?" He then left, his anger unabated.

I could not stop crying when I went to see our team leader. Meizhao, his wife, was a kind-hearted woman. She and some of the other peasant women tried to soothe me. "Little Liang," she said, "please stop crying. You'll go blind from all those tears." The women stayed with me, chatting. Some of them spoke about the village accountant. Calling him a freeloader, they denounced him for taking advantage of the *zhiqing*.

Back in my living quarters, I latched the door and continued to cry, all alone. One of my roommates, Liu, had gone back to her Xiamen home, awaiting approval for traveling abroad. The other two girls, Qiu and Chen, who had just turned sixteen when they came to the countryside, had departed to join their elder brothers working in other villages. Because of my dubious overseas family background, I was never offered any urban jobs or other opportunities to return to the city. Although I was rated as a good commune member every year, the rewards given me were actually very poor. During my first year there, I was given two work-points for a day's backbreaking toil, which was worth a mere fourteen cents. (An able-bodied male peasant usually earned ten work-points a day, while a peasant woman earned from six to eight work-points -- ed.). While they continued to heap praise on me for my hard work and outstanding ability, they raised my earnings only one work-point each subsequent year, and stopped raises altogether when my work-points reached six. During the busy season, especially during the hot summer when we had to plant the second crop right after reaping the first, I had to get out of bed hours before daybreak and return late at night. I never dared to relax even when I had to work under the scorching noonday sun with my feet steeping in the hot water of the paddy fields. Moreover, I was sometimes an object of ridicule and mischief by individual peasants. When I recollected these unhappy events, I cried like a baby until I was exhausted and fell asleep on the floor.

The next morning, I was awakened by a knocking at the door. It was a female *zhiqing* from the neighboring village. She seemed relieved to find me still alive, but she could not help shedding tears for me when she saw that my eyes were so swollen from crying they looked like walnuts.

Tempered through labor, I was not afraid of hardships in farm work. It was mental trauma that made me cry. I had a profound love for life. On ordinary days, when going to work with villagers, I liked to walk through the forests on mountain paths, and was delighted to see the vigorous greenery all over the mountain slopes. I liked to listen to the murmur of water in the small brooks by the mountainside and smell the fragrance of wild flowers. I used to gather a bundle of the flowers to take home. I liked to follow small birds just learning to fly.

Sometimes we had to work in fields deep in remote mountains, where I would feel more relaxed seeing squirrels scampering on tree branches, or pangolins and Chinese water deer scurrying by. The sights and sounds of the open country often prompted me to sing a song with a light heart. Several villagers said I was like a child. While a stinging remark could make me cry, a beautiful flower or a small bird could put a smile on my face.

Once we were sent to work in a swamp. A young man smiled and said, "Little Liang, come over here. I will show you how to break up the soil and remove the weeds." He then led me into a waterlogged field. I found myself sinking into the mud until it reached my breast. I let out a loud cry. Amused by my plight, all the peasants standing on the field path roared with laughter. Only Qiu, a timid, young *zhiqing* girl, was frightened. She pleaded tearfully with the peasants to save me, but no one paid any attention to her. They were just enjoying a good laugh. Soon I realized that my feet were touching solid ground. No longer in fear, I hastened to assure Qiu that I was all right. All the peasants around me were still enjoying the joke, some laughing so hard they had tears in their eyes, others clutching their stomachs.

I had never seen such scenes of mirth among the country folk. I had been feeling pity for them, the way they had to work from dawn to dusk to attain minimum survival. They had no entertainment, no cultural life. Their burdens left few smiles on their faces. Laugh to your hearts' content, I thought to myself. Stuck in the mud, I joined them in laughing at myself.

Eventually, the young man who had tricked me reached out a hoe handle to help me out of the mud. Another villager said that the young man was standing on the trunk of an old pine tree that had been put there by their ancestors as a safe place to step, which was why he was in no danger of sinking into the mire. Fun-loving by nature, I decided to take my revenge. I asked him to grasp the other end of the hoe handle so I could rely on it to get onto the tree trunk. But when he did so, I gave it such a yank that he fell right in. This stirred another round of laughter among the peasant crowd.

To work in muddy fields was not to be feared. The really horrible experience was to be attacked by leeches. Once attached to your body, they would suck your blood until they were full. They would not budge when you tried to pull them off by hand. The villagers taught me how to scrape them off with the back of a knife. The leeches often made me bleed all over. Once when harvesting in paddy fields, I found twenty-seven leeches on my legs. The wounds would continue to bleed through the next morning.

During the slack season, I would join the villagers collecting the dung of wild pigs to spread on the fields. This was supposed to be good for my "re-education." I bought a dustpan and made myself long bamboo tongs for the job. The more pig dung I turned in to our production team the more points I accrued on my annual work record, which would bring me more food grain.

One early morning, taking my implements with me, I walked

along the side paths around the village and then up the mountain slope looking for pig dung. An old granny who was a habitual pig dung collector had not yet arrived. Some small children watched me using the tongs to pick up the lumps of pig dung and put them in my dustpan. They followed me wherever I went, laughing at my clumsiness. It took me a whole morning to fill my dustpan with a large heap of dung. I unloaded it on the ground beside the toilet outside my landlord's house, thinking that I could deliver it to our production team later. The following morning, I found out to my dismay that the landlord's hen and chicks had eaten the whole pile.

Discouraged, I took up my implements and again walked up the mountain slope. This time the old granny had arrived there before me, carrying her small grandson on her back. Whenever she saw a pig coming, she would follow it and pick up any dung it produced. She did not like competition. When a small boy walked alongside her and attempted to pick up some dung, she used her tongs to strike his dustpan. Hoping to avoid the scramble, I went in another direction in search of new sources of pig dung. Much to my surprise, however, she caught up to me and complained: "Little Liang, why do you try to grab our rice bowl from us? I am getting old and useless. This is the only work I can do. If I fail to collect pig dung, I will get home with nothing to eat. You've got money. Why do you come to collect pig dung?"

I was stunned by her words and felt a surge of sadness, both for the old granny and for myself.

Perspective of a Returned *Zhiqing*

by Jia Pingwa

Coming back from school in the county seat to my rural home at Dihua, I became a full-fledged peasant. Yet among the peasants, I was considered an educated youth, or a returned *zhiqing*. Later I became a professional writer. For a long period of time, literary works on the *zhiqing* stole much of the limelight on China's literary scene, but I didn't write a word on the subject. In the minds of most people, "*zhiqing*" referred to those young educated people who had originally lived in the cities, often in prosperous circumstances. They showed up in the countryside all of a sudden, amidst the beating of drums and the crashing of cymbals,. Their job was to learn how to be a peasant. Since my home was in the countryside, I was born a peasant. So, their situation had nothing to do with mine. There was a saying in journalistic circles: "When a dog bites a man, that is not news. But if a man bites a dog, that is news." We rural-based educated youth were no Cinderellas. No one cared about us, not the government, not the public, not even writers of literary works.

I have read many novels on *zhiqing*. Those youngsters were sent to places far away from their kin and their comfortable urban homes. They went through many hardships and ordeals. They were justified in cursing those days and pouring out their grievances. Their works distressed and moved me to tears. Those young people should not have been sent to the countryside. But after reading their experiences, I often wondered why we should have been born here to endure all the pain and suffering.

Ceramic tiles can surface kitchen counters as well as toilet walls. When ceramic tiles on a kitchen counter are removed to be used on toilet walls, cries of agony might be heard from the kitchen counter. But who would pay attention to the sobbing of the ceramic tiles that had always been on the toilet floor?

An aphorism says: "Stationary barracks, flowing soldiers." It implies that the constant flow of new talent is what makes an institution stable and strong. The necessity for constant change is also well expressed in other adages: "Wealth never survives three generations" and "The wheel of fortune always keeps turning."

A city is a place where survival of the fittest applies. Some people leave the city for the countryside, while capable rural folk enter the city. The city is always the center of civilization in society.

Back in those years, how deeply I admired the urban *zhiqing* who came to our village. Escorted by a few officials, they arrived with much fanfare. They were given important but undemanding jobs such as barefoot doctors, substitute teachers, tractor drivers, work record keepers and art troupers. They enjoyed fixed grain quotas that were slightly above the norm. They could return to cities at regular intervals, bringing back transistor radios, books, flashlights, tiger balm, biscuits and candies. Wearing Western-style pants, nylon socks and canvas waistbands, they ignored the air pollution and left their surgical masks hanging loose on their necks. They were knowledgeable and eloquent, and didn't have any scruples about stealing our chickens or slaughtering our dogs. Sometimes several of them would encircle one of us and beat us up. The most discouraging thing was that they would attract the prettiest girls in the village, who looked upon them as their first choice and we came in second.

The song Little Fragrance was very popular several years ago. It portrays an urban educated youth missing his old flame in the countryside, a village girl he abandoned when he returned to the city. While it expresses some repentance, it says, "Thank you for the love you gave me. You kept me company all those years." The young man in the song struck me as a typically shallow, self-centered *zhiqing*. Having suffered a stroke of bad luck in those tumultuous times, they came to our land to eat our grain, vegetables and chickens, and to subvert our love affairs, making our desolate land even worse. Our girls chose them because they were sophisticated urbanites even though they would finally return to the cities.

German shepherds are by birth superior to ordinary dogs – they are stronger and more valuable. We male villagers also think this way. When the army, government or factories needed new recruits, sooner or later the urban *zhiqing* were all enlisted. We rural-based *zhiqing* found this state of affairs to be fully justified. We were like bricks fired in the same kiln as tiles. The tiles would be put on the roof, whereas the bricks would be laid as wall foundations beneath the ground.

We were truly upset, however, by the success of our schoolmate nicknamed Pursed Mouth, a village boy who always had a runny nose and used to catch lice on his body in the presence of other people. Why was he recruited by the local geological prospecting team? After plotting for some time, I and several other *zhiqing* sent a letter of accusation to the relevant authorities. We also spread rumors to damage his reputation and block his path to becoming a worker.

Our scheme ended in failure, however. We found out that his sister had had intimate relations with a commune official, which meant we had no means to dislodge him. Nevertheless, a few persimmon trees in Pursed Mouth's courtyard soon withered and died because someone had cut a groove around the trunk of each tree.

Around this time, a pig castrator was visiting our village. He rode a bicycle with a shop flag in front made of iron wire and a piece of red cloth. He seemed to have a nice income that required little effort. I was watching him castrating a boar at the roadside when I saw the commune official coming out of the house of Pursed Mouth, who was holding a farewell dinner for his buddies. His face glowed red with drink.

"Several of your schoolmates are drinking here," he said to me. "Why didn't you come?"

"I was too busy," I replied

"I was told that you were the best student in their class," he said with a smile. "Are you content to stay in the village all your life?"

"I'm learning how to castrate boars," I quipped and walked away, thinking: If I really do learn that skill, I'll castrate you first of all!

Twenty years later, I was sitting at my desk reading a novel about *zhiqing*. My daughter had finished reading it several days before and was very much moved by it. She asked me about *zhiqing*'s sufferings in those years. I said to her:

"If you travel a whole day without seeing a restaurant, my child, you might feel very hungry. But that hunger would be very different from what you would feel if you didn't know where your next meal was coming from!"

The Price of Dignity

by Wang Lingling

I was a naive girl of eighteen when I was sent down to work in a village of the Red Flag Commune, Dechang County, Sichuan Province. It was about 500 kilometers south of Chengdu, the provincial capital that was my home. The workers' propaganda team that had come to our school to recruit us described the Dechang countryside in glowing terms. They made me believe that, despite my undesirable family background, I could temper and reform myself through re-education and become a trusted member in the revolutionary ranks led by the Communist Party. This could be accomplished, they argued convincingly, by living and working among the poor and lower-middle peasants of the land reform period, who were to be my teachers.

Hoping to be absolved of misfortune linked to my family background, I decided to change the unsociable bent I had exhibited during my school days and adapt myself to the new circumstances. I tried to do my best in all farm work despite hardship, exhaustion and the dirtiness of certain jobs. After a day's work, I would teach singing to children of commune members on the village threshing floor, and show them how to do *zhongziwu*, a type of dance that expressed people's loyalty to Chairman Mao. In the evening, under the light of a pine-seed oil lamp, I would read newspapers or Chairman Mao's writings to commune members.

Commune members had high praise for my hard work. People in our village, who made up a single production team, soon recommended me to attend meetings of activist representatives, where we learned Chairman Mao's works at both the brigade and commune levels. They even nominated me as a candidate for membership in the revolutionary leading group of our production team.

In the meantime, a commune official named Wan Yande had been assigned to work for a time in our village. His job was to help "consolidate" the leading group by educating and re-shuffling its membership. My good performance as a *zhiqing* soon attracted his attention. He showed concern for me and was very warm to me. He frequently approached me in the name of discussing ideological questions. Initially, because of his official status, I was respectful toward him. But he be-came increasingly open in expressing his carnal desires, and I felt a strong aversion to him. As a young, unworldly girl far away from home, I didn't know how to deal with the problem.

One evening in late autumn of 1969, Wan appeared like a specter at our abode. With a mischievous grin on his face, he came over and again tried to pressure me. Already in a bad mood due to another unpleasant matter, I pushed him away and shouted, "Get away from me!" I never imagined what a disaster would await me for taking this action to defend my dignity.

A few months passed, and the 1970 new year festival was in the offing. It was a year since we *zhiqing* had come to the village, and many of us were planning to go home for fami-ly reunions. Having to support five children, two as *zhiqing* in the countryside and three at school, my parents were in financial straits, so I decided not to go home during the peak travel season when fares were high. Before long, some *zhiqing* working in other villages brought me bad news from the commune office: Wan the official was spreading word among them, saying, "Wang Lingling does not dare to go back to Chengdu for fear of losing face. Her illicit relations with some male *zhiqing* have landed her in trouble."

Confronted with this slander, I decided to leave for Chengdu, hoping this would prove that I had no scruples about returning there. At home, however, I heard a fresh rumor spread by Wan among *zhiqing* who had remained in their villages after my departure: "Wang Lingling had no choice but to leave the village. Her belly would have betrayed her if she had stayed." I was in a dilemma. I could not explain things to people to dispel their suspicion, nor did I have any means to prove my innocence. There wasn't any place to lodge my complaint or anyone to protect me.

To intensify persecution of me, information about my family background was deliberately revealed and spread throughout the commune. "Wang Lingling has contacts overseas. Her maternal uncle is in Taiwan. Her father is a counterrevolutionary." Furthermore, our village leadership was instructed that the political performance of any *zhiqing* in the village should be judged by his or her relations with me. Some of the *zhiqing* working in our village were my former schoolmates. Younger than me and unable to stand the pressure, they all promised Wan or other officials that they would make a clean break with me. Slanders, suspicion and discrimination against me also affected the villagers, who began to distance themselves from me. Only then did I realize the true cost of offending someone with power. What a price I had to pay to defend my dignity!

For a time, I lost the will to live. I would go out alone into the open fields and shout to my mother, "Why did you bring me into this world?" Who could rescue me, a weak girl born into an ideologically suspect family? I thought of suicide and wrote a will. I wanted my death to prove my innocence. What saved me was help from my dear friend Wu Xinhui, another *zhiqing* who is now the chief physician at Huili county hospital.

She spent many nights urging me to consider the consequences if I were to commit suicide. People would say that I had killed myself to escape punishment or that I was discontented with the society. My suicide would subject my younger siblings to even more humiliation and discrimination than they were already experiencing as children of suspect parents. My friend persuaded me to let the passage of time prove my innocence. With her help, I was able to survive the most difficult period of my life.

My Country Mother

by Zhu Jifei

Granny Peng was the head of our host family when, in 1969, ten other *zhiqing* and I were assigned to work at Peng Family Hamlet, a poor mountain village in Jingxian County, southwestern Hunan Province. We all lived on the top floor of her house, which she had used as a storeroom.

Granny Peng was a widow. Her two elder daughters were married and living in other villages. The elder son was recruited by the army, leaving Granny Peng to take care of her youngest daughter and her younger son.

Operating as a single production team, the village had little cultivable land, averaging about one-sixth of an acre per head. Nominally, we were sent there "to change the backwardness of the countryside". The actual fact was that we were joining a scramble for food with the local peasants. Seeing no hopeful future, all *zhiqing* except me had left before the end of the following year. Some had been recruited by the army or local factories, others had returned to Changsha, the provincial capital, to visit their families and just never came back.

My father had been labeled a "bourgeois Rightist" and had few connections. So, I had no alternative but to stay in the village working as a farmer. I was only seventeen when I first arrived. I didn't know how to grow vegetables, or how to raise pigs. After a day's hard work, I had to cook my own meals. Seeing the difficulties of my life, Granny Peng suggested that I eat with them. I hesitated, fearing it would be too much trouble for her. But she persuaded me by saying: "It would only be a matter of putting another pair of chopsticks on the table. I can take care of the plot of land allocated to you for growing your own vegetables. You put your waste in my night soil pail. We can put our quotas of grain together." From then on, I became a member of her family.

Each day, I went out to work with her youngest daughter, Guizi, who earned 8 work-points a day whereas I earned 10. Xianzhong, the younger son, who had just graduated from primary school and started working as a young team member, earned 5 work-points. During the midday break, I went with Xianzhong to collect firewood, while Guizi gathered wild plants for pig food. After a day's work, I returned to my room upstairs to enjoy reading. When supper was ready, Granny Peng would stand at the threshold of the house entrance and shout: "Zhu Jifei, come down for supper!"

My dirty clothes and bedding used to be washed for me by Guizi. When I felt tired and hungry working in distant fields, I would invariably see Granny Peng appear at the turn of the road, tottering along in my direction, carrying my lunch in a basket. There was a general shortage of food back then, and people could seldom eat their fill. Nevertheless, Granny Peng would fill our bowls with rice--once, twice and often three times while we ate dinner by the fireplace. Only after the three of us, the working members of the family, had finished our meals would Granny Peng begin to eat whatever remained, sometimes only a scorched crust of rice at the bottom of the pot. But she never uttered a word of complaint.

Young and inconsiderate, I knew only that I was hungry and I ate a lot to satisfy my big appetite. I never considered whether Granny Peng would go hungry. In the spring, which was usually a season of serious grain shortages, Granny Peng would go deep into the mountains to gather wild chestnuts, bamboo shoots, kudzu and other wild plant roots to supplement our food supply. I would invariably suffer a stomach-ache if I ate sweet potatoes and pumpkins, so Granny Peng would bid her children to eat them, along with other food made from coarse grain, and leave the rice to me.

There was a big chestnut tree by the side of Granny Peng's house. She had always let the villagers gather the ripened chestnuts each year, but when I became the only *zhiqing* in her house, she would allow villagers to gather them only after she had selected the best chestnuts for me. She wanted me to take them back to Changsha during my home leaves.

Once when I was sent by the team leader to participate in a railway repair project, Granny Peng asked Guizi to make a pair of cloth shoes for me. In a word, she treated me as a member of her family. Villagers soon began speaking about me as her *dazai*, meaning, "eldest son".

During my spare time, I ran a literacy class for children whose parents could not afford to send them to school. Guizi was one of my students. Once she asked me to write the Chinese word "loyalty" for her, and I reminded her that she had learned that word in my class. She said that her writing was no good. When I realized that she intended to embroider the word on a pair of shoes she had made for her fiancé, I took time to write in calligraphic style the word "love" for her, which she said she could not recognize. I told her it was a variant form of the word "loyalty".

Xianzhong, Granny Peng's younger son, and I became good friends. We went to work together every day. He taught me many things about mountain life: where to gather firewood, where to go for waxberries, how to set traps for small wild animals, etc. In return, I told him stories from popular novels. It was in such a warm and harmonious atmosphere that I spent four years with the Peng family, who were typical of the kind-hearted, unsophisticated peasants I knew.

In 1975, I was recruited by a trade cooperative in a small town not far from the village. When I told my colleagues that I would be going home for the next holiday, they questioned how I could possibly do a round trip in a single day to distant Changsha. I explained that by "going home" I meant I was going back to the nearby Peng Family Hamlet.

Once Granny Peng sent me a message inviting me home for dinner in celebration of her birthday. I went with great pleasure, taking with me some pork meat and a piece of black corduroy for making her a short gown. By that time, her eldest son had been honorably discharged from the army and had returned to the village. Their standard of living had improved, and they now had enough to eat.

Later I was transferred to Changsha, where my parents had been sent to work for several years, and eventually we returned to Beijing in 1984. I lost touch with Granny Peng. In 1995, when I was made responsible for exploring potential trade opportunities at my work unit, I decided to go to Jingxian County and purchase several train carloads of Mandarin oranges -- a local product of the county -- and have them sold in Beijing. My primary motive in fact was to revisit the Peng Family Village and see Granny Peng and her family. In the fifteen intervening years, many highways had been built in the countryside, so I could get to the village by car.

Granny Peng looked much older this time, and her hair had turned white. She still lived in her old house and wore the short black corduroy gown I had given her for her birthday. She insisted on my staying for dinner. I responded, "Then, let me fetch you two pailfuls of water with that old shoulder pole. Is that fair enough?"

I walked along the narrow path leading to the well I had

helped dig. I found the familiar old scenes very moving.

Granny Peng's eldest son was married now and living in his own house. Her youngest daughter, Guizhi, had married outside of the village. Xianzhong, the younger son, had found a job in a lumber company in the county seat. Life was difficult for Granny Pang living all alone. I was seething with anger when I met Xiancheng, the elder son, and his wife. I told them that if they continued to leave Granny Peng cooking her own meals and living by herself in the old house, I would disown him as my brother. I would take her to Beijing to stay with me. Then the whole village would despise and denounce him.

Upon learning of our conversation, Granny Peng said to me, "Don't talk to them like that. I will not go and live with them. I don't deserve that kind of good fortune. My life is much better than it was in the past. I have enough to eat now." What low expectations my poor granny had!

Some villagers told me Granny Peng was approaching eighty. In the past few years, she had been sick several times. She had long been looking forward to seeing me.

When I was leaving the village, Granny Peng stood at the threshold where she used to call me for supper and shouted, "Zhu Jifei, come back again!" Tears ran down my cheeks as I drove away, unable to utter a word. In the summer of 1996, Xianzhong, the younger son, phoned to tell me that Granny Peng had passed away soon after my visit.

Since the Mandarin oranges from Jingxian County had sold very well in Beijing, I decided to make a second trip to Jingxian County in mid-November when the fruit ripens. Xianzhong accompanied me to Granny Peng's grave on a mountaintop, surrounded by wild grass. I dug a hole in front of her grave with my bare hands and, with the utmost care and respect, I buried there a pair of cloisonné wrist rings I had purchased in Beijing. Granny Peng had never worn any jewelry. The closest thing was a hair clip that she had bought for five fen. I burned a bundle of incense sticks before her grave. With streaming tears, I felt sorry that I had not taken her with me to Beijing during my first visit. My pitiful granny had never traveled on a train in her life!

All told, I stayed in Jingxian County for twelve years. I managed to survive many hardships there thanks to the kindness of Granny Peng and her family. I will never forget them. Her children and grandchildren continue to think of me as kin. When Xianzhong's son came to Beijing as a migrant worker, the first thing he did was to visit me. Granny Peng's grandchildren would tell friends of mine visiting from Changsha that they had an uncle working in Beijing. That uncle's name, they said, was Zhu Jifei.

The Visiting Cicada

by Wang Xiaoqiang

毛主席是各族

人民的大救

224

I was sixteen when I was sent down to a small mountain village in Zhidan County, some ninety kilometers west of Yanan, a sacred place in the history of the Chinese Revolution where the Chinese Communist Party had established its headquarters after the epic Long March. Within two years, I learned all sorts of farming skills and became a real farmer. In the third year, the village head gave me a new job -- teaching at the village's primary school.

On my first day of teaching, I met a frail, little eleven-year-old girl named Laichan'er (literally, "Visiting Cicada"). She had unkempt yellow-brown hair and unusually large eyes out of proportion to her small, innocent face. I have forgotten the names of all my students at the village school, except that of Laichan'er, which was her family nickname. Her formal name was Duan Yuqin.

Children in this area had a lot of work to do outside of school -- to herd the goats, feed the pigs and look after their younger siblings. They had little interest in schoolwork, but, like many of her classmates, Laichan'er enjoyed the stories I used to tell the class. I remembered many stories from my own childhood and was good at telling them. After my resources were exhausted, however, I found teaching these rural children to be a great challenge. Their progress depended entirely on my efforts. I had to teach them the basics from scratch--even how to handle a pencil. It was Laichan'er who often gave me consolation and courage. She was the first pupil who learned to count to 100, and she worked hard on every assignment. She was always the first to raise her hand when I asked a question. Smart but mischievous, she liked to climb to the tops of trees and to charge down the nearby slope at full speed. While she could reduce the naughtiest boy in class to tears in a fistfight, she was able to grasp a new subject sooner than the others.

For all these reasons I was particularly fond of her. When the children were playing on the school ground, I used to gaze at her big eyes. Each time she discovered that I was watching her, she would respond with a sweet smile.

As a token of my fondness for her, I once kept her after class and gave her an exercise book and pencil. I asked her several times to keep the gifts to herself in order to avoid giving people the wrong idea, but as soon as she got out, she was surrounded by her classmates. She showed them the gifts, which were passed from hand to hand. Upset, I never gave her another thing after that.

I left the mountain village two years later on short notice, unable to say goodbye to Laichan'er.

Another eight years passed. As a young scholar at the Chinese Academy of Social Sciences, I was investigating the effects of rural economic policies in Gansu province. On my return trip to Beijing, I made a detour to visit the village where I had worked for four years. I thought of Laichan'er and my other pupils. She must now be twenty, the customary age for rural girls to get married.

I did not see her on the first day. I learned from her parents that she would marry someone in another village during the winter. Her parents also told me that she had stopped going to school after I left. She was working on a remote plot of land that day, so I initially missed seeing her, to my regret. It was already afternoon when I finished my lunch at a peasant's home. I went to take a look at my former cave home not far from the gateway to the village. When I raised my head, I spotted a girl standing before the cave.

"What's your name?" I asked when I came close.

"Laichan'er," she answered.

"Laichan'er!" I exclaimed in pleasant surprise.

She wore a brand new Dacron shirt with a yellow silk-laced collar. Coming face to face with her, I tried to find traces of the little girl I had known, but she was now all grown up, her face full and suntanned. Her big eyes, though, remained bright and attractive. I embarrassed her with my staring.

She led me to her cave home. Her parents were away, so she took it upon herself to boil water for me to drink. I sat on the kang, a kind of brick bed warmed from beneath by cooking fire, and noticed that she stole a few glances at me when she was refueling the stove.

"Do you remember me?" I asked her.

"Yes, I do."

"What do you remember?"

"I remember everything."

After this brief exchange, several young men came in, three of whom had been my students. They were eager to talk with me.

Half-jestingly, I said to Laichan'er, "They tell me you're going to get married this winter. How much is your groom giving you as a betrothal gift?"

She denied any such thing, her face reddening. A young man squatting at the threshold stuck out his little finger and said, "She's getting a thousand yuan."

We drank hot water and chatted for a while. I suggested taking a picture of Laichan'er with my camera. She said I should do it on the highway.

A crowd of women and children accompanied us down the highway and out of the village. Laichan'er surprised me by asking if I had a photo of myself that I could give her, but unfortunately I did not have any. I took some pictures of her as we walked along. It was getting late for me to visit friends at the next village, so I waved to the crowd and bade farewell to them. My shouted "zaijian" (goodbye) was mainly for Laichan'er, who was looking at me with sorrow-filled eyes.

Despite my farewell, Laichan'er caught up to me at a turn of the highway. I urged her to go home, saying she must have other things to do, but she murmured, "No, nothing." Her attachment was contagious -- I really wanted to stay with her at that moment.

After meeting my friends at the neighboring village, I walked back along a 200-meter country road which connected the village to the highway. Soon I spotted Laichan'er hiding behind a jujube tree, waiting for me. I was about to ask her again to return home when I saw her big, melancholy eyes. At a loss for something to say to her, I slackened my pace.

"Do you really have no photos on you?" She asked.

"No, I really don't," I said.

She heaved a faint sigh, which stung me.

"I used to go to Laiwa's all the time to see your picture," she said. I looked at her, puzzled. "Laiwa put some of his pictures in a frame and hung it on the wall. It had a picture of you."

Now I saw what she meant. I hastened to say, "You're a clever girl Laichan'er. It's a shame you didn't stay in school."

"A bit more schooling wouldn't have changed a life doomed to hardship," she said, obviously uncomfortable with the subject. Then she said softly, "My mom told me yesterday that you were coming. I couldn't sleep all night." She had made up an excuse, she said, to leave work in order see me. "When I got home, they told me you were probably leaving this after-noon. So, I was hanging around in the village. I would have felt terrible if I had missed seeing you." She sounded ready to cry.

Moved, I said with difficulty, "I've never forgotten you, ei-ther."

This seemed to calm her down.

After a while, I said with some hesitation, "I'll bet you're marrying into a nice family."

"Nice? A family of farm laborers, like mine."

"Have you visited them in their village?"

"I went there once last year."

Laichan'er seemed to have a lot she wanted to say, but she was having trouble getting it out. We walked slowly, neither of us venturing to break the silence.

Eventually, we had to separate. Standing on the side of highway, she said, "Send me a photo so that I have something to hang on to."

I cast one last glance at her big eyes and departed. After walking a long distance, I turned around. She was still stand-ing there.

Only then did it occur to me how she had arranged ev-erything for our possible encounter. She had changed into a new shirt after going to work in the morning. She had taken great pains to put her house in order so that I would feel com-fortable. She had proposed taking pictures on the highway so that she could have a chance to talk with me. I had been so numb and stupid. I should have said more to soothe her -- but what could I have said? I should have given her all the money I was carrying, plus my watch as a souvenir. But she had only asked me for a photo. Did she understand that, given the things that separated us, we could never have a seri-ous relationship? Surely she did not. Nor did she need to. Her attachment was so pure that nothing could desecrate it. Still, I had to ask myself if I was worthy of such an attachment.

Someday, I am sure, I will go back to see her. But as to her attachment, my position can only be that of a sympathetic bystander. My real regret is that there is nothing I can do to change her destiny.

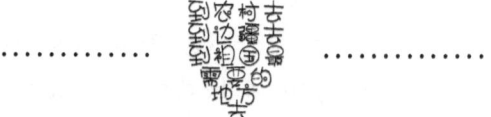

Life in Rural Mingshan

by Tian Ziyi

The arrival of my *zhiqing* group stirred ripples in the daily life of our host village, a remote hamlet that sat like a pool of stagnant water between the hills.

For several days after our arrival, we were surrounded by villagers who would gape at everything we did. In the early mornings when we were brushing our teeth, a dozen people or more, both males and females, would stand watching us from afar in rapt attention. One young boy with a runny nose said loudly to the others, "How strange! They are stirring tiny sticks in their mouths. Look at all the bubbles coming out!" They might as well have been watching a magic show.

A girl with braids laughed at him. "You dope!" she said. "Don't you know about tooth brushing?" She looked to be sixteen or seventeen and was more neatly dressed than the others. She was surprisingly attractive, with fair skin, a set of snow-white teeth, and a ruddy face like a flowering Chinese rose. Under long, black eyebrows she had big eyes that sparkled like spring water. When we got to know her later, we learned that her name was Wang Cunfen. She had graduated from primary school but then discontinued her studies. As the eldest of three daughters, she had to look after her young siblings in addition to earning her own livelihood.

Wang Cunfen soon became a faithful follower of our female *zhiqing*, working alongside them in the farm fields and visiting them during off hours. As her visits grew more frequent, she seemed to feel increasingly comfortable with them. She dropped in on us boys as well. Once inside our room, she would pick up a mirror to look at herself, sniff a bar of soap, strike up a conversation, and even crack harmless jokes with us. To be honest, if she had not been a peasant girl, one of us boys might have fallen in love with her.

One day after work, we heard Cunfen's mother screaming at their front door. Some of us went to investigate. The quarrel soon drew a small crowd of villagers. Shouting all the while, Cunfen's mother was trying to seize a roll of white cloth from her daughter's hands, causing the girl to fall on the ground, but Cunfen had the cloth in her grasp and wouldn't let go.

Cunfen's mother, we learned, had recently purchased a roll of cloth at the rural market in order to make two bed sheets. She wanted the cloth to be dyed cyan blue, but Cunfen was strongly opposed to the idea.

"You're crazy," her mother shouted, obviously used to having her way. "Everybody in the village has blue sheets."

"Yes, but all the *zhiqing*'s bed sheets are white and clean," Cunfen responded, speaking clearly but softly.

"White bed sheets are too hard to wash," the mother said, her voice somewhat lowered, though she was still gripping one end of the cloth.

"Well, I'm the one who has to wash them," Cunfen said. "I do all the washing, don't I? I'll never wash the sheets if you dye them blue." Cunfen got up from the ground still gripping the roll of cloth as if she were defending her own purity.

"How can we emulate the *zhiqing*?" The mother asked. "They can afford soap. What can you use for washing white bed sheets?"

All the male *zhiqing* present assured Cunfen's mother that they would provide her family with soap when they needed it.

The mother finally let go of the roll of cloth. Looking at us, Cunfen swept aside the hair on her face, her big, beautiful eyes glistening with tears.

Setting Up A Fence

With *zhiqing* having their own dormitory, villagers now had a place for entertainment.

After supper, many villagers came to visit. They would listen to us singing songs, playing musical instruments, or talking about odd events that had happened in the cities. They would also listen to broadcasts on our transistor radios. Visitors included young and middle-aged peasants, and sometimes elderly people as well. Once Mrs. Sun, a widow in her 70's, staggered along with her bound feet to visit us. All the other members of her family had starved to death during famine years. She was supported by our production team, which was in charge of all public affairs in the village. She brought us a bottle of broad-bean butter she had made, and sat for a while before leaving. Probably inspired by her example, other villagers started bringing small gifts when they visited -- a bundle of fresh vegetables, a bowl of home-made bean curd, and whatnot. As welcome as these gifts were, they were far from the amount of non-staple food the seven of us *zhiqing* needed. We had to rely on our own vegetable garden for such supplies.

The vegetables in our plot grew much better than anyone had expected. Villagers marveled at our shiny green plants, but they didn't know our secret -- we had applied on them some urea fertilizer we stole from the public warehouse.

One day, going to water the vegetables, we were enraged to see a flock of chickens making havoc of our garden. Young shoots had been uprooted and eaten up. The bigger plants were full of holes. Shouting angry curses, we picked up stones and earthen clots to throw at the chickens, which scattered in all directions.

We decided to replant the vegetables but wondered how we could prevent future intrusions by the chickens. I proposed a vicious scheme -- go to the rural market and buy an infected chicken, kill it and then spread its entrails, blood, and feathers on our vegetable plot so that any intruding domestic fowl would become infected and die of bird flu. My scheme was approved by all and was soon carried out.

Several days later, while working in the fields, we heard peasants saying that some of the villagers' chickens were dying of bird flu. Their talk made us laugh in secret.

When passing by Mrs. Sun's publicly owned house, we saw the old widow weeping over the loss of her chickens. A dead chicken was lying on the ground, its legs stretching stiffly out. By its side, two hens were dozing, their heads tucked under their wings -- a typical symptom of bird flu infection. Wiping her eyes with a dirty apron, Mrs. Sun pursed her deeply wrinkled lips as if she were mourning the death not of chickens but of her own children.

We hurried away from this distressing sight, but our team leader followed close behind us and came to visit. He said with a wry smile, "Did you buy an infected chicken on purpose?" We didn't know how to reply. "Well done! Well done!" he continued. "Our superiors are always telling us to curtail capitalism in the village, but I haven't been able to think of a way to do it. It's hard! Commune members' only cash income comes from the sale of their chickens, so they just ignore the instructions. Mrs. Sun is a good case in point. She relies on our production team for her staple food, but she needs money to buy salt and vegetable oil. For that, she depends on her chickens." He heaved a long sigh. "Doing away with them is a good thing. There won't be any chickens to ruin our crops."

All the *zhiqing* present were confused, wondering what he was driving at.

The team leader walked off, but after a few paces, he turned back and said, "Go and gather some fir branches to build a fence. It will prevent future intrusions by the chickens."

When the hunchbacked team leader disappeared into the distance, one of my companions grumbled, "Fir branches? What a stupid idea."

Building a fence made of fir branches was indeed no easy task. Their needles stung us like hornets, and the pain lasted for days. Encircling our entire plot would be a huge job.

Coming back from work one day, I saw a distant shadow moving about on our vegetable plot and found that Mrs. Sun was building a fence for us. Indeed, the weak old widow had almost finished the job. I wondered where she had gathered all the fir branches. The sight of her thin, childlike figure filled me with such shame I wanted to cry. I hastened to help her complete the job, ignoring the pain of the fir needles.

Gasping for breath, the old lady murmured, "Without my chickens, where can I get the money to buy salt?"

I wanted to take her hands into mine and ask her forgiveness, but I lacked the courage to do so.

From then on, a few young men were the only visitors to our dormitory. People no longer came to listen to music or chat. An invisible fence seemed to have been erected between us and the villagers.

A Terrible Voice

Zhiqing were recruited in great numbers by urban factories in 1971. Their departure evoked a general feeling of insecurity among those of us who stayed behind. People with connections stepped up their efforts to make backdoor deals, with the result that even more *zhiqing* returned to cities. Procedures regarding their selection were kept secret.

In 1973 came the disturbing news that within three years no more *zhiqing* would be recruited by urban enterprises. In an entire row of rooms at the *zhiqing* dormitory, I was the only one who remained.

Recruiters had repeatedly refused me because I had failed to pass political vetting. For many years, my undesirable family background had been a sore spot for me -- a source of pain that could break out at any time. Refusals by recruiters were like pinches of salt sprinkled on my bleeding wound.

Our team leader, seeing me alone in a row of empty rooms, approached me with his advice. Puffing on his pipe, he said, "Go back to Chengdu. Try to find some channels that can help you out."

My trip to Chengdu proved useless. My family had no connections with any key persons in organizations that were actively recruiting. I was tormented by my mother's sighs and by her new white hairs and wrinkles.

Friends and acquaintances I met on the streets would ask me warmly where I was working. When I said that I was still working in the countryside, they would invariably ask, "How come almost all *zhiqing* have returned home but you?" Their words felt like a stab in the heart. I wanted to magically disappear from their sight and avoid having more salt smeared on my wound.

I returned to our village in low spirits under cover of night and sneaked into my room at the pine-shrouded *zhiqing* dormitory. I knew that our team leader and villagers would ask me about the results of my public relations efforts in Chengdu, but any show of concern by others carried a nuance of pity if not sarcasm. I shut myself up in my room, like a bruised animal that has escaped to its mountain cave to lick its wounds.

For almost two weeks on end, I didn't go back to work in the fields, nor did I go out to visit anyone. I spent most of my time reading and practicing Chinese calligraphy, but mental agony and despair never left me. I cooked once every three days. For each meal, I would pour boiled water in a bowl of cold rice, put in a small spoonful of chili sauce, and finish eating in no time. I didn't see or speak to anyone.

During the day, I would occasionally hear distant voices and laughter when villagers came back from work, or giggles from cowherds in the forests. Everyone else seemed happier than I was. At night, I listened to the sighing of the pine trees and the cries of owls. I had a hazy feeling that I had entered a different world.

Two weeks of self-isolation seemed like long years to me. They did not alleviate my mental agonies but increased my confusion and sense of uncertainty and helplessness.

One dark night when everything was quiet except the far-off barking of a dog, I reclined on my bed watching curls of black smoke rising from a flickering kerosene lamp. My mind was wandering aimlessly when suddenly a strange voice reached my ears and spoke a few indistinct words. I was startled and sat up. Looking around my room, I found no one but myself.

The kerosene lamp flickered more unsteadily, and the

rustling of pine trees came in waves from the forest. I jumped off my bed to check the latch on my door. Picking up a hoe handle, I muttered to myself, Let's see what kind of strange things might happen tonight. With this utterance, I began to laugh at myself. Only then did I realize that the strange voice was my own, that I was thinking aloud. After two weeks of complete silence, my voice had become unfamiliar even to myself.

I was seized by fear and wondered if I was having a nervous breakdown. Was I going mad? I sweated profusely and soon my hazy brain began to clear. To stay behind in the countryside was not so terrible, I thought. The real terror was to go mad, as a few of our fellow *zhiqing* had done. I should not isolate myself. As a *zhiqing*, I must mix with the peasants and communicate with them.

The following morning, I took up my hoe, opened the door, and went to the fields to restart my life as a *zhiqing*.

The Middle School Principal

By 1975, I had spent six years in the countryside. Sometimes after a day's work, I would go the commune-run middle school to see a teacher friend and borrow books from him.

The school had a new principal. On learning that I was a high school student back in the late 1960's, he made a special trip to our village to visit our team leader and ask him to allow me to transfer to a teaching job at his school.

The principal's name was Zhang Kequan. He was a native of the area in his late thirties, a graduate from Sichuan Normal College majoring in mathematics. He had a thin face and always wore a serious expression, constantly knitting his thick eyebrows. I soon found that his pointed criticism of people could be merciless, and I was a bit afraid of him.

The school was built on a small hilltop and had only partial walls to seal out the weather. Classroom windows were framed but had no glass. This posed no problem in summer, but was awful in winter. One day when I was writing on the blackboard, I heard a stamping sound behind my back. When I turned around, the sound stopped and all the students were sitting straight. There were no signs of mischief. When I resumed writing on the blackboard, the sound started up again. I guessed that several students must be stamping their feet. This happened a few times and was beginning to annoy me. The next time the sound started, I whirled around to catch some of them in the act. They looked at me nervously. All rural children feared censure by their teachers.

Looking beneath their desks, I felt a shiver go through me. Their bare feet looked like dirty red radishes. These were children of the poor and lower-middle class of peasants, and though most of them wore cotton-padded jackets to ward off the severe winter chill, below the waist they had on only thin trousers and no shoes.

I was wearing a woolen sweater beneath my overcoat, and sweat pants over my cotton trousers, but my hands and feet were stiff from the cold. I could well imagine what the children must be suffering.

"Do you feel very cold?" I asked them as gently as I could.

"Yes, Teacher Tian," they answered in unison with grateful expressions.

"All right," I said without hesitation, "go outside for a five-minute break. Get some exercise and come back when you've warmed up."

With a loud hurrah, the children scampered outside.

Principal Zhang rushed out of his office and shouted at me, "What's going on, Teacher Tian? The recess bell hasn't rung yet."

I explained to him what had led up to my quick decision, fully prepared to accept his criticism, but he just patted me on the shoulder and said slowly, "You did the right thing, Teacher Tian. You did the right thing."

He knitted his eyebrows more tightly than usual, looking anxious and contemplative.

The following spring, I was recruited by the factory where my father had worked. Before I went to the county seat for my physical exam, Principal Zhang called me into his office and tried hard to persuade me to stay. "The native teachers are not as high as you in their educational level," he said. "It would not be good for the children if you were to leave. I guarantee that you will be kept on the government payroll as long as I remain principal here. Mingshan County isn't too far from Chengdu. It will be convenient for you to go home during vacations. And if you want to settle down here, I can be your match-maker. Country girls have high respect for teachers. Think of a little wife bringing you a basin of hot water to wash your feet. Please stay with us, Teacher Tian."

He all but begged me to stay, and I could see it from his point of view. Unable to resist the temptations of urban life, however, I failed to live up to his goodwill and expectations.

Please forgive me, Principal Zhang Kequan. I will never forget you!

Ah, Guifang

by Qi Yushan

Guifang was the first country girl I got to know when I went to work in a village in Inner Mongolia. To quote her words, she and I "were destined to become bosom friends."

On the first day of our arrival, I and several other girl students from Beijing were surrounded by a group of country girls who gathered beneath the windows of our dormitory. While watching us with curiosity, they were chattering away. Only Guifang stood aside in silence against a wall.

Later, Guifang became a frequent visitor. While we were reading, chatting or washing our utensils, she would sit speechless in a corner of our *kang*[3], her black eyes sparkling.

That winter I didn't return to Beijing. In our village, the remuneration for a day's work was a mere five fen. Financial straits prompted me to stay behind. Moreover, I didn't want to spend a leisurely winter at home at the expense of my widowed mother. When the Chinese New Year was drawing near, I was the only *zhiqing* in our group who remained in the countryside.

I will never forget the wintertime on the Inner Mongolian grasslands: the raging windstorm, the rustling withered grass, the gaping cracks in the frozen ground. In the evening, when curls of smoke from kitchen chimneys shrouded the whole village, the neighing of horses and the barking of dogs echoed from a distant forest in the west, and a freezing gale ripped into me like a knife. I felt miserable and alone. Staying by myself in a row of empty rooms, I felt afraid and very cold.

One night, Guifang came to visit me. When she saw me in a daze, gazing at the flames in the kitchen stove in the central room, large teardrops ran down her cheeks. She had

3. Raised brick or clay platform bed heated from beneath used in northern China and Manchuria.

brought her bedding, ready to stay with me to keep me company. During the long nights, she would do her needlework while I was reading. We found consolation in being together. She was such a nice, understanding and empathetic girl.

One night, my vegetable oil for lighting was exhausted. I did not have enough money left to buy a catty of vegetable oil. I suggested to Guifang that we retire early so that I could tell her some tales in bed. That was how I started to spend several cold wintry nights telling her stories in a lightless room of our dormitory.

I recounted episodes from Chinese classical works like Dream of the Red Chamber, Romance of the Western Chamber, and tales about love and urban life in ancient times from a collection of short stories by a noted Ming dynasty writer. When I ran out of Chinese stories I could tell from memory, I started to entertain her with tales from foreign classical works, such as *La Traviata, Eugénie Grandet, Jane Eyre, Home of the Gentry* . . . Completely absorbed, she used to say to me when I had finished a story, "Elder sister, please tell me another one." She was three years younger than I was. Though an illiterate peasant who had never been to school, she was extremely clever. She was able to tell her young siblings the same stories in their entirety that I had narrated to her the previous night.

During those long wintry nights, a sisterly relationship was formed between the two of us. Because of poverty and cultural backwardness, the 19-year-old Guifang handled all problems of puberty in a very primitive manner. From what I knew, I explained physical hygiene to her in simple terms, made her a sanitary pad, and recommended that she buy a kind of rough tissue paper she could afford, telling her how to sterilize it before use. I also gave her a bra as a gift. She always listened closely to me, her big eyes open wide in wonderment. She followed my instructions conscientiously, giving me the impression that she was extremely earnest in emulating us *zhiqing*.

Probably because I felt lonely and needed someone to listen to my outpourings, or because I thought that Guifang was the one who could understand me, I opened my heart to her without reserve, telling her about my longings for my family in Beijing, my nostalgia about the days I had spent together with my schoolmates and friends who were now scattered in different parts of the country, my yearnings for love, and my impressions and observations of the state of affairs in the countryside. She listened to me with full attention. Sometimes excited, sometimes dejected, she seemed completely submerged in my world as if sharing my fate with me.

One day, she walked in with red eyes. I asked her what had happened. She told me tearfully that her elder sister had returned home after being badly beaten by her husband. The man, whom Guifang called a beast, lived far away from their village. Her elder sister had never met him before the wedding. A betrothal gift of 300 yuan plus the sweet words of a match-maker induced her to fall into the trap that ended in an inhuman life. As far as I knew, however, this was the path traversed by almost all the girls in that locality. That night, I didn't tell her any stories. Guifang sat there dazed, obviously musing over her own worries. When bedtime came, she got on the bed and said softly to me over the pillow, "I would rather die than follow in the footsteps of my elder sister." By the moonlight that shone through the window, I detected a strange, extraordinary sparkle in her eyes.

The following day, she brought some lamp oil and a language primer that had been used by her younger brother. She became the first student in my life. Working very hard, she finished the lessons in the primer within a few days. I was pleased and praised her, saying that she could finish all language lessons in an elementary school in a short time. She seemed to have changed into a different person. Her pale face turned rosy, and her eyes became brighter. She was probably experiencing the happiness of starting a new life.

Although late in coming, the spring was nice and pleasant. My fellow students were returning reluctantly to our village like a flock of seasonal birds flying northward from the south. The period when Guifang would keep me company came to an end. During the summer, I contracted acute lymphangitis, which became increasingly serious owing to lack of medical service. I decided to sell the grain I had earned and buy a train ticket back to Beijing. When I returned to the village after my recovery several months later, it was already late spring of the following year.

On the very day of my return, I learned the news about Guifang's betrothal. In the winter of the year when I had left the village, the leadership of our banner[4] had sent a work team to our village to start a political movement mainly targeting the so-called counterrevolutionaries. Guifang's father was classified as one of those. He disagreed with the label put on him and wanted to lodge a complaint with the government at a higher level, but he lacked the money to pay for travel expenses. In return for a 300-yuan gift, he promised Gui-

4. A banner is an administrative division of the Inner Mongolia Autonomous Region in the Peoples Republic of China, corresponding to the county level (Wikipedia, Banners of Inner Mongolia).

fang's betrothal to a peasant who lived some 50 miles away. Guifang was firmly against the deal that would marry her to a man she had never met. Her parents and five young siblings knelt down before her, imploring her to do so. She finally nodded her acquiescence in tears.

On the first night after my return, someone called me outside the enclosure wall. I went out and found it was Guifang's mother, a kind, gentle peasant woman. She said timidly to me that Guifang was to be married in a few days. She knew that I was Guifang's best friend, believing that her daughter would follow my advice. She asked me not to discourage the marriage, saying, "I know that this arrangement is unfair to her. She has been thinking all along of marrying someone of her own choice, in the manner you *zhiqing* do. But her father has fallen ill and has a counterrevolutionary label on his head. Her siblings are all too young. We have used the man's money and have eaten his grain. What can we do but let Guifang marry him?" It was distressing to hear her words amidst sobs. I didn't sleep well that night.

The following morning before I went out to work in the fields, Guifang surprised me by sneaking into our bedroom. The luster in her big eyes had been replaced by listlessness. Her ruddy face had turned languidly yellow. She quietly told me she would be getting married in two days. She brought me a blue flowered cloth jacket and a pair of black flannel shoes, which she had made for me as keepsakes.

I didn't ask her to be compliant as her mother had wished me to do. Nor did I suggest that she run away from the wedding as I had originally intended to do. After all, I had lived in the countryside for five years and had been through many vicissitudes. I was no longer a young girl full of romantic dreams.

I helped her to cut her braids and trimmed her hair into a bob. Gazing at her haggard face in the mirror and recalling the miserable evening when she came to visit me with a roll of bedding, standing in the central room and shedding tears for me, I could not but embrace her in my arms. Both of us erupted into loud crying.

Not long after Guifang got married, her father and the whole family were forced to flee Inner Mongolia and moved to Heilongjiang Province. Guifang never returned to our village. In the meantime, I was transferred to work in a rural clinic further away from Guifang's new home. I missed her very much. Later I had a chance encounter with her elder sister. She told me tearfully that Guifang, out of protest, had refused to sleep with her husband and remained a virgin for more than a year. Her husband, a short, timid man, had beaten her in order to subdue her. But her strong resistance thwarted his attempt, leaving him at the end of his rope. His relatives, enraged, decided to take collective action. They bound her up, and gave her a sound beating, leaving many bruises on her body. She could only lie there exhausted and motionless. On that very night, she became his real wife.

Her elder sister's words shocked me. My desire to see her was so strong that I waited on the country road for a whole morning until I got on a farm cart going in the direction of her village. By the time of my arrival, night had already fallen and the sky was full of stars. A warm-hearted old man escorted me to her door. On hearing my voice, Guifang rushed out barefoot, embraced me and pushed me into her house. Probably because her room was too dark, it took me some time to discern in her distorted face some remaining traces of the Guifang I had known so well. Her husband greeted me politely though betraying some perplexity and alarm. He hastened to bring in some kindling for preparing a meal. I took Guifang's hands into mine and said, "Are you all right?" Choked by sobs, I couldn't go on. Then I saw tears streaming down her thin cheeks.

I stayed two days with Guifang, during which time she told me the rest of her story. After going through both mental and physical agonies, she no longer wished to live. She kept so quiet that her husband and his relatives believed that they had subdued her. After resting a couple of weeks, she forced herself to get out of bed. Taking a big mirror down from a wall in her room, she scraped the silver film from the back of the mirror, mixed the powdered fragments in water and drank them. She said to me with a forced smile, "I tried to kill myself, mistaking the powder for mercury, which I knew to be a sure killer." After this episode, her husband's family began keeping a tighter watch on her. Once, when her sister-in-law was off her guard, Guifang broke a window pane and used the broken glass to slash her own wrist. But she didn't get to the blood vessel. She also tried to swallow the tiny broken glass pieces…. While desperately trying to find a way to commit suicide, she discovered that she had become pregnant. For the first time, her desire for death was suddenly driven away by tender feelings of a would-be mother expecting the birth of a new life. It was hard to tell whether she was experiencing joy or sorrow. In any case, she managed to survive……

Sitting on the bed, her jacket thrown over her shoulders, Guifang looked at the silvery moonlight outside the window and said to me, "Elder sister, do you believe in destiny? If you are destined to miss a certain thing, you won't succeed even if you go out of your way to get it. It was so stupid of me to try to follow your example. Like what was described in the books, I only wanted to find someone I really loved, not for his fine looks or his wealth. That would be a life worth living. But I was not destined for that."

Unable to utter a word, I felt extremely remorseful over the things that I had done that winter. I shouldn't have told her those stories: I shouldn't have taught her how to read. If all that had not happened that winter, probably she would have lived a more contented, peaceful life without going through such great suffering.

In 1979, I returned to Beijing under the government policy for *zhiqing* suffering from various illnesses. Before departure, I asked someone to pass a message to Guifang, asking her to come to the banner seat to meet me before our final separation. When she came to meet me, she looked much better. Occasionally, she would smile at me, her 3-year-old son at her side. She said to me, "When my son grows up, I'll let him go to Beijing to see you. I hope he can study there."

"Certainly", I responded.

Her son Xiaodong is now in his third year in one of the best junior middle schools in the banner. In a letter to me, he wrote: "From my mom, I've long heard about you and other *zhiqing* who once lived in her village. Though she hasn't got much education, she thinks a lot and is very strict with me in my studies. She has high hopes for me. I'm determined to live up to her expectations."

I invited him to come to Beijing and have some fun in the capital. He wrote me a reply, saying, "I'll certainly come to Beijing. Not for fun, but to study at a college there."

Guifang, I am glad for you for having such a son. I know you'll try your best to help him get what you missed out on. l am convinced of that.

The Death of Mei

by Meng Liwei

There is a misty drizzle outside. People rush in both directions along the nearby road. The long, hard winter is over. Everyone is marking the traditional Qingming Festival by visiting the graves of their ancestors and departed loved ones. I think of Mei, a *zhiqing* companion and close friend since childhood, and I cannot restrain my tears. Where are you, Mei? Does your soul rest in peace? Can you hear my affectionate call? Do you know that your *zhiqing* companions still remember you with fondness and recall your misfortune with grief?

I burn a small bundle of incense sticks and pray for you, raising toward Heaven a cup of wine diluted by my tears. Through the incense smoke, the tragic scene reemerges before my eyes.

One afternoon during the Qingming Festival of 1970, there were few people working in the fields. Most of the villagers had gone to visit the graveyards. The broad farm fields looked dismal and deserted in the misty rain. The five *zhiqing* in our production team, wearing bamboo hats and raincoats, were tilling the fields alongside a few elderly men and women. There were no gossiping housewives, no teasing farmhands telling dirty jokes. The sky was gloomy with thick clouds, and a chilly wind was blowing. We felt lost and depressed. Every one of us was silently doing his or her job, hoping to finish it quickly and go home.

At about three o'clock, a peasant woman from a nearby production team ran wildly toward us, yelling: "Help! Help! Something terrible has happened to one of the *zhiqing*." Dazed, we threw away our shovels and ran toward the adjacent production team. But it was too late. Peering through a window of a dark, stinking cowshed, we were astounded to see Mei hanging from the rafters, her face a yellowish brown.

How did this happen? Why? We were seized with fear, not knowing what to do. "Hurry and let her down!" Someone shouted. Having come to my senses, I tried to break into the cowshed. I noticed that there was already a gap between the door and its frame. Someone had obviously tried to break in before me, but a big water vat had been placed behind the door to block the way.

"She is beyond saving. We have to protect the crime scene," a village cadre said. He prevented us from going inside.

"Who made her kill herself?" "Is this a place for human beings to live in?" We *zhiqing* roared angrily, with tears running down our faces.

Last evening, Mei had come over to our living quarters when we were taking supper. She seemed heavy-hearted. I consoled her by saying: "Don't worry. I will ask our group leader to hold a meeting and see how to relocate you to a different village." Precisely at this time, the head of the militia came to inform us that they had discovered airdropped reactionary leaflets and asked us to start a search of the fields right away. I asked Mei to stay with me a while, but she insisted on going. She said a village woman would accompany her that night. I knew that she was worrying about the safety of her several pounds of grain, which she had earned by hard work and now stored at her "home". I never realized that our separation that night would be eternal.

Mei had graduated from junior middle school in 1966. Our parents had worked in the same hospital and we had grown up together. In 1969, she and I came to work as *zhiqing* in this same village, which was located in Guangxi province of southern China. But she alone was appointed to work in a different production team and lived with a peasant family at the far end of the village. The host family was quite big--an aged couple living with their five sons. All but the eldest son remained unmarried.

Back in the late 1950s, Mei's father had been labeled a "bourgeois Rightist" and sent to his home village to be re-formed through labor. Mei's mother was re-assigned to a county hospital, where my mother was also sent to work. Mei and I seemed to have shared the same fate. We became home-less and were forced to feed ourselves by earning seven fen a day. In the second spring after our arrival, all *zhiqing* except Mei moved from peasants' homes into new abodes, which had been built for us with a special fund from the government. We had our own kitchens where we cooked our meals. The pro-duction team to which Mei belonged had received their share of a government fund but did not build a home for her, which meant she had to continue living with her host family.

One day in mid-March of 1971, Mei, who was introverted and seldom mixed with other *zhiqing*, came to visit us. She told us that she had suffered frequent harassment by the 35-year-old son, the second in her host family. Because of her repeated refusals, a drastic change had taken place in their attitude, and they often threw sarcastic or slighting re-marks at her. While working in the fields, she began hearing gossip about herself from villagers, which also gave her great stress.

Mei asked the team leader to arrange a new place for her to live, but time and again, he used various pretexts to delay a solution. We all understood why at the start the peasant family had taken the initiative to ask for a female *zhiqing* to stay with them. Since all families in the village belonged to the same clan, it was clear whom the team leader had chosen to side with. After consultations, several of us *zhiqing* agreed that the only alternative was to continue negotiating with the leadership of the production brigade and asking them to relocate Mei.

About two weeks after her visit, a pale-faced Mei again came over on a drizzly day, which was typical of the spring weather in that part of China. She told us that her host family had thrown all her belongings out of their house. She asked us to help her move her things to her new place. In a persistent rain and foul wind, several of us picked up her sacks of grain and other belongings, which lay strewn on the ground, and we moved them to her new abode -- a cowshed from which the cattle had just been led away. Surrounded by pigsties, toilets, and abandoned shanties, the cowshed we saw was a damp, dark and stinking shelter! Mistreatment of Mei and the scene at the site aroused our indignation. The meek, good-natured Mei tried to calm us down. She said she had just sent in an application for relocation to the production brigade headquarters. Until that could be processed, she had no alternative but to stay here and continue to work in the production team in order to earn a living. We understood her. She didn't want to make a big issue of her problem because she felt so miserable and helpless.

The first few days after she had been driven out of the peasant's home, she had stayed with me. She had showed me a love letter the man had written her. He was using both carrot and stick, trying to pressure her into submission. The following words are still fresh in my mind: "If you refuse to marry me, I will follow you wherever you go. I will make you lose face before all folk. You shall die a painful death." The open threat contained in the letter made me angry. I asked Mei to show the letter to the leadership of our production brigade but she refused, saying that things would be settled after she was transferred to another commune where her elder sister was working as a *zhiqing*.

But she was rejected by that commune on the grounds that they had too many people for their small area of cultivable land. Probably, this was what had driven her to despair. Another possibility was that the peasant woman who had promised to keep Mei company that night had changed her mind, so Mei might have been sexually assaulted on her way home or at the cowshed. The door of the cowshed could not be firmly latched, and the walls of the enclosure were so low that it was very easy for any intruder to climb over.

An even more outrageous episode happened when Mei's mother came to the village after being informed of her daughter's death. Some villagers blamed her for having intervened in Mei's marriage affairs, saying that it was her intervention that had led Mei to commit suicide. With deep sorrow and indignation, Mei's mother complained to us, saying: "Not long ago, when I learnt that a son of her host family was seeking love from her, I only advised her to think clearly over the matter, saying that I would raise no objections if she decided to start a family in the village." As a matter of fact, Mei's sister had married a peasant without intervention from her mother. Now that Mei had died such a miserable death, some people wanted to shift the blame to her mother. This was what made her angry. "Where can I find justice?" She asked.

Mei had died suddenly, leaving many puzzles behind. There were more than one hundred *zhiqing* scattered in different villages of the production brigade. We had not yet managed to get together for a discussion of Mei's death when we were informed of the Brigade Party branch's instruction on this matter: The joint conclusion of the police, prosecutorial and legal departments was that Mei had committed suicide because of her bourgeois outlook on love affairs. The Party branch warned us *zhiqing* against stirring up turmoil over the matter.

How absurd it was! Should a girl *zhiqing* be blamed for having a bourgeois outlook on love affairs just because of her refusal to marry a peasant? Should she be subjected to abuse and discrimination because of such a refusal? We *zhiqing* were not convinced, but we had no evidence of homicide. Not even the love letter Mei had shown me was found after her death. Mei's pitiful mother abandoned any legal pursuit, probably convinced that she could only resign herself to her fate.

Whenever I think of Mei, my heart is filled with pain. She was terribly wronged, and her death still calls out for justice.

Mei, I often sing the popular *zhiqing* song Remembrance for you. It expresses the deep sorrow I feel for all the *zhiqing* who sacrificed their lives, for different reasons, during the Sent-down movement.

In the subtropical forest lies your worthy young life.
–Why did you depart so hastily, all alone,
Leaving behind a lingering remembrance,
–And deep grief to your family and friends?

Chasing Away the "Black Households"

by Zhao Chao

不如社会主义好

That wintry morning, I was still deeply immersed in a sweet dream of sharing Chinese New Year dinner with my family back in Beijing. When I was about to put a piece of chicken into my mouth, I was awakened by a knocking at the door.

"Old Zhao, get up now. I need you to do something."

I knew from the low, muffled voice that it was Party Secretary Yang of our Production Brigade. He put the word "Old" before my surname as a sign of respect even though I was still a teenager.

Damn! There was no farm work in winter. Why was he coming so early to disturb me? I got up and opened the door. A draft of cold air made me shiver.

"Old Zhao, here's what I want you to do. The commune sent someone here, ordering us to cut off the tail of capitalism, and chase the 'black households' away from the gullies behind the mountains. You go with Ma Shifa and Yang Liwa to complete the job."

"How should we chase them away?" I asked.

"This is an assignment from above. We are required to chase all the 'black households' out of Ganquan County within three days. When the inspection team comes, the 'black households' must not be there. Do it by force if necessary. If people refuse to leave, tie them up and string them together."

He fumbled about in his pocket as he spoke, pulling out a handful of hard nuts and thrusting them into my hands. "Get started right after breakfast," he said. "It's almost thirty li[5] from here."

Having lived in the village for almost a year, I was quite

5. About ten miles.

familiar with the term "black household". Yulin Prefecture in the north had suffered droughts for several consecutive years, leaving some areas with no harvests at all. People had to rely on state relief but still could not fill their bellies. Some of them came to the deep gullies in our Yan'an region and opened wasteland to grow crops. At the start, only men came. They grew crops in spring, harvested in autumn, and then took the grain back home. Later, they brought their families and settled down. In official language, they were classified as "unauthorized migrants" (*mang liu*), but the local people called them "black households." Since they didn't encroach upon the land of our production brigade, we lived in peace with them. Sometimes, when our villagers went to work in fields not far from their settlement, they would offer us boiled water or thin grain soup. People of our production brigade were never concerned about their reclamation of the wasteland, adopting the attitude that they were toilers just like us.

I kindled a fire to cook my breakfast. I had barely finished my meal when Ma Shifa and Yang Liwa arrived. Ma was the deputy leader of our production brigade, while Yang was head of the militia.

"No more lolling in bed, Chao," Ma said with a smile and a playful punch, calling me by my given name.

"I couldn't 'loll' if I wanted to," I said, returning his punch. "All the other *zhiqing* have gone home to Beijing, and I'm the only one left. It doesn't matter where I go. You're the one who had to crawl out of a bed with someone in it to warm your feet. Anyhow, let's go."

Yang went ahead, humming a local folksong:

My fancy man, you went toward

the Western Pass of the Great Wall;
Leaving your sweetheart behind
with long streaming tears.

Yang was very good at playing and singing folksongs. I liked to work beside him when we were hoeing in the field, where he would endlessly sing lovely melodies that echoed across the hills.

Walking along the mountain trail, we reached an elevated place on a gentle slope. Before us stretched a vast expanse of bare earth after the harvest, with patches alternating between gray and yellowish brown. Only the sky was blue, a sort of deep and crystal blue that made you want to plunge into it.

Ma walked very quickly in his grass sandals. He casually collected some kindling from both sides of the path, and used withered straw to make bundles, which he placed beside the path for pickup on our return trip. Ancient folkways still prevailed in these mountainous regions. No one would take away anything left beside the path.

"Old Ma, how shall we drive the 'black households' away?" I asked. "They keep coming back every year."

Before Ma could reply, Yang said, "We just walk all around the area, yell at a few people, and return to report a job well done." Yang was familiar with many of the "black households" from his work on the pig farm of our production brigade, which was close to their settlement.

"Do you think it'll work?" I was still not convinced.

"Sure it will," Ma said, taking his pipe from his mouth. "The authorities are really serious this time, and we should be, too. We have to 'grasp revolution'." He nudged Yang and said, "Chao will give these 'black households' a good lecture and explain the basic principles to them."

I felt that something was not quite right. I didn't know what the two of them were planning. Ma and his brother were well-known in the area for their shrewdness. Ma himself sometimes expressed ideas that stunned all of us *zhiqing*, even with our high school educations. He once confided to me, "We'll be going to war soon. We can't do without wars. We've got too many people." A few days later, a battle with the former Soviet Union broke out at Zhenbao Island on the northern border. From then on we called him "The Malthusian prophet" or just "Prophet Ma," a nickname he gladly accepted.

There was a lot of singing and blathering along the way. It was already noontime when we reached Mali Village, where more than twenty "black households" were concentrated, people of both sexes numbering nearly a hundred.

Many young men and housewives greeted Yang as we passed by. I was the only stranger to them, and they looked at me with curiosity. Yang escorted us to a big, neat cave home, where we were warmly received by a man of about fifty who grasped our hands and led us inside. He invited us to sit on a kang.[7]

In the absence of any furniture, the room looked quite spacious and clean. On the *kang*, torn pieces of matting were arranged neatly, and over them a lambskin was placed beside two patched quilts. A few jars sat on the kitchen counter, which was also made of clay like the *kang*. In one corner there were several sacks of grain and two hoes. These were probably all the assets of the cave home's owner.

Ma grandly crossed his legs and sat in the center of the

7. About 0.3 kilogram

kang. "Old Ji," he said to our host, "summon all your people together. We have an urgent matter to discuss. Old Zhao here was sent down to work in our production brigade." Ma pointed at me.

"Right, right," Ji replied humbly with a nod and a smile, well aware that as "black households" they were in a weak position. He then addressed Ma by his title: "Production Brigade Leader, it's already noontime. Let's take lunch before our meeting."

"Take lunch? That sounds like a good idea. What kind of lunch did you have in mind?"

"We have some fresh meat to go with buckwheat noodles."

Before long, two women carried in some meat soup and hot sauce along with plates and bowls. On the kitchen counter was placed a wooden noodle-making device. A strong young man got onto the counter and pressed the lever at one end of the device. Then with a squeaky sound, buckwheat noodles came slowly out of the openings of a grid on the other end and fell into a big pot of boiling water. These "black households" appeared well-equipped, I thought to myself. In the official propaganda, it was alleged that production by individual households would nurture capitalism, which should be eradicated. What I saw seemed to justify this statement. A lenient policy would not work in dealing with these households based on private production. I regretted that we had not waited till armed militia could come with us. I nudged Ma, who was chatting quietly with Ji, and said to him, "Old Ma, we can't eat here. Let's have a meeting and leave."

Not waiting for Ma's reply, Ji hastened to say to me: "Old

Zhao, do you think our meal isn't good enough? It's a shame we do not have any wheat flour as we didn't grow wheat. What should we do?"

"Your meal is fine. We just can't eat here. We've got work to do."

"Even great missions can't prevent people from eating their meals. An emperor wouldn't dispatch hungry soldiers. Please take the meal even though it is not good."

Ma echoed our host. "He's right, Old Zhao. Let's eat before we do other things." Ma normally addressed me by my given name, Chao, without formality, but now he switched to "Old Zhao," as I was called by Party Secretary Yang and a few elderly housewives who didn't know me well.

Setting bowls filled with noodles before us, a woman said, "It's paradise for us to eat like this. People don't know how poorly we ate back in our Yulin region."

"What did you eat?" I asked. I had heard about their hard life back there, but I wanted to know the details.

"Leaves of poplar trees, vines of sweet potatoes and chaff. It was the best food we could get," the woman responded, her eyes glistening, though I wasn't sure whether it was from tears or the kitchen steam. She described to me how they had processed those famine foods.

"Didn't you have relief from the government?"

"The local authorities provided each person with six liang of grain per day. But you had to buy it with cash. We had no harvests from fields, and no side occupations to earn any money. Where could we get the cash to buy grain?"

I could hardly believe my ears. The press was full of good news every day, reporting bumper harvests everywhere and painting a rosy picture of the overall situation. Although the nation's self-inflicted setbacks during the Cultural Revolution had already made me dubious about many things, the political ideology imbedded in my mind over long years prevented me from accepting the harsh reality: In socialist China, some people still lived in dire poverty!

"Natural disasters have hit our region for six consecutive years," Ji said. "Last spring saw a serious drought. With the little rain we later had, we planted our crops. Then the drought resumed and persisted. Several years earlier, political movements started with the persecution of landlords, rich peasants and anti-revolutionaries, and then armed conflicts broke out. In the past two years, people were asked to cut off the tail of capitalism. Chickens and piglets were taken away from us and became publicly owned. Collecting medicinal herbs was also forbidden. To avoid starvation, we had no choice but to come here," Ji said. Lowering his head and filling his pipe with tobacco, he started smoking in silence.

Others present joined the conversation.

"As long as we toilers had some grain, no one wanted to desert our homes. People say that we Northern Shaanxi folks are particularly fond of our homeland."

"We were so miserable. Adults still had some endurance, but without food, the children would cry their hearts out."

The more I heard, the sadder I felt.

A big crowd had gathered on the empty ground outside the cave, some standing, some squatting, while others drew together for warmth. All of them wore somber expressions. Once we came out of the cave, they all turned their eyes on us, like a flock of sheep waiting to be slaughtered.

Ma was the first to speak. "Dear folks, today we come

here on the instruction of the county and commune author-ities to solve the problem of unauthorized migration. Now, let Old Zhao explain the official policy to you." He pushed me forward to confront the crowd. All eyes were riveted on me.

Facing a crowd dressed in ragged clothes, and look-ing at their eyes full of worries and expectations, I found it hard to bring myself to say the words that boiled down to chasing them away. I knew that to speak official jargon, such as "going back home to grasp revolution and promote production," "cutting off the tails of capitalism," and "sup-porting the world revolution" would have no relevance or effect on them. How could I ask them to go home, knowing what awaited them were droughts and starvation? Yet be-hind these official statements were armed militiamen. What would happen to these "black households" if they refused to leave?

I stood there, knowing perfectly well what I should say according to official policy. What I actually said was:

"Dear folks, people here are very clear about the calam-ities and hardships in your district. We don't want to drive you away. But...."

Then an idea came to me. I turned to Ma and said: "Shifa, shall we persuade these folks to leave for a few days just to evade the forthcoming inspection? It should be OK so long as inspectors from the commune don't see them. They can come back when the inspection is over."

"What'll we tell the Party Secretary?" Ma asked me with a shrewd smile.

"You can say this was my idea. Our task is completed once these folks leave here. No one can prevent them from coming back."

Both Ma and Yang broke into hearty laughter. Ma said, "Excellent, Chao. I guess I had the right idea about you." Then he whispered to me: "Before your speech, I reached an agreement with Ji that the old folks and children would leave and go past the commune headquarters before turning back. The young people would hide in the ravines behind the mountains to keep an eye on the crops. I didn't tell you about it because I was afraid you might not go along with the arrangement."

"What do you think I am—some kind of idiot?" I gave him a blow to the chest. Everyone burst into laughter.

Ji then said, "All right, so everything is worked out in the interest of us toilers. If there's nothing more to discuss, the meeting is dismissed. Everybody hurry and pack your things."

Someone in the crowd shouted, "Let Old Zhao sing a song for us."

I waved away the idea. "I'm no singer. Let Yang Liwa do it."

The crowd stirred and another voice shouted at me, "Old Yang knows he can't get away without singing. But you, too, sing a song for us, please. What do you say, everybody!" The crowd applauded.

Ma gave me a push and said, "Come on, Chao. People here need entertainment. They don't even have radios."

With expectant gazes fixed on me, I started singing an aria from a popular modern Peking opera. Once I had sweated my way through that demanding piece of music, I turned to Yang Liwa.

He started singing folksongs of Northern Shaanxi. One song after another flowed out from his vast repertoire. The "black households" people seemed to be enjoying his performance tremendously. Some of them hummed the tunes along with him. As I watched them and imagined them roaming about the following day in the freezing cold with their old folks and children, I began to feel very sad. Unable to stay there any longer, I left the crowd and walked into the hills. I wanted to find a place where I could have a good cry.

Behind me, voices sang in unison:

In the middle of nowhere, wild lilies grow,
Their red flowers reflected in the pools.
We toilers are looking forward
To a happy, prosperous future.

Cruelty beyond Words

by Zhu Jihong

A man with unkempt hair and dressed in rags was escorted to a struggle session with the high-sounding title "Striking Hard at the Spontaneous Forces of Capitalism" – an expression targeted at people engaged in individual productive or commercial activities. In those days, such outlaws were regarded as dangerous people trying to restore capitalism in China.

As a *zhiqing* working on a paramilitary farm in China's Northeast, I followed our battalion instructor to the struggle session, which was held by one of our companies. The targeted man was very thin and had a yellowish, wrinkled face that looked like dried walnut meat. "Shrunken Man," the nickname people gave him, seemed to fit him perfectly.

Being an unworldly young student, I could not help wondering why such a man was selected to represent the spontaneous forces of capitalism. In my mind, capitalists were all grotesquely fat.

The meeting was held in a highly charged atmosphere. Following a prearranged schedule, speakers started denouncing Shrunken Man one after another, letting out angry shouts, with saliva flying from their mouths. His crime: going down to the river to catch fish, climbing up to the mountains to gather Chinese medicinal herbs, and paying special attention to managing his own private plot of land. But Shrunken Man seemed totally unmoved. He only stood there in silence, his head bowed.

Several similar struggle sessions had already been held against Shrunken Man prior to this, but without tangible results. He continued to go his own way, working on the farm during daytime, attending meetings where he was denounced in the evening, and going to the river to catch fish late at night.

It remained a puzzle to me why Shrunken Man was so single-minded. He seemed to be running down a dark road like a man possessed.

The farm leadership now cited the recent tragic example of another farm employee to warn Shrunken Man and enlighten others. That employee had stealthily gone fishing at night but had never returned. A month later, his body was discovered at the riverside, with so much of his face eaten by fish that it was hard to identify him. This presumably showed the dire consequences of "capitalist pursuits." But Shrunken Man remained defiant. He suddenly roared: "If you had a family to feed, you would outdo me in such pursuits!" Once more, he refused to plead guilty.

Armed militiamen led him away, pushing and roughing him up. People were astounded to see how crazy the "spontaneous forces of capitalism" could be.

But the man's fate proved to be unpredictable. Barely a month after the Striking Hard session, a public funeral was held to mark Shrunken Man's untimely death.

I tried my best to find out the details of his story.

One day, Shrunken Man was driving a horse-drawn cart heavily laden with lime for the farm. Having climbed to the highest point of a sandy road, his cart started going down a steep slope. He soon spotted a group of small children playing in the middle of the road and shouted at them to move, but two of the children were so frightened they froze. At this crucial juncture, Shrunken Man jumped ahead of the horse and quickly threw the two children to the roadside. The wheels of the cart ran over him, splashing his blood on the ground.

People flocked to the spot and found him beyond rescue.

Shrunken Man seemed more shriveled. His face looked like a sheet of yellowish paper. With no more blood flowing from his body, he lay there still, his eyes opened and his face wearing a painful expression.

More *zhiqing* and farm employees came to the scene. Among them were the eloquent revolutionaries and warriors who had thundered and shouted at him with raised arms. One could see exhibited a whole range of reactions--indifference, puzzlement, lamentation, sobbing and loud cries. Most of the people present expressed sympathy and admiration. Those farm employees who had more or less traveled the same "capitalist road" along with Shrunken Man remained silent as they proceeded to carry his body away.

The funeral was plain and without ceremony. There was no eulogy. People just watched his shriveled body in silence, and then dug a small grave for him. But in the calm of the day, I felt a deep, overwhelming emotion that shook my heart.

After the funeral, I went to visit his home. I pushed open the shaky door of a wretched thatched hut. What greeted my eye was a mottled kitchen stove connected to a *kang,* an earthen bed which was heated from beneath by kitchen fire. The *kang* was covered by several pieces from a broken bamboo mat. Lying on it was a woman with unkempt hair, a dirty face and dull-looking eyes. Beside her were seven or eight small children, their eyes wandering about aimlessly. They evoked the image of a horde of mice in a straw nest. Though their upper bodies were in rags which could barely hide their skinny arms, the white pants they wore were all brand-new. Their dozen-plus small feet were as black as charcoal.

Faced with an unexpected visitor, the woman struggled to sit up, wiping her tearful eyes with a corner of her shirt.

She murmured in a faint voice: "Our company office sent me thirty chi (a length slightly more than a foot - ed.) of white cloth for making a mourning dress. I used it to make pants for them. Now they can go about without showing their buttocks. Many thanks for this."

Pointing at a child whose feet were wrapped in corn sheathes, she said: "I was expecting my old devil to shoot a wild duck and get a pair of shoes for him. I have been sick in bed for four or five years. Our family of ten relied on his monthly pay of thirty yuan. How can we make ends meet? I don't know if he was a good person or a bad one. Anyhow, my children and I often talk about the good things he did for us. Now, he is no longer alive. He lived a miserable life and suffered a painful death."

I wandered out of the thatched hut in a daze. I knew no comforting words that could soothe her broken heart. Much less did I know what I could do to help her.

Images of the woman and her family stayed with me for a long time -- her yellowish face, her listless eyes, and her swarm of helpless children.

I now came to understand why Shrunken Man had been so determined in going his own way. To live as a worthy family man was all he wanted!

III. Love, Marriage, and Family

....

Love at the Floodgates

by Guo Mengwei

294

In 1969, I was sent to work as a *zhiqing* on a farm in North China. It was one of the many paramilitary farms managed by the so-called Production and Construction Corps of Inner Mongolia.

On an irrigation canal that ran through our farm, there was a floodgate that was probably the grandest structure in the territory. Close by stood a small watchman's hut with earthen walls. It was less than three square meters in size, and most of it was occupied by a single *kang*. The wall facing the canal had a tiny window—a hole--for overseeing the water flow during flood seasons. None of us ever imagined that such a poor shelter would be turned into a romantic trysting place for young lovers.

A Three-Year Taboo

A three-year ban on *zhiqing* love affairs was already in place when we arrived. Some of the older ones among us tried to evade it by "going underground". However, once discovered by company leaders or ultra-revolutionaries, violators would be subjected to severe criticism. They would lose face in public as if they had been caught stealing in broad daylight.

The first time I attended a political meeting, I saw a male companion from Zhejiang coming under heavy fire just because he had sent a love letter to a female *zhiqing*. The letter had somehow landed in the hands of a company leader. The young man was reprimanded for having committed what sounded like an unpardonable crime. A silly boy from Beijing went so far as to compare him to the two infamous high officials in Tianjin who had been executed for corruption in the early 1950s. In retrospect, this vehement denunciation seems ridiculous and deplorable.

A female *zhiqing* from Baotou who had been appointed a squad leader was found to be using a warehouse under her authority for rendezvous with her boyfriend. She was denounced and disgraced. There were people full of ultra-leftist ideas in both the rank-and-file and the leadership. They would kick up a big fuss over nothing and subject young *zhiqing* to humiliation and insult in the name of "class struggle".

Place for Rendezvous

We lived in harsh conditions year after year, subjected to heavy physical labor and provided with no cultural diversions. Despite the extreme cruelty of the regulations, the dismissals, and other disciplinary measures put in place by the ultra-left, the seeds of love continued to sprout. A gesture of goodwill from, or a chance encounter with, a member of the opposite sex -- a lunch brought to a sickbed, the offer of a piece of corn bread or toffee or a handkerchief -- might spark passions that caused many of us to fall into the river of love.

After the three-year ban on love affairs was lifted, *zhiqing* lovers no longer had to go underground. We all lived in dormitories without access to theaters or cinemas or rooms for private meetings, which meant that young lovers had to go out into the wilderness or the sand dunes to be alone together. Inner Mongolia had windy weather more than 200 days of the year. In a big gale, the air would be thick with sand and dust, and people could hardly open their eyes or see where they were going. The small hut at the floodgate thus became a much-treasured place for lovers to meet. Virtually all young lovers on our farm must have spent some time there.

Witness to Joys and Sorrows

Struggles would ensue when demand for the hut was at its height. Generally, it was first come first served, but a few mischievous boys found ways to override this rule. A *zhiqing* boy from Baoding, Hebei Province, too impatient to wait his turn, set off some firecrackers close to the hut. The two lovers inside soon fled and the Baoding boy went in triumphantly with his sweetheart. Two pairs of Beijing lovers found another way to occupy the love nest. They formed a mutual-aid team. One pair would enter the hut at midnight while the other pair would lock the door from the outside so others couldn't get in. Sometimes one pair would keep watch for the other until it was time for them to take over. Their maneuvers enabled them to monopolize the hut for a period of time.

The hut thus performed as a kind of marriage agency, but it oversaw divorces as well. A senior male *zhiqing* from Zhejiang, whom most of us respected as an elder brother, once took on the role of a tragic figure in that tiny hut. On hearing that his lover was to be transferred to teach in an urban school, he took the initiative to end their relationship. Assuming that he would probably spend the rest of his life in the countryside, he did not want to be a hindrance to her. I still remember how he and his lover went to that little hut for their last meeting. He came back with his eyes red and brimming with tears. I felt helpless listening to him pour out his feelings.

That "divorce" was far from being the only one. Many people who had to stay behind acted in the way our Zhejiang elder brother did, but sometimes, the one who had a chance to leave simply abandoned the other one.

It has been said that *zhiqing* had a void in their lives in the realm of love—that, living in a suffocating political climate and working under harsh physical conditions, we had no chance to enjoy love as young people should. As I see it, however, despite the bitterness and helplessness we experienced, that little hut at the floodgate still offered many of us a bit of the sweetness and romance of love we longed for.

A Tearful Wedding

by Ren Guoqing

我们的共产党和共产党所领导的八路军、新四军，是革命的队伍。我们这个队伍完全是为着解放人民的，是彻底地为人民的利益工作的。张思德[1]同志就是我们这个队伍中的一个同志。人总是要死的，但死的意义有不同。中国古时候有个文学家叫做司马迁的说过："人固有一死，或重于泰山，或轻于鸿毛。"[2]为人民利益而死，就比泰山还重；替法西斯卖力，替剥削人民和压迫人民的人去死，就比鸿毛还轻。张思德同志是为人民利益而死的，他的死是比泰山还要重的。因为我们是为人民服务的，所以，我们如果有缺点，就不怕别人批评指出。不管是什么人，谁向我们指出都行。只要你说得对，我们就改正。你说的办法

白求恩同志是实践了这一系列宁主义路线的。我们中国共产党员也要实践这一条路线。我们要和一切资本主义国家的无产阶级联合起来，要和日本的、英国的、美国的、德国的、意大利的以及一切资本主义国家的无产阶级联合起来，才能打倒帝国主义，解放我们的民族和人民，解放世界的民族和人民。这就是我们的国际主义，这就是我们用以反对狭隘民族主义和狭隘爱国主义的国际主义。白求恩同志毫不利己专门利人的精神，表现在他对工作的极端负责任，对同志对人民的极端的热忱。每个共产党员都要学习他。不少的人对工作不负责任，拈轻怕重，把重担子推给人家，自己挑轻的。一事当前，先替自己打算，然后再替别人打算。出了一点力就觉得了不起，喜欢自吹，生怕人家不知道。对同志对人民不是满腔热忱，而是冷冷清清，漠不关心，麻木不仁。这种人其实不是共产党员，至少不能算一个纯粹的共产党员。从前线回来的人说到白求恩，没有一个不佩服，没有一个不为他的精神所感动。晋察冀边区的军民，凡亲身受过白求恩医生的治疗和亲眼看过白求恩医生的工作的，无不为之感动。

One day in 1974 our company leader came back from the regimental headquarters with news about a decision that would have major significance for our future. It had been made by the Party Committee of the Production and Construction Corps of Inner Mongolia, an umbrella organization that supervised the operation of all paramilitary farms in the region.

Most of us *zhiqing* had long since lost interest in decisions made by the leadership, so only a few of our group went to the meeting to hear our company leader give a briefing. What we later learnt from them caused a great uproar. To encourage us *zhiqing* to "strike roots in the border region", the Corps Party Committee had decided to lift the ban on love affairs and marriage for *zhiqing*. All the regiments and companies were instructed to prepare housing for young couples who had plans to get married.

Everyone became heavy-hearted on hearing the news, feeling that the nightmare prospect of staying in the border region for life had become a reality.

Though we greeted this Party decision with resentment and fear, the prospect of being allowed to pursue love awakened our long-suppressed interest in the opposite sex. About 60% of *zhiqing* in our regiment were 1969 graduates from junior middle school and were all around the age of twenty. The rest were two or three years younger. Most of them had graduated from junior middle school in 1971.

Until then, love affairs had been strictly prohibited. Even love novels and love songs were forbidden. Many *zhiqing* were criticized for singing love songs. Young lovers were severely reprimanded for their "roguish behavior" and disciplined accordingly. In such a repressive atmosphere, male and female *zhiqing* had little contact and were afraid of arousing suspicion if they even spoke to each other.

What was love? How could one start a love affair? They had only the vaguest idea. Now everything changed. The Corps leadership not only allowed but encouraged love affairs. Suddenly you could have love if you wanted it.

It was as if a dam had burst. Boys and girls who had never spoken to each other started going out as couples. Driven by instinct, most would follow the example of those disillusioned, freewheeling Red Guards of the late 1960s whose attitude toward love was anything but serious.

Skills in love-making became a subject for open discussion in the dormitories. Many of us had had love affairs and enjoyed love-making but refrained from getting married. According to government policy, wedlock required a local marriage license and household registration, which meant a personal decision to settle down and make a commitment to stay in the border region for the rest of one's life.

My close friend W came to see me one day and confided, "My girlfriend is pregnant. What should I do?"

I knew he was speaking about a girl named L.

"What are you planning to do?" I asked him.

"Quite a few people have induced abortions by beating the pregnant girl's belly. I just don't have the guts to do it."

"No, you really shouldn't do that. She could be maimed for life if something went wrong. Don't worry, I'll help you to find a way out."

I went that evening to see the farm physician, Dr. Han. He said, "I have a prescription handed down from my ancestors that is very effective in inducing abortion. It won't do any harm to the pregnant woman, but it requires a special herb that you may not be able to buy at any Chinese medicinal herbs store. If you cannot get it, don't bother making the prescription. Any concoction without it would be useless."

My friend and I went to a Chinese medicinal herb store in Wulateqian Banner. The old man behind the counter looked at the prescription and then sized us up with a strange expression in his eyes. It was easy for him to identify us as *zhiqing* from a paramilitary farm. He then lowered his head to take another look at the prescription and said, "This store does not carry one of the herbs. Please look for it at other stores." I asked him which of the herbs he meant. He pointed his finger at precisely the one Dr. Han had said was essential.

We traveled to Baotou, the largest industrial city in Inner Mongolia, and Hohhot, the regional capital. We visited all Chinese medicinal herb stores in both cities and got the same answer.

L's belly grew bigger with each passing day. W came to me and said, "We have to get married. I don't want my child to be born out of wedlock."

Their wedding took place in the auditorium at the regimental headquarters. It was the first celebration of marriage between two *zhiqing* lovers on our farm. All their former fellow students attended. The presence of the regimental commander and the commissar added a strong political color to the ceremony. The commissar made a speech saying, "We come to celebrate the wedding of Comrades W and L. They have taken concrete action in response to the call of Chairman Mao to 'strike roots in the border regions'. They have played an exemplary role for all members of our Corps." Calling theirs a "revolutionary, glorious marriage," he urged us all to learn from their example and devote the rest of our lives to the construction of the border region.

The bride and her friends were already hugging each other and crying bitterly before the commissar had finished his speech. "I will never be able to return home!" Wailed the bride. One of her tearful companions observed that she was the first to take this step and that, sooner or later, they would all meet with the same fate.

There were a number of *zhiqing* who resisted the temptations of love, including some who worked hard learning English. The majority of these people were 1966-68 graduates of middle or high school, the so-called *laosanjie*. They were a few years older and more sensible than other *zhiqing*. Biding their time for opportunities to leave the countryside, they determined never to "strike roots in the border region."

Women Captives

by Lin Xiaozhong

1974 was my fourth year of working as a *zhiqing* in Arong Banner, Hulunbei'er League of Inner Mongolia. I was leader of our production team, giving assignments to people gathered on the threshing ground one autumn day, when a team member in charge of guarding our harvests came running to inform me that he had caught a new bunch of thieves. I looked up to find several young villagers armed with shotguns and spears escorting a dozen or so captives who turned out to be women dressed in rags.

Autumn was the most beautiful season on this vast expanse of black earth. It was also the season when work was most difficult and exhausting. The sorghum and soybeans were ripe and ready for harvest. But the unpredictable weather posed a major threat. A snowstorm might blow in at any time to destroy all the crops. What was worse, in those tumultuous years, many migrants came from south of the Great Wall to seek a means of survival. Along with starving peasants in adjacent areas, they sneaked onto our fields and stole our harvested grain. Soybeans on large tracts of land were clubbed down and the beans collected by the marauders, leaving behind only heaps of empty stalks.

Despite a shortage of hands, I had to allocate a sizable portion of our labor force to guarding the harvests. Fights between guards and marauders, sometimes with weapons, broke out from time to time.

The capture of women thieves created a sensation in our small mountain village of slightly more than two hundred people. Adults and children alike flocked to see the spectacle. The dozen or so females surrounded by the crowd appeared desperate and panic-stricken, like a pack of lambs waiting to be slaughtered.

The youngest among them were only fifteen or sixteen, the eldest around thirty. Most of them had ropes in their hands for binding crops. I felt pity for them, but I had to punish them in some way as a warning to future marauders. I ordered them to be escorted to the threshing ground where a big pile of corn cobs was covered by snow. "Don't let them leave until they have unsheathed all the cobs," I instructed.

At noontime, the leader of our women's team came up and told me that one of the captives was a *zhiqing* from Beijing, my hometown, who lived in another village. Like me, she had come to this rural area in 1968, but since then most of her companions had left her village, mainly through backdoor deals, leaving only seven or eight of them behind. Since local girls married at an early age, female *zhiqing* soon became the only women working with the male villagers in the fields, doing all kinds of heavy labor. Most of them developed gynecological and other diseases. Not surprisingly, they rushed into marriage one after another for the simple purpose of survival. The woman *zhiqing* captive from Beijing was one of them. She and her husband didn't get along well, and this was complicated by a faultfinding mother-in-law. Life remained truly difficult for her. Her attempt at theft was obviously forced upon her by these circumstances.

I recalled the *zhiqing* captive clearly. She was tall and slender, with big, melancholy eyes and a pale face. She wore a cotton-padded jacket with a checkered covering and blue raglan sleeves. On her unkempt hair hung blades of withered grass. To look at her, you would never guess that she was an educated person from Beijing. Our chance encounter was an embarrassment for both of us. The rest of the women captives must also have had their own sorry tales to tell. I asked our woman leader to arrange a lunch for them, have a soothing talk with them, and then send them away.

During my nine-year stay in the countryside, few of the male *zhiqing* got married, and still fewer of them married peasant girls. Among the female *zhiqing* who married locally, most had come from workers' families rather than from families of officials or intellectuals. I did know of one village in a nearby commune where most of the *zhiqing* girls married local peasants. These were girls who had no prospect of returning home, and living alone was simply too hard for them. Their fiancés and in-laws usually treated them very well during courtship, but once married, they had to behave as peasant housewives -- doing all the household chores and waiting upon their husbands and parents-in-law. Long accustomed to urban living, they found the way of life in a remote, backward mountain village barely tolerable. Problems proliferated with the birth of children. More often than not, when their first children were still toddling around, *zhiqing* mothers were already nursing new babies at their breasts. Life was so hard and monotonous that they became numb and depressed. The dual burden of physical hardship and mental distress made them the most unfortunate *zhiqing* group. When their counterparts returned to the cities by the millions toward the end of the 1970's, they were left behind and forgotten.

Two years after the capture of the women during the autumn harvest, I heard from a dependable source that the Beijing *zhiqing* had committed suicide. Owing to many hardships and a bad relationship with her husband, she swallowed a bottle of insecticide, leaving behind a barely one-year-old baby.

I could hardly believe it. She was too young to be laid to rest beneath the black soil of the northern wildness. To this very day, her image as a frightened captive remains alive in my mind.

How I Disappointed the Village Girl

by Xu Zhendong

316

Seventeen-year-old Ying'er was the only child of a peasant family in a village of Jurong County, Jiangsu Province. Like her thin, tall father, she stood at about 1.7 meters, taller than the average village girl. Narrow-shouldered and with two slender braids reaching down below her waist, she had a white face with a yellowish tinge, probably a sign of malnourishment.

I was a sturdy boy at the time. As a *zhiqing*, I proved stronger than most young villagers in carrying loads by shoulder pole or pushcart. Whenever a peasant family was building a new house, I was invariably invited to help transport bricks and tiles. The host family would treat all helpers to a simple dinner at the end of the workday, and we would enjoy plentiful liquor made from dried taros. I never feared that anyone could out-drink me.

During breaks in our farm work, villagers used to ask me to tell them news about the rest of the country and the world, and we would often lose track of the time, sometimes not resuming work until sunset. Once I told them the story about the lunar landing by a three-man US crew on Apollo 12. An old peasant refused to believe it. He said that the moon was a great treasure. How could men tread on such a treasure? Whenever I spun a yarn to the villagers, Ying'er would sit close to me, listening with rapt attention like a small child.

One day during that summer, I was carrying two loads of rice seedlings with a shoulder pole and tried repeatedly to step onto a slippery footpath from a paddy field. Suddenly, a small, thin hand stretched in front of me. I grasped it instinctively and managed to step onto the footpath, only to discover that it was Ying'er who had helped me. For the rest of the day, I found myself wondering how the hand of a peasant girl could be so soft that I almost didn't feel any bones! This reminded me of the great Chinese writer Lu Xun's most popular novella, The True Story of Ah Q. The protagonist pinches the cheek of a young nun and later can't forget how soft and smooth it was. The obvious parallel made me laugh at myself.

That winter, our commune mobilized its members to build a reservoir near Mount Gaolun. Our production team leader sent me and several young villagers to participate. He also dispatched Ying'er and a few other girls to serve as cooks and cart-pullers. The carts we used were wheelbarrows, each with two projecting shafts at the rear for handles. We put our bedding, rice and firewood on the carts and hung a bottle of pickles on the handle of one. It took us half a day to reach the mountain.

After two weeks of hard work, we had a day off. The others spent the day sleeping or playing cards, but I thought about an old villager who had asked me to buy him two big vats for making pickles. Leaving early in the morning, I pushed one of the carts to an earthenware factory near our worksite. I bought the two vats and had them loaded into the cart, which I was pushing out of the factory gate when Ying'er emerged from nowhere and stood in front of the cart. She took up the pulling ropes, ready to go with me. I asked her to return to the worksite, saying that I could manage by myself. She answered, "I will go back when we have covered the mountain paths...." She then bent her slim body forward and started pulling the cart. Our village was about ten miles away. Two-thirds of the trip was on mountain paths with many ups and downs.

Ying'er was an experienced cart puller. When we were going up a mountain slope, she would pull the cart with all her strength. Going down, she would prevent the cart from accelerating by blocking it at the front. Her assistance saved me a lot of energy. Thanks to her help, I managed to push the cart through the narrow, rugged mountain paths. I might not have been able to safely transport the vats to our village without her. We did not speak a word along the way.

Eventually we came out of the mountains. The rest of the journey was three miles of smooth road. Stopping at the foot of the mountain, I thanked Ying'er and asked her to go back to our worksite. She lowered her head, her hands playing with the rope. She did not utter a word or show any sign of leaving. Growing impatient, I went to the front of the cart, took the rope from her hands, and wound it around the front of the cart. Again I asked her to go back. Then I lifted the handles, stood upright and started to go. She raised her head to look at me in silence, her eyes glistening with tears.

Alarmed, I now realized that Ying'er must be fond of me. But she was not aware that I had all along avoided love. Neither the concern showed me by a female *zhiqing* in an adjacent village, nor the extreme kindness of Ying'er, moved me beyond causing a warm feeling in my heart. I had always pretended to be a blockhead who knew nothing about love.

The pitiful Ying'er did not know that her seed of love would never bud in my heart because I did not want to live a life of poverty like hers in the countryside.

With my teeth clenched and my face expressionless, I said only, "I'm leaving."

I walked a few dozen paces and turned around to find her still standing there, motionless. I stopped for a few moments and shouted at her, "Off you go!" I never looked back again.

Several decades have passed since then. I cannot help thinking of Ying'er from time to time. Where is she now? How is she doing? I wish her well. Needless to say, what she had been offering me was her first love.

My First Love in the Countryside

by Sheng Zhongyi

Bo and I were middle school graduates of 1975 though we came from different schools. Because both our parents worked in Changchun Film Studio, we went as *zhiqing* to the same production brigade in Shuangyang County, which was only an hour's drive by car from Changchun, capital of Jilin Province, where the studio was located and where our families lived.

She was sent to the fourth production team while I was sent to the second. Though we had grown up together as children of studio staff members, we had never spoken to each other. In the countryside we got to know each other and soon fell in love. It all began with rehearsals of an entertainment program prepared by our brigade for presentation at a joint performance sponsored by our commune.

The headmaster of the village primary school was put in charge of the rehearsals. Since the Chinese New Year was drawing near, we had plenty of time during the winter vacation. Bo and I were selected to do an *errenzhuan*, a form of song and dance duet popular in China's Northeast. Its title was The Young Eagle Learns to Fly. Bo was the most beautiful girl of all *zhiqing* in our production brigade. She looked like Wen Qing, a popular TV hostess. Many male *zhiqing* adored her and sought her attention. Several of them were participants in the rehearsals. They were envious of me for being able to do a duet with her.

An introvert with a sedate, sensible personality, I did not expect to win her heart. She was a celebrated figure in our group, with her parents working in important positions at the studio. I was homely, and my father was just a physical laborer. Thinking that the two of us were really no match, I always reminded myself to keep my distance. Other male *zhiqing* would try to approach her during rehearsal breaks, but Bo did her best to avoid them. Sometimes, she came over and sat by my side, perhaps to create the impression that she belonged to me, much to the others' disappointment.

Two weeks quickly passed and our program was beginning to take shape. One day, our production brigade's leaders were scheduled to review our program. They had arranged the order of appearances, and players could leave when they had completed their presentations. Bo and I were the last to perform, which meant our presentation would be the finale of our program.

During the rehearsals, a heavy snow started. Looking outside, some of the female *zhiqing* worried aloud about bad road conditions on their return trip. Bo said half-jokingly that she needed my company all the way back home. I nodded in response. In fact, our two teams were separated only by a mountain peak. She lived about 3 miles away from the brigade headquarters where we did the rehearsals, and I lived a mile further away on the other side of the peak.

Night had fallen by the time the brigade leadership had reviewed the whole program. The snow was still falling when Bo and I left the brigade office, but after some time, luckily for us, it gradually stopped. Very soon the moon rose, shining over a vast expanse of glittering snow. We seemed to have entered a fairytale wonderland.

All was quiet that night. We talked about our ideals and our thoughts of the future as we walked along. Suddenly, a black shadow rushed out from behind willow trees on the roadside. Bo cried out and threw herself into my arms. This was the first time I had been so close to a beautiful girl and I was at a loss what to do. I soon discovered that the shadow was a wild dog. I shouted at it and it ran away without uttering a sound. I pushed Bo away from me, telling her that she had no need to fear. She dropped her head in embarrassment.

In China of the 1970s, young people were not so open as they are today. They would even feel shy when discovered walking hand in hand. Probably because both of us felt a bit embarrassed, we just walked in silence, with only the sound of snow under our feet.

After walking quite a long distance, Bo broke the silence by asking me hesitantly: "Zhongyi, do you mind my asking you a question?"

"No, not at all," I said.

"Do you have a girl friend?"

"No, I don't. Why?"

"Never mind. I was just wondering," she said, looking embarrassed. "Let's not talk about it anymore.....Zhongyi, you have such a good voice. When will you go to the brigade broadcast station again and read some more stories for us?"

"You really like my broadcast stories? How were my readings?" I asked her seriously.

"No need to ask me that. Your readings were really wonderful," she answered.

Bo's parents worked as voice actors at the studio. Under their influence, Bo must have developed good judgment on such matters and her comments carried weight. Pleased by her praise, I smiled and said, "You flatter me. They only asked me to do it because our studio supervisor told the brigade leadership that I had broadcasting experience."

"I thought the broadcasts were being done by some professional voice actor. Later I learnt that it was you. The villagers were obsessed with your readings. You really did a good job and made all of us *zhiqing* look good. Why did you stop?"

"I had to work in the fields during the day and walk to the broadcast station at night. The brigade leader saw how tired I was and stopped asking me to do the job."

I saw Bo to her dormitory. When we separated, she said to me: "You're a nice guy, but kind of a nerd." Then she turned and ran inside.

After this, our relationship seemed to change subtly. We plunged into the rehearsals with greater energy and enthusiasm.

On the day of the performance, our song and dance duet was a big success. Afterwards, the brigade leadership held a dinner for the entire cast. The Party secretary went from table to table to drink a toast to us. Coming to our table, he patted me on the shoulder and said, "The two of you played very well in The Young Eagle Learns to Fly.....Not to mention the fact that offstage you two make a good couple." His remark left us both red-faced.

We walked back to our dormitories down the long, winding road. I took out my harmonica and started playing the popular love song that begins: "In a faraway place, there is a nice girl......" When we were about to separate in front of her dormitory, she thrust into my hands a small parcel and said shyly to me: "This is for you. Don't open it until later." Then she ran off with a laugh.

I opened the parcel and found a pair of woolen socks she had knitted for me. In the severe cold of Northeastern China, these socks would help keep me warm. I stood on the snowy ground and watched her disappear into the darkness. I felt a warm, sweet glow in my heart. It was probably the sweet happiness that came with a first love.

From then on, our love only deepened. We tried to keep it a secret.

To avoid being discovered by our companions, we set up a contact point at a villager's home where we exchanged our love letters and messages. But as the Chinese saying goes, "There are no airtight walls in the world." News about our relationship soon spread.

One day, a male *zhiqing* named Yu who had been transferred to the brigade headquarters for a temporary job came to visit me. He told me that Bo had been his girlfriend for a long time and warned me not to come between them. He showed me a photo of the two of them together. Indeed, I had heard rumors that Bo and Yu had an unusual relationship, but only later did I learn that Yu's father was a skilled manipulator of photographic images. Yu had studied photography from him since he was a small boy. He brought a camera with him to the countryside, and frequently snapped photos of other *zhiqing* as well as villagers. A camera was a rarity at the time, and people envied him for it. He was particularly welcomed by female *zhiqing*. I began to blame Bo for having a foot in both camps and decided to end my position as "the third party" in the middle of a committed relationship.

After Yu's visit, I went to Bo's living quarters. I thrust the previously treasured socks into her hands, and walked off, not even bothering to look back. I could faintly hear her sobbing. I thought to myself: we had performed The Young Eagle Learns to Fly together. Now that we had taken our curtain call, it was time for us to end our love.

Afterwards, I learnt that Bo had been recruited by an army song and dance ensemble. Before departure, she asked a *zhiqing* companion to pass on a brief letter to me in which she had written: "Zhongyi: Before leaving here, I must make it clear to you that there has never been a love affair between Yu and me. It was all in his mind. I am not a fickle girl. You blamed me wrongly. Proud of myself, I seldom beg forgiveness of others, especially when I am not at fault....Since we have lost the chance that once brought us together, why should I try hard to retrieve it? My warm greetings."

Reading her letter left me deeply shaken. I realized that my rejection of Bo was the stupidest thing I had ever done in my life. Looking out of the window at the world of ice and snow, I suddenly felt the deep chill of winter.

Thirty years have passed since then. Whenever snow-flakes flutter in the air, I can't help thinking of Bo, my first love in the countryside.

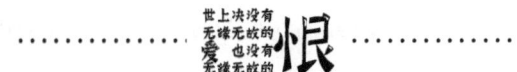

Wild Man and His Wife

by Jia Hongtu

332

He was a 1968 graduate of a middle school in Beijing who went to work on a paramilitary farm in Heilongjiang province in China's Northeast. People ignored his real name and just called him Wild Man. Normally quiet and well-behaved, he was known for his bad temper and his intolerance for injustice. He won some fame when he organized a protest against the harsh living conditions that he and his fellow *zhiqing* were forced to endure.

They were then on assignment opening up a large swath of swampland in a remote county. Sleeping in tents pitched on a damp, grassy field, they sometimes went without meals because of food shortages. Wild Man mobilized his companions to pile logs on a highway in order to block the passage of their regiment commander's jeep from Beijing. After they had explained their situation to him, the regiment commander apologized and took measures to improve things for them. Their company later became known as the best new unit in the whole division in terms of living conditions. After the event, Wild Man became a popular figure in his company and was frequently consulted on matters of common concern.

Like Wild Man, his future wife was better known by her nickname, *Liufeng'er*, which literally meant "adding the finishing touch". A 1969 middle school graduate from a coal city of the province, she was a girl of plain looks and few words who got along well with people. She would sit silently amongst a group engaged in conversation, listening to their talk, and adding a few humorous "finishing touches" that ended things with a roar of laughter.

No one knew how the relationship between Wild Man and Liufeng'er had developed. Love affairs were strictly prohibited among *zhiqing*. Young men and women in love had to meet in secret. But people began to note that Wild Man and Liufeng'er would disappear simultaneously, first in the early mornings of spring when the grass started to turn green, and then in the late evenings of summer when flowers were in full bloom.

Little Ma, a village girl who shared a bed with Liufeng'er, was the first to notice the changes in her companion. Her belly appeared to be getting bigger, and she would wrap a band of cloth around her waist. She would go out of her way to do heavy physical jobs, dancing and jumping. Ma also discovered that Liufeng'er was frequently followed by the gaze of Wild Man, who wore a sullen, worried look on his face. It soon became obvious that Liufeng'er had become pregnant with Wild Man's child. News spread fast on the farm. Company leaders were upset, while rank-and-file members, instead of discriminating against them, showed them concern and care.

The company leadership, however, would not allow love affairs among *zhiqing*, let alone children born out of wedlock by them. A tractor transported Liufeng'er to the regiment headquarters for an abortion. An angry Wild Man followed the tractor, seized Liufeng'er and brought her back. He declared, "I will fight to death anyone who tries to kill my child!" The matter finally ended with Liufeng'er being ordered to leave the Young Communist League and Wild Man being given a demerit by the farm management.

No one could stop their offspring from coming into the world, but its arrival was untimely. The severity of winter was aggravated by a raging snowstorm. Huge in her pregnancy, Liufeng'er could only stumble around in the snow and was incapable of doing any work. Totally unprepared, she couldn't even determine the expected date of delivery.

One day, the company held a full session in one of the big rooms of the female dormitory. The girls all sat on their beds while the boys sat on wooden logs. Feeling sick, Liufeng'er reclined on her bed beneath a quilt. Hu, a female *zhiqing* who served as the deputy instructor in the company, sat beside her. The deputy commander was giving a lecture on discipline, citing many violations and criticizing the offenders severely. Suddenly, Liufeng'er began to feel birth pains and couldn't help groaning. Wild Man, who sat close by, asked her to lower her voice. But her pains became so acute that drops of sweat began streaming down her face. Grasping Hu's hand in desperation, Liufeng'er said: "Oh, no. I can't stand it anymore. The baby is coming."

Only after repeated requests from Hu did the deputy commander adjourn the meeting.

Liufeng'er uttered a shrill cry and delivered a baby right on her bed. When it cried out, her boots turned into pools of blood.

One of the girls standing nearby shouted, "It's a boy, it's a boy!" Wild Man just stood there, stunned.

All the female *zhiqing* gathered around and formed a partition with their bedding. Then Hu noticed that the new mother's belly remained round and there seemed to be a second baby trying to wiggle out. "There's another baby!" she shouted. "Get the medical orderly!"

The second baby had already been born by the time the medical orderly arrived. "It's another boy!" Someone shouted. Wild Man let out a deep cry, clasping his hands to his head. It was hard to tell whether he was overjoyed by the birth of twins or distressed by his wife's ordeal.

The company leadership decided to turn the big room into

a temporary abode for the mother and her twins. The female *zhiqing* who evacuated that room left behind many things Liufeng'er needed -- sugar, clean bed sheets, towels, tissue papers, etc. -- and Hu donated her white goose down quilt.

A tearful Wild Man bowed in thanks to his companions. It was only after their departure that he took a careful look at his twin sons. They were cute and chubby, with better looks than their parents'. Liufeng'er, in the meantime, had fallen asleep in exhaustion.

The following morning, Hu was awakened by someone shouting, "Terrible! Terrible! The first baby is dead!" Hu ran to the big room where Liufeng'er was staying. The first baby's pale face had a purplish tinge and his body was cold. He was indeed dead. Liufeng'er was crying her heart out, the dead baby in her arms.

Wild Man later carried the baby's body to the forest behind the farm. The ground was so deeply frozen that he could not dig a grave. He had no choice but to leave the tiny corpse behind. Perhaps the wolves would eat it.

Hu and the medical orderly got together to analyze the cause of the baby's death. Most probably, the thick bedding that the inexperienced parents had put on him had suffocated him. They had been fast asleep because of fatigue and were unaware of the danger.

Hours passed, and Liufeng'er was not producing milk for her second baby. Deputy instructor Hu came to her aid again. Going from door to door in the village, she collected seven eggs from the peasants. Eggs were rarities in those days when chicken or pig raising by individual families was labeled "going down the road of capitalism." After eating the eggs, Liufeng'er became capable of nursing the baby, but the infant just cried and refused the nipple. After a few days, the baby began to look like a skinny monkey. He was clearly starving to death, his eyes taking on a forlorn gleam.

The medical orderly was a hardworking, conscientious young man, but he could not explain why the hungry baby refused to nurse. Fortunately, a medical team from the general headquarters came to the farm on an inspection tour. A surgeon examined the baby and discovered a slender tendon under the baby's tongue connected to his lower jaw, which prevented his tongue from curling up. After the tendon was cut, the baby immediately started suckling. Day by day, the baby grew fatter and fatter and became a handsome little boy. After a day's work, the *zhiqing* girls used to pass him around, hugging him as if he were a big toy.

It was difficult for *zhiqing* to set up a family on a paramilitary farm and even more so for them to rear children. Wild Man worked as a farm hand while Liufeng'er joined the team in charge of the company's vegetable garden. Both of them worked hard to support their family, not daring to miss a single working day. During off hours, Liufeng'er would look after the baby while Wild Man tended their small vegetable plot. Collecting firewood for the long winter was also his job. In the year that followed, they had another baby, a cute, healthy girl. Many people on the farm observed that the two children were much better-looking than the parents.

The couple lived and worked ten years on the farm. In 1979, when most *zhiqing* were returning to their urban homes, they decided to swim with the new tide for the sake of the children's education. Government policy stipulated that *zhiqing* could return only to their home cities and married couples could live together only if they remained in the country. Thus, Wild Man returned to Beijing, taking their son with him, while Liufeng'er returned to her coal city home with their daughter. Both found jobs as low-paid manual laborers, and their separation only served to aggravate their difficulties, making mutual visits hardly affordable.

Eventually, Wild Man managed to exchange jobs and residencies legitimately with a man in the coal city who was anxious to return to Beijing. As part of the deal, he took the man's job in a Peking opera troupe in the coal city. Knowing nothing about his new trade, he could only perform odd jobs backstage. Later, he decided to retire on a monthly pension of a little over 1,000 yuan. When Liufeng'er retired, she received even less.

What consoled them was that both their children had grown up and were doing well. Their handsome son became a businessman in Beijing and set up his family in the metropolis. Their lovely daughter, who also married, became a teacher in a suburban school. Wild Man and Liufeng'er lived by themselves in peace, though not without occasional squabbles due to his bad temper. As always, it was the good-natured, humorous Liufeng'er who turned tensions into laughter.

Lanlan and Her Brother Wan Sheng

by Liu Tianqing

I went with my family to the countryside after my father was labeled a "counter-revolutionary" during the Cultural Revolution. He was exiled from a port city in northeastern China where he had served many years as a government official. This was how I became a *zhiqing* in a small mountain village 100 kilometers away from the city. North of the village was a small hill, the lush summer greenery of which was truly beautiful. Down in the south was a level stretch of land that reached out to the sea. From a height, one could see golden sunrays dancing over the waves.

There was a young man named Wan Sheng in our village. His younger sister, the 22-year-old Lanlan, was generally recognized as the prettiest girl in the whole township. She was a good singer and dancer, and would sometimes join performance tours organized by the township art troupe. People were captivated by her stunningly beautiful face, her slim body and her lively dancing. The peasant boys of the village were always looking for opportunities to talk to her or to help her complete her farm work. Bachelors from miles around would find excuses to come to our village, approach her through acquaintances, and try everything they could think of to attract her attention.

Matchmakers came to visit from outside the village. Plied with proposals from wealthy people, handsome young men, factory workers, or young government officials, Lanlan remained unmoved. She always kept a distance from her horde of admirers in the village, though they all had the advantage of coming from families free of the capitalist taint. She would smile at them, showing her charming dimples, but she would never allow them to touch her.

My family lived next door to Wan Sheng and Lanlan. Wan

Sheng and I were good friends. We went to work in the fields every morning, helped each other in our daily life, and had a lot of fun together. During our spare time, we would sit over a Chinese chess board or talk about books we had read. Since we were separated only by a wall, and even the private plots of our two families lay side by side, my contact with Lanlan became more frequent. We soon fell deeply in love.

As the ancient Chinese saying goes, "No wall under the sky can completely hold back the wind." News about our love soon spread throughout the village. On hearing the news, Wan Sheng flew into a rage. He had never dreamed of his sister falling in love with me. What angered him even more was the rumor that Lanlan had taken the initiative: she had first expressed her fondness for me through a mutual friend.

"What a stupid girl Lanlan is!" Wan Sheng exclaimed to everyone he met. "Sure, Liu is a nice guy – clever, capable, honest and trustworthy. But marriage is a matter of lifelong importance. How could Lanlan marry a man whose father still wears a 'counter-revolutionary' hat? Even if the old man eventually succeeds in removing this label, his whole life is already ruined. Their only property is a shabby three-room hut. They have no money and no social position. They don't even measure up to an ordinary peasant family. How could Lanlan have chosen a man with such a family background, a man destined to toil on the farmland for life!"

I was surprised to learn that the young male villagers, most of them of politically untainted families, had launched a smear campaign against me, using the vilest words to slander and abuse me. Was this a product of their envy or of the epoch itself? Did it mean that a man of my family background was not entitled to marry a beautiful girl? That whatever vestiges of rights left to people like me would be taken away from us?

One day, an exasperated Wan Sheng asked me to come to his home. He instructed Lanlan to bring me a cup of drinking water and ordered her to leave the house.

"I was told that you and Lanlan have fallen in love," Wan Sheng said.

I nodded, not wanting to hide our relationship any longer.

"When did it begin?"

"Three months ago."

"Do you have someone who can vouch for that?"

"Yes, Chang Qing."

Wan Sheng fell silent.

Chang Qing came from a landlord family. If he had not had such an undesirable family background, he would have entered college instead of working as a farmer. He was very bright--the top student in his high school. He had come back home after graduation but failed to find a wife until a *zhiqing* girl agreed to marry him when he was thirty.

Wan Sheng knew that Chang Qing and I were best friends and talked freely about everything. Sometimes Wan Sheng himself would join us. He knew both of us as knowledgeable, sensible persons, but he must have reasoned that Lanlan could never expect a decent living if she were to marry me.

"Please try to put yourself in my shoes," he begged. "You know my father committed suicide. The official judgment was that he did it to escape punishment for his past crimes. So, my family was considered not to have a clean historical record. That's why my mother remarried outside our village. I won't hide the fact that there is tremendous political pressure on me. I'm the eldest child in my family, and I only have the one sister living with me." His only wish now, he said, was to marry Lanlan into a family of reliable political standing.

"I'm in a very difficult position," he continued. "I hope you'll understand and pardon me. Please end your relationship with my sister. I implore you to give her up."

He looked at me intently, obviously hoping that I would agree to his request.

I would not do that, of course, because I would never abandon the genuine love that Lanlan had given me. Since the day she poured her heart out to Chang Qing, telling him that she loved me, he often praised her by citing the example of his own wife, who had plainly said, "I married this person, not his class status." He said that I should treasure Lanlan's love, that I should feel fortunate and honored to have it under the current political circumstances, not to mention that she was such a beautiful girl.

That night, Lanlan called me to the edge of our private plot of land beneath a wall, where we hid behind a bundle of straw. Her brother had been spewing venom these past few days, she said. He was totally opposed to her marrying me. I could see her eyes brimming with tears. She had become noticeably thinner.

"Since I have promised to marry you," Lanlan continued, "I am not afraid of any hindrance from others. We can go together to a faraway place, maybe to the Great Northern Wilderness in China's Northeast..."

I took her hands in mine and said: "I love you, Lanlan. With your love, I feel content and will be grateful for the rest of my life." I then cupped her tearful face in my hands and continued, "Since our arrival here, I have come to know your family, and you also know our family. You understand that my father is going through a terrible ordeal. I can't possibly leave him for the remote Northern Wilderness now. I love you, and would sacrifice everything for you, but it would be too hard for me to leave. I think our only way is to fight back."

"That is bound to fail," she said, shaking my hands fiercely.

Her mother had come to see her, she said. Her elder sister and her aunts had also visited or sent messages. All of them wanted to know whether news about her love for me was true.

"I told them it was true. My mother threatened to commit suicide as my father had done. Now that my father is no longer with us, my brother's opinion is what counts most. Unless you can convince him, it would be too hard--no, impossible."

"Why impossible?"

I assured her that I would do my best.

"Don't you know that my father committed suicide for fear of punishment? My brother is under great pressure. He cried when he talked to me. He said so many politically pure young men were seeking my hand, why couldn't I choose one of them? He couldn't stop crying. I know he means well, but he doesn't understand me."

Lanlan was sobbing uncontrollably. She felt the entire community was against us, she said. We would never be able to marry here. She was bent on our leaving the village for someplace remote.

"My brother is the mainstay of our family. He bears all the burden," Lanlan continued. "I pity him and really don't want to upset him. The only way is for us to leave. After our departure, he will have to reconcile himself to the accomplished fact. Leaving is our only option."

Her brother was not the only one under enormous pressure. I thought of my wronged father. He had to undergo labor reform every day from dawn to dusk, doing heavy and sometimes dangerous jobs under surveillance. My mother was in deep agony. She had quit her job in order to follow my father and move our whole family to the countryside. She once said to me that she would never believe that my father was a counter-revolutionary.

"After so many years of marriage, how could I abandon him at this crucial time?" she said.

If she had not believed my father would be rehabilitated sooner or later, she would never have moved the family to this place where, she said, "even a rabbit would not bother to relieve itself". The important thing was to stay with him, to give him confidence in the future and the courage to live on. The villagers were of course unaware of all this. They treated him harshly as a class enemy. But she would warm his heart with love and care.

Lanlan knew nothing of this situation, nor was I prepared to give her the details. In the darkness of the night, I still hoped that something good would turn up

"Lanlan, you are the best girl in the world," I said to her, "But have you ever thought that I am only twenty-three? There are still three more years to go before I reach the legal marriage age for males.....What should we do in those three years? I definitely cannot leave my parents and this poor home. Of course, I can wait. But can you wait three years?"

When I said this to Lanlan, my heart suffered sharp pains like deep knife cuts.

"Even if you can wait, can you stand the pressure? After three years, my family will remain as poor and downtrodden as it is today". I shook my head in deep sorrow, trying to ask her to think twice and be sober-minded.

Lanlan continued to cry, tears streaming down her face. For a long, long time, as a heartbroken young couple deep in love, we racked our brains to work out a way to save our love.

In the end, we failed. Lanlan went to marry the son of a production brigade leader in a commune some ten kilometers away from our village. The marriage had been arranged by Wan Sheng, their mother and aunts.

Someone saw Lanlan on her wedding day when she left her house with red eyes. She had obviously been crying all night. Again and again, she looked back in the direction of my house. Since the day we parted at the back wall, she had never had a chance to talk with me alone, because I tried hard to avoid her.

It is now many years since our family moved back to the seaport city after my father was rehabilitated. I was admitted to college in 1978.

I often think of Lanlan, my unforgettable first love. I like to think about the days I spent in the countryside, with all its bitterness and sweetness. Because of Lanlan, the dull, painful life of those days was sometimes flooded with bright sunlight.

IV.
The Go-Home Campaign
And Afterwards

....

Solidarity Brings Us Home

by Ye Feng

....

Mengding Farm, where I was sent to work as a *zhiqing* in 1969, was located in Gengma County, Yunnan Province, southwestern China. It was one of the 34 paramilitary farms in Yunnan that enrolled more than 100,000 teenagers like me from Beijing, Shanghai and other big cities during the Cultural Revolution. Our assignment was to plant rubber trees and other cash crops then much in need in China. Because many of these farms were grossly mismanaged, however, and could not provide us with a secure livelihood in a harsh environment, we soon lost hope for our future. From late 1978 to early 1979, *zhiqing* working on Yunnan farms launched numerous protests, demonstrations and strikes in a powerful go-home petition campaign that eventually forced the central authorities to reassess the Sent-down movement and change their policy. Thousands of young people on our Mengding Farm played such a significant role in the campaign that Mengding came to be known as the place where the curtain was closed on the entire Sent-down movement. As a participant and leader, I feel it is important to record for posterity this crucial chapter in the *zhiqing* history of China.

Our story began on December 23, 1978. At the end of another day's backbreaking toil, we were informed by our company instructor to gather at 8 o'clock for the broadcast of an important official document called the "40-Point Program for Work on *Zhiqing*" produced at a recent national conference. The document stated that from then on, all *zhiqing* working on the country's paramilitary farms would become farm employees and no longer be treated as *zhiqing*.

This policy statement caused a huge uproar among all *zhiqing* in our company because it meant that we had to stay on the farms for the rest of our lives. Our dream to return home was completely shattered. Burning with indignation, many of us left the site before the broadcast ended.

Almost all the male *zhiqing* in our company came to the room I shared with several others, and a heated discussion ensued.

"We have been here eight years. Even the war of resistance against Japan ended after eight years."

"As veterans, we should be demobilized and sent home."

"We came here as *zhiqing*. Why should they change our status to that of farm employees?"

Some suggested that we draft a letter of petition, collect ten thousand signatures, and send the letter to the Party's Central Committee. Since Yunnan Province still had more than 75,000 *zhiqing* working on paramilitary farms, and our Mengding Farm alone had several thousand, collecting a significant number of signatures in support of our petition would not be difficult. Others said that we should write to the Office of *Zhiqing* Affairs under the State Council, asking them to change the decision and reconfirm our status as *zhiqing*. Still others proposed that we should send a delegation to Beijing to plead with the authorities.

My instinct told me that the best way to attain our objective was to stay together where we were, because strength came from solidarity. A letter of complaint could be ignored by bureaucrats and might fail to reach decision-makers. A Beijing-bound delegation, which would consist of a small number of people separated from the broad masses of *zhiqing* and their power base, could be easily dismissed. By staying on our farms, we could make our protests heard, not only by the central authorities, but also by people throughout the country.

I then took out a copy of the PRC Constitution and read

aloud the paragraph on the rights of citizens to demonstrate and strike. We all agreed to hold a demonstration the following day at Mengding Street, which was the administrative and commercial center of the area. Two teams were dispatched that very night to inform all *zhiqing* in our battalion about our decision and urge them to join us.

All twelve other companies responded enthusiastically. About seven to eight hundred people -- more than half of the total *zhiqing* population in our battalion -- went to Mengding Street to take part in the demonstration. We walked back and forth three times along the 200-meter street, waving flags and shouting slogans.

"We veterans should be demobilized after serving eight years."

"We are *zhiqing*, not farm employees!"

"Give back our urban residency! Give back our youth!"

"We'll fight to the death to go home!"

"Give back our youth" was a slogan that openly challenged the Sent-down movement, which had deprived us of the best years of our lives, but "Give back our urban residency" was the indispensable key to achieving our goal of returning home. Without that official change in residency, we would not have the coupons we needed to buy rationed food, let alone find a job.

It was a market day when we marched on Mengding Street. The crowds of local people had never seen a demonstration before and didn't know what to make of it. All the shops closed and people scattered in every direction.

We improvised a podium by tying several bicycles together. One after another, *zhiqing* climbed onto the "podium" to pour out our long-suppressed grievances.

One *zhiqing*, nicknamed Old Devil Wu, described how he

and his fellow students from Chengdu had been deceived years before by recruiting officers from Yunnan. They had promised that we would be given military uniforms and weapons, which were much sought after by young people in those days. They had described Yunnan as a wonderful place "where bananas hang over your head, pineapples lie at your feet, and if you trip and fall, you'll harvest a bunch of peanuts from the ground."

Instead of living in two-story houses with electric lights and telephones as the recruiters had promised, we *zhiqing* lived in thatched shanties which provided little shelter from the extreme weather of southwestern Yunnan. Long hours of hard labor overtaxed our strength, but all we were given to eat was rice mixed with coarsely ground corn. We had no vegetables or meat except on a few holidays.

Another *zhiqing* spoke about the mistreatment and persecution we had suffered at the hands of farm officials. *Zhiqing* who had committed minor transgressions or simply offended those men were trussed up, beaten savagely, and taken into custody. Cases of rape were not uncommon.

The speakers' sad outpourings evoked a strong echo among the *zhiqing* audience, many of whom burst into tears. We decided to set up a petition committee that very afternoon.

Early the following morning, our company's petition committee started a strike. Around 10 o'clock, representatives from other companies arrived, and we set up a petition committee at the battalion level. On December 29, the founding of a General Committee for Strike and Petition (abbreviated as General Strike Committee hereafter) was proclaimed and a declaration formulated for our entire regiment. I was appointed chairman of a committee of some dozen members.

Two days before this, a male *zhiqing* from our regimental

headquarters had come to inform me that top officers of the farm had worked out a frame-up against me. They were going to charge me with theft in a hotel room on Mengding Street, where a Shanghai female *zhiqing* had stayed overnight on her way home. Telling me no details about the source of his information, not even his own name, the visiting *zhiqing* warned me to take precautions and then left. As a preventive measure, I led a group of *zhiqing* to the hotel, where we found that no theft had been reported at the hotel in recent days.

In the morning on December 29, an officer named Tang from regimental headquarters came to our company in a Beijing jeep, accompanied by four policemen. He ordered me to go with them to headquarters to clear up a case of theft allegedly involving me at the Mengding Street hotel. Since we had made investigations beforehand, it was easy to give the lie to their charge. Embarrassed by our rebuttal and scared by a large crowd of *zhiqing* surrounding and glaring at them, they soon departed in defeat.

On January 5, 1979, in compliance with a resolution of the General Strike Committee, thousands of *zhiqing* on our Mengding Farm -- originally from Beijing, Shanghai, Chengdu and Kunming -- rose early to attend a mass rally at the regimental headquarters. Since we were organized on a company basis and lived in settlements scattered over a 20-mile-long, narrow area, most *zhiqing* had to walk up to twenty miles to reach the headquarters. It was indeed a spectacular sight: traveling down the highway leading to the Sino-Burmese border were thousands of *zhiqing* of both sexes, some on horse-drawn carts, some on bicycles or tractors, but most of them on foot. By 10 o'clock, they had all arrived and gathered in front of the auditorium near the office buildings of the regimental headquarters.

In my opening speech, I gave a brief account of our activities during the previous two weeks, pointing out that through intensive publicity and organizational work, almost all *zhiqing* on the farms had been mobilized. The mass rally demonstrated our solidarity and determination to win back our legitimate right to return home. We should continue to fight until we were able to take our destiny into our own hands. Then I declared a general strike and a staff member of the General Strike Committee read out the disciplines to be observed.

Prior to the meeting, committee members had reached a consensus on the importance of discipline. The principle of voluntariness was emphasized, with absolute prohibition on attempts to stop farm employees from going to work. Thefts, fistfights, gambling, destruction of public and private property were all strictly prohibited. Other taboos included acts of revenge against farm officers who had persecuted us.

By the time we held the rally, most regimental leaders and officers had deserted the headquarters. Only a handful who had been on friendly terms with us had remained. After the whole event was over, it was commonly acknowledged that the best period of our farm life, in terms of public order, were the days when we *zhiqing* were on strike. Not a single transgression took place.

The rest of the rally was taken up by free speakers. Some *zhiqing* recounted their painful experiences on the farm, while others exposed the evil deeds of certain farm officials. There were also *zhiqing* who recited their original poems on homesickness or our current struggle. The speaker who impressed me most was a tall young man in blue overalls wearing a cap. Later I learned he was a *zhiqing* in the engineering company named Zhou Xingru.

Zhou argued, "If we came here as *zhiqing*, we should be treated as such. If we were enlisted as servicepersons, as our recruiters told us, we should be demobilized after serving eight years." He cited many examples to demonstrate how our living standards and conditions had deteriorated in the eight years since our arrival. "The only way for us to change our destiny," he concluded, "is for us to go home."

Zhou stressed that we should make returning home our sole objective and refrain from raising other demands, which could give farm management excuses for brutal suppression.

The audience was held spellbound by his passionate, insightful speech delivered at a time when cries for democracy were still much in the air after the fall of the Gang of Four. Many of us admired Zhou all the more when we later learned that he had already received permission to return to Chengdu, with a job waiting for him. He had chosen instead to remain on the farm to join the struggle, casting his lot with his *zhiqing* comrades. With strong recommendations from me and several others, Zhou soon became a member of the General Strike Committee.

In the afternoon after the rally, the General Strike Committee held an expanded session which all committee members at the battalion level were invited to attend. Their reports showed that farm leaders were intensifying their effort to break our strike. They had sent teams to show entertainment films to many battalions and companies as a measure to woo and distract. They also relaxed controls over home and sick leaves, and tried hard to dissuade *zhiqing* from joining the strike. Calling strike leaders "bad elements," they warned *zhiqing* to keep away from us, lest they face serious consequences.

While our discussion was still going on, we saw a long line

of cars, followed by an ambulance, speeding down the highway toward our regimental headquarters. We took them to be a delegation sent by the central authorities, never having seen such a large fleet visiting our farm before. Many of us jumped and shouted for joy and hugged each other in tears, thinking that a ray of sunlight had eventually fallen on us.

Our meeting with the newly arrived officials the following morning (January 6), however, only served to disappoint and infuriate us. They turned out to be a working group dispatched by the provincial authorities to tamp down the fires we had started. Unable or unwilling to address the issues we had raised, they tried to persuade us to end the strike by lecturing us on the importance of stability and unity. Seeing that we would get nowhere by talking with them, we walked out of the meeting.

Immediately after their departure, the General Strike Committee called an emergency meeting, at which we reached the following conclusions:

1. Since we were scattered widely on the farm, it would be easy for the farm authorities to divide and conquer us one company after another;

2. Along with farm management, government authorities from county to provincial levels were stepping up their efforts to break our strike. We would certainly fail unless we adopted countermeasures and upgraded our struggle.

3. We must assemble all *zhiqing* on the farm at the regimental headquarters, stay together and hold a hunger (and thirst) strike.

We chose the hostel at the regimental headquarters as the site of our hunger strike. The hostel had a courtyard surrounded by rows of rooms on four sides that formed an enclosure.

It had an entrance with an iron gate, and a back door leading to toilets outside. The first batch of 211 hunger strikers were selected from hundreds of volunteers. At one o'clock in the afternoon, I was at the head of the column as we filed past the iron gate, marking the start of our hunger strike. We all stayed under the roofs of the corridors on four sides, sitting or lying on the cement ground covered with straw and bedding.

Zhou Xingru and other General Strike Committee members, together with several hundred *zhiqing* from companies farther away from regimental headquarters, stayed outside the hostel around the clock as support and reserve forces. To prepare for a long strike, they had brought plastic sheets for making tents, as well as daily necessities. Hundreds more *zhiqing* from companies closer to the headquarters came to join their ranks during the day.

In the meantime, each of us hunger strikers had sent a telegram to our families informing them of our action and resolution. Our families responded promptly by sending back telegrams that expressed serious concern and anxiety. News about our hunger strike spread to relatives and friends and the society at large. We soon received numerous telegrams and letters showing sympathy and support, many of them coming from middle school students.

My father was a kindhearted, calm old man with a firm will. His telegram in reply read, "I believe you are a good young man. Think three times before taking any action. Commit no transgression under any circumstances. Remember my words!"

In addition to Zhou Xingru and some others, those leading the general strike outside the hostel were Chen Xianfu and Shi Yong, the only female General Strike Committee member whom foreign reporters called the woman general. A special division was formed to coordinate food and other supplies for all battalions and companies. Pickets were dispatched to protect the arsenal, the room for keeping confidential files, and the deserted offices and living quarters of the farm staff at the headquarters. Measures were taken to guard against fire and other potential hazards.

On the following day (January 7), a *zhiqing* who had served as a signalman in the army, succeeded in getting in touch by phone with an officer on duty at the Central Military Commission, who in turn transferred our phone call to the General Office of the State Council. Speaking with the official at the other end of line, Zhou told him about our protest petition and our hunger strike in particular.

The official asked Zhou to hold on and returned after twenty minutes, saying: "You have opened the arsenal and seized arms and munitions. You have threatened and beaten up farm officers and destroyed state property. Your actions amount to misbehavior of the gravest nature ....."

Shocked and enraged by these false accusations, Zhou hastened to explain that nothing of the sort had happened; they must be slanders spread by people with ulterior motives. He expressed the hope that the central authorities would quickly send an investigative team to Mengding Farm to find out the truth, handle our petition, and save the lives of the hunger strikers.

The official at the other end then softened his tone and asked us to end the hunger strike. He told Zhou that an investigative team sent by the central authorities was already in Yunnan, and that he himself would immediately inform the Yunnan provincial authorities about our situation.

Slanders against us were quickly debunked by twenty-five

zhiqing who were members of the Communist Party. In an urgent telegram to the Disciplinary Commission of the Party's Central Committee, they refuted the alleged seizure of arms and other false charges against us, and called for a prompt investigation to uncover and punish those guilty of spreading such misinformation.

News about the conversation between Zhou and the official at the State Council was a consolation to everyone on strike, especially to the hunger strikers. At long last, we had established direct contact with the central authorities.

Meanwhile, I began to feel an acute headache and severe discomfort in my stomach. Some other *zhiqing* showed more serious signs of dehydration. Li Xuehua, my roommate for eight years, was the first to fall into a swoon. I lost no time in inviting Zhou and a few other leaders for an urgent consultation across the iron gate. We decided to send for an experienced paramedic from our regimental hospital. His job was to perform a physical check-up on Li and other hunger strikers whose lives were in danger and, when absolutely necessary, take measures to prevent them from dying. We wanted to prevent even a single death from taking place.

Since January 8, 1979 was the third anniversary of the death of Premier Zhou Enlai, the General Strike Committee decided to hold a simple but solemn memorial service on the site of the strike. By ten o'clock that morning, more than twenty hunger strikers had lost consciousness. They were lying quietly just beyond the iron gate of the hostel, with the rest of the hunger strikers behind them. The highly emotionally charged atmosphere on this memorial day, combined with the pathetic sight of the hunger strikers, evoked strong feelings of grief and despair among the crowd. When a female *zhiqing* stepped forward to bow before the portrait of the late premier, she broke into a flood of tears. Instantly, the whole site resounded with wails and cries.

Then a shout suddenly erupted from the crowd:

"Give back our comrades-in-arms!"

The shout immediately produced strong echoes among the crowd. Driven by an impulse to save hunger strikers from the threat of death, many *zhiqing* surged toward the iron gate, trying to break in and bring out their comrades-in-arms. Some of the pickets rushed forward trying to restore order.

Grasping the crossbars of the iron gate, I summoned up all the energy I had left and spoke in a faint voice through a microphone: "Please control your emotions. Don't attempt to bring out our comrades on hunger strike. Otherwise our previous efforts will be wasted. Our serious hunger strike would turn into a farce. If you don't listen to my advice, I'll dash my head against the iron gate and kill myself in front of you."

On hearing my words, the crowd gradually calmed down. Urged by other General Strike Committee members, *zhiqing* from different companies gradually returned to their original locations.

After the short commotion was over, Zhou made an urgent phone call to the State Council, reporting to them that the lives of more than twenty hunger strikers were hanging by a thread, and that the masses of *zhiqing* had become so emotional that it was hard to keep the situation under control. The official at the other end asked our General Strike Committee to end the hunger strike and do our utmost to prevent things from getting out of hand. He told Zhou that the central investigative team then staying in Xishuangbana had already been instructed to make an urgent, non-stop trip to our Mengding Farm. Their job was to investigate and solve our problems.

The written record of these telephone messages was read to me by one of my comrades. But he had not finished reading them before I fainted. Later I learnt that with the arrival of the Beijing official team in sight, Zhou and other leaders had decided to call off the hunger strike, but to continue the general strike. The iron gate was opened and hunger strikers in critical condition were promptly sent to the hospital while the rest of the hunger strikers who had regained consciousness, including myself, started eating sugared rice soup or other nutritional fluids. According to doctors' advice, this was the proper way to achieve a gradual recovery.

On the night of January 9, the central investigative team headed by Zhao Fan, Vice-Minister of Agriculture and Forestry and deputy head of the leading group in charge of *zhiqing* affairs under the State Council, arrived in Mengding after traveling by car a whole day and night.

The following day, we arranged a warm welcome for Zhao Fan and his team. At a mass meeting held in the afternoon, Zhao spoke to about two thousand *zhiqing* gathered on the ground outside the hostel where our hunger strike had taken place. As chairman of the General Strike Committee, I sat behind him when he spoke.

At the beginning, there was some contention between Zhao Fan and us *zhiqing* as he spoke in the spirit of the official document. For example, he opened his speech by addressing us as "young farm employees." Alerted by his use of this controversial term, I immediately stood up and led the crowd in shouting: "We are *zhiqing*, not farm employees!"

Then he spoke about Yunnan being a nice place with rich natural resources and other advantages. We again interrupted him by shouting the following slogans:

"We veterans want to be demobilized after serving eight years!"

"We want to go home!"

"Give back our urban residency! Give back our youth!"

"We'll fight to the death to go home!"

The continual slogan-shouting by the large crowd of young people clothed in rags, steeped in sorrow, and driven by utter helplessness and despair, seemed to shock him. I was standing by his side when he faced the shouting crowd. Unable to utter a word, he looked intently at them, his face ghastly pale, his teeth clenched, and his whole body shivering. As a revolutionary veteran, he had joined the Communist-led armed forces in 1937 and fought against the Japanese invaders until victory in 1945. After WWII, he had worked underground in Beijing until the city was peacefully liberated in 1949. He had gone through fire and water numerous times, yet he had never faced such a pathetic multitude of young people.

Suddenly, a female *zhiqing* in the front row knelt down before him and started crying bitterly. Almost the entire *zhiqing* audience spontaneously followed suit, kneeling down and letting out loud wails. The profound sadness that hung in the air was overwhelming. Even the Dai minority villagers and some farm employees who watched the scene from some distance started shedding tears out of sympathy.

No longer able to restrain himself, Zhao Fan sobbed loudly over the microphone, his tears spilling down his cheeks, "*Zhiqing* comrades, I have three sons working as *zhiqing* in rural Shaanxi, and a daughter in a factory. As a *zhiqing* parent, I understand and sympathize with you. Your demand is legitimate. Your wish can be realized."

The *zhiqing* crowd greeted his words with thunderous applause and shouts of joy. No longer regarding him as a high official on an investigative tour, they saw him as a family member coming to see and console them, a fatherly shoulder to cry on. The meeting ended in a joyous atmosphere.

A day later, Zhao Fan called a smaller meeting to which close to thirty *zhiqing* delegates were invited. He asked them to say all they knew and to say it without reserve. Listening to their complaints and sad stories, he sat there speechless, his eyes slightly closed, tears rolling down his cheeks. At the end of the meeting, he admitted that he had come with the idea of attempting persuasion, but after seeing the real situation, he had changed his idea. He assured us that he would report our real situation and his own views to the central authorities and that we should allow some time for them to consider and work out a solution.

About a week after Zhao's departure from our farm, a decision was made after consultations between Yunnan, Shanghai, Beijing, and Sichuan that greatly relaxed the previous *zhiqing* policy. The decision was soon approved by the State Council. Its essence was to grant the wish of all *zhiqing* who wanted to go home. Those who wanted to stay were welcome to do so. Thanks to this new policy, not only the 75,000 *zhiqing* then in Yunnan, but millions of others throughout the country soon rushed to join their families in the cities. This new shift of population, which went in the opposite direction of the Sent-down movement, was called the "back-to-city wind" (*fancheng feng*) that swept the whole of China at the end of the 1970s.

....

Love Cemented by Hunger Strike

by Chen Xiaoyi

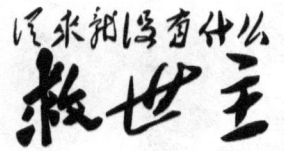

....

December 23, 1978 is an unforgettable day for all *zhiqing* who worked on paramilitary farms in Yunnan. That was the day a group of *zhiqing* on our Mengding Farm started a petition for returning to their urban homes. The movement spread to the entire farm and soon escalated into a hunger strike that alarmed Beijing and forced it to end the unpopular Sent-down movement.

One of the things we *zhiqing* feared and hated most was the so-called "voluntary labor" required on "customary commemorative days" -- a euphemism for the extortion of extra hours of hard toil from us in the name of commemorating special occasions. Like imprisoned criminals, we *zhiqing* couldn't refuse such "voluntary labor" without getting into serious trouble. The extreme extraction of our labor in total disregard of our legitimate rights was nothing less than a wicked invention of the ultra-leftists.

I was a 17-year-old girl when I came to the farm. I cursed those loathsome days when, after a day's backbreaking toil, I still had to work more hours. Why should we have so many events to commemorate? I wondered. Whenever a commemorative day ended, I used to count the days we had left until the next one . I felt like a convict who silently counts the number of lashings he has endured, waiting for his flogging to end.

Fortunately, just three days away from the 85th anniversary of the birthday of our late great leader Chairman Mao--a date on which "voluntary labor" was anticipated-- we went on strike. At long last, we no longer needed to work!

I was grateful to those strong fellow *zhiqing* who had called the strike. We were so desperately in need of a good rest!

A whistle summoned people to go to work the next morning, but nowhere in sight was the army of *zhiqing* marching in a long column with scythes in their hands or hoes on their shoulders. I saw only a few shadows moving in distant forests and thought these must be some timid individuals. After living in isolation for eight years in deep mountains, the existence of a few diffident souls was only to be expected. People could understand and forgive them. But they should not be allowed to affect the morale of the army of us strikers, or hinder our brave fight for a change in our destiny. Our strike would become truly powerful if all *zhiqing* would join in.

I went with my companions to talk with the few *zhiqing* who had gone out to work. We easily persuaded them to join our ranks.

In the afternoon, there was no more whistle blowing. The absence of the damned whistle signaled the end of a gloomy period of my life and the advent of a new era for us *zhiqing* on the farm.

Though the strike spread quickly and irresistibly like a tidal wave, our dream to return home appeared far from becoming a reality. Because our entirely reasonable demand remained unanswered for several days, we decided to escalate our struggle.

In the initial stage, strikes were organized on a company basis, and actions were scattered and limited in scale. Very soon, meetings of protest and accusation against the farm management were held at the battalion level. Finally, *zhiqing* from all battalions assembled and camped on the grounds at the regimental headquarters. With thousands of people gathered at the encampment, we felt the power of our strength. The flow of information became faster and more people came forward with good ideas. More importantly, all *zhiqing* were united as one. Our solidarity was best expressed in our favorite song, "Solidarity Means Strength!" Again and again we sang the lines:

"Our strength is like iron,

Our strength is like steel--

Even harder than iron,

More solid than steel..."

We had never sung so passionately, movingly and tearfully. For the very first time in my experience, I felt a real surge of life and saw the value and power of solidarity.

For a time, however, our protests produced no tangible results. Many of us began to doubt whether our struggle could succeed. And in fact, such doubts were by no means groundless. We were well aware that what we were fighting against was a policy of the central authorities, though no one dared to spell it out openly. We had to pretend that we were fighting the bureaucracy of farm management and of the local authorities. But these bureaucrats were no blockheads. They were cruel, scheming and totally untrustworthy, and would fight to protect their power to the bitter end.

When our efforts bore no fruit, we decided to launch a hunger strike. Two hundred eleven brave fighters were selected from hundreds of volunteers. I was deeply shaken by their heroic action -- waging this last-ditch struggle at the risk of their own lives for the sake of all *zhiqing*.

In this courageous group were many women like myself, including a young mother who had been holding her baby in her arms until the moment she joined their ranks. I shed tears of admiration for their determination and noble spirit.

I wanted to join the strike, but was dissuaded by my boyfriend who was a resolute hunger striker. He said to me, "One of us should stay behind. In the worst case, one of us should remain to remember the other and explain things to our families." He asked me to stay outside the hostel at the regimental headquarters, which was the site of the hunger strike. I could join thousands of *zhiqing*, he said, at the encampment in supporting the hunger strike.

On the second day of the hunger (and thirst) strike, the health of the participants quickly deteriorated due to dehydration. Many began to have stomachaches, loss of consciousness and blood in their urine. My boyfriend, who stood at over 1.7 meters, weighed only a little over 40 kilograms. A group of medical personnel ran to their aid but were refused by these brave people.

I experienced a kind of agony that I had never known before, suspended between hope and despair, fear and resolve. My boyfriend was risking his life, but I knew I should not hold him back. I was determined to join him if the need arose.

On the third day of the hunger strike, I gave a small candy to a male *zhiqing* comrade, asking him to hand it to my boyfriend when he came out to the toilet. "Make sure he eats it," I said to him. One piece of candy could not make much difference, I knew, but I hoped it would help him survive a little longer and make me feel somewhat better.

I waited a long time until I saw my boyfriend in the distance coming out of the toilet. He refused the candy a few times when the comrade tried to thrust it into his hand. But when he turned around and caught a glimpse of me, he hesitated for a moment before quickly taking the candy and putting it into his mouth. He then rejoined the other hunger strikers without another glance at me.

Only then did I realize how wrong—how seriously wrong--it was of me to do such a thing. Done in the open, it might have led to grave consequences or even the abortion of our movement. But then, I thought, perhaps people could understand me: all I had wanted was for him to persevere a little longer! Standing outside the site of the hunger strike, I consoled myself time and again with that idea.

At long last, the hunger strike ended in success. A central government team was rushing at full speed toward our farm to handle our petition.

The iron gate of the hostel opened. Though feeble and exhausted, many of the hunger strikers came out wearing expressions of indescribable happiness.

Large crowds of *zhiqing* rushed toward the gate to greet the heroes and heroines, bringing the choicest foods to their dear comrades.

Later, my boyfriend thanked me for my deep concern for him. He told me that he had not eaten the candy, but had spit it out once he turned around. He could not go back on his pledge, he said, asking me to pardon him.

His words were a shock to me at first. I could no longer restrain my tears. It took me some time to find the right words to say to him: "You are a real man!"

He later became my husband. His name is Yang Guoding.

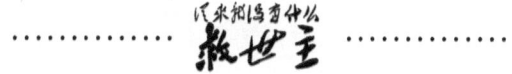

Misery of a Blind *Zhiqing*

by Wang Xiaomei

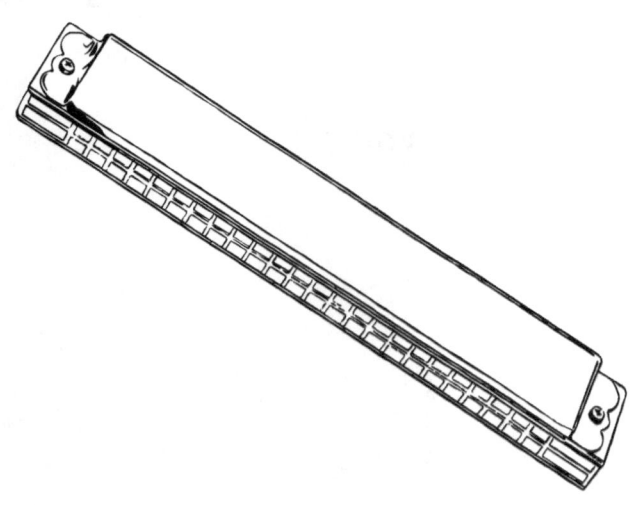

I worked for eight long years, 1971-1979, in Plantain Grove, which was part of a big farm at Mengding in Yunnan Province. I was only one of thousands of teenagers there, most of whom came from my home town of Chengdu. After my years as a *zhiqing*, I went back to Chengdu and entered Sichuan University, but I spent part of my 1985 summer vacation visiting Plantain Grove. I was warmly received by the Grove manager, who surprised me at dinner by mentioning one of my fellow *zhiqing*, Ruan Dangsheng.

"Ruan Dangsheng is still here?" I exclaimed. Ten years had passed, and tremendous changes had taken place in our country. Almost all *zhiqing* on the farm had returned to their hometowns, yet Ruan was still here!

"How can a blind *zhiqing* manage to live here by himself?" I asked

"We hired an elderly man to take care of him," he answered, sighing. "It was all we could afford." He sighed again and said, "Can you ask his family to take him home? He's so miserable!

"But I must see him," I answered.

The manager hesitated. "He's living in a place that belongs to the Third Production Team. His room is so dirty you can hardly step inside."

When I insisted on seeing Ruan Dangsheng, the Grove manager promised to have someone take me there the following morning.

I couldn't sleep that night. A thunderstorm was raging outside. Memories of past events at the farm rushed back to me more quickly than I could sort them out, but foremost among them was the tragedy of Ruan Dangsheng.

Back then, I had been working as an assistant in charge of youth affairs in the Grove's office, which we called the battalion headquarters. My colleagues and I were shocked to hear that Ruan had been gravely injured in an accident. We had just seen him the previous evening when he came to our room for a drink of water after playing basketball at the headquarters.

Soon we heard shouts and cries coming from the highway that led to the headquarters. We rushed outside to see a small group of *zhiqing* in ragged clothes carrying Ruan with their bare hands and moving in our direction. Ruan's voice was hoarse from crying, and his hands flailed upward as if he was trying to grasp something. His companions tried to keep his hands down, fearing they would touch his open wounds. The doctor at our clinic immediately decided that he be sent to the army hospital in Gengma County. We saw him off with heavy hearts.

It was one of the first workdays after the 1975 New Year holidays. Ruan had been trying to remove the stump and roots of a giant tree with dynamite, which was normal practice at the farm to level the ground for planting rubber trees after the virgin forests were destroyed. The dynamite had exploded prematurely in his face.

His family came from Chengdu to see him some days later. I and a leader from our farm were present when they were at his bedside in the ward. The doctor said his life had been saved but his vision could never be restored.

Ruan had been a popular figure at Plantain Grove. An excellent basketball player, he was tall and handsome, with large, almost feminine, eyes. Now, alas, his big, bright eyes were replaced by two dark holes.

The day after I met the Grove manager, the daughter of a farm employee took me to Ruan's abode. On the way, she told me many things about Ruan. He was an odd fellow, she said, spending most of his pension on liquor. He had a short temper, often making a row for no reason at all, throwing things on the ground, and sometimes tearing his own clothes. No one dared to approach him, or cared to be his neighbor. When we arrived at the place, the young woman pointed at his door but refused to go in and hurried away.

I gently pushed open the door of the hut, the walls of which were made of bamboo strips and earth. A repulsive smell struck me in the face as I spotted a pail of human excreta near the door. Although mentally prepared, I was stunned by what I saw inside the room: Wearing dark glasses on his expressionless face, Ruan was sitting on the edge of his bed. His clothes were filthy beyond description. He looked somewhat bloated, as though with edema -- shockingly changed from the neatly dressed, dashing boy I had known. A tattered mosquito net hung over his bed. The cloth of the bedding was torn and shredded, the cotton stuffing exposed and crumbling. A most striking sight was the empty liquor bottles lined up on an improvised table near the bed. Dirty clothes dangled from a rope hung across the room. At the far end of the room was a heap of firewood that also stank. This was the sum total of Ruan's belongings.

The place was totally unfit for human habitation. I had seen neater pigsties and chicken coops. Even in our *zhiqing* days we had lived under tiled roofs, but this thatched hut had been used for storing firewood and other assorted junk.

"Who is it?" Ruan asked.

"It's me, Wang Xiaomei. Do you remember me?"

"Wang Xiaomei! I know you, of course. Why are you here? To see my misery and to ridicule me?"

I was certain that any of his old *zhiqing* companions would be heartbroken to witness his dire circumstances. How could I laugh at his misfortune? But for a while, I didn't know how to respond.

"I heard that you are still here," I said at last, "so I came over to see you. I would like to find out if there is anything I can do to help you."

He fell silent.

Just then, the door was pushed open and a somewhat hunchbacked old man came in. Without uttering a word, he handed me a stool, picked up two empty bowls on the ground, and fetched some kindling before going out. Ruan told me this was his caregiver, groaning that the old fellow was practically mute and that his cooking was terrible. Even such a person had to be persuaded to do the job, he added. The manager had told Ruan that the farm had to pay the old man a regular salary.

We became more relaxed as our conversation went on. Ruan complained, though with some restraint, that he was in poor health, that he had difficulty even in standing up and walking; that doctors at the hospital were irresponsible, always ready to send him off before giving him any serious treatment; that payment of his pension was often delayed; and that no one would speak with him.

I asked him whether I should talk with his family to request that they bring him home, but he again fell silent. After some time, he said he missed the spicy beef jerky made in Chengdu, and asked whether I could have his family mail him a parcel of the beef, along with some sausages and salted pork. Finally, he expressed his wish to get married, saying that he wouldn't mind if I laughed at him for blurting out such a wish. He wanted me to ask the manager to help him find a wife.

Tears streamed down my cheeks as I listened to him. Ruan had had many admirers among the *zhiqing* girls in the old days. After the accident, one farm leader tried find out which of the girls was closest to him and promised a good job for any girl who would take care of Ruan. As time went by, however, all the *zhiqing* left the farm and married. Only Ruan stayed behind, spending the long, dark nights by himself.

As we parted, I advised Ruan to pay more attention to his health, and to cut down on his alcohol consumption. It was all I could think of to say.

When I mentioned Ruan's wish to the manager, he shook his head fiercely and expressed doubt that any woman would want to marry him. He asked me several times to contact Ruan's family and suggest they take him home. I complained that Ruan's abode wasn't a fit place for anyone to live in, let alone a sick, handicapped man like Ruan. He deserved much better care than he was receiving. The manager promised to move him to a different abode, but at the same time said that, as I must know, the resources of the farm were very limited.

Back in Chengdu, I was surprised to learn that Ruan's family had actually brought him home some years before after he was released from the army hospital. His parents and siblings had taken turns caring for him. They were tolerant of his bad temper and would forgive him for his outbursts. Some of the *zhiqing* who had worked in the same company with him would drop in occasionally and sometimes take him to the cinema so that he could listen to a film. After a few years, however, as his parents grew older and his siblings set up their own families, it became increasingly difficult for them to keep Ruan in Chengdu. They eventually sent him back to the farm in Yunnan, which was why I found him there on my visit.

Notwithstanding this background, I decided to see Ruan's parents. I reported to them on their son's health and his situation in general, and conveyed the farm manager's message asking them to bring him home again. The old couple, looking very weak and sad, listened to me in silence. Ruan's father finally said, "This is a big issue. Our whole family have to discuss the matter in order to make a decision. I will give you a responsible reply." Seeing the sorrowful, helpless expression on their faces, their eyes glistening with tears, I regretted having played the role of a cruel messenger.

Several days later, I received a recorded message on the phone stating that the decision of the whole Ruan family was not to bring Ruan Dangsheng back to Chengdu. Their decision was not unexpected. It explained why Ruan Dangsheng had fallen silent when I mentioned the idea to him.

I visited Mengding again in the spring of 1991 as a member of a small work group collecting materials for an exhibition in commemoration of the 20th anniversary of Chengdu *zhiqing* going to Yunnan. That was when I learned that Ruan Dangsheng had died a few years before of complications arising from his injury.

I learned also that the manager had kept his promise. Soon after my first visit, he had ordered Ruan moved into a house with a tiled roof close to the battalion headquarters. People there used to hear the blind man singing in a husky voice. He would ask anyone he met to help him find a wife, but he remained a virgin to the very end.

Life Trajectory of a Shanghai *Zhiqing*

by Liu Xiaohang

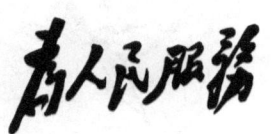

I first met Jin in 1972 when we worked as *zhiqing* in the countryside of Nanling County, Anhui Province, in eastern China. We lived in different villages, but we got to know each other at a short-term training class on literature and art run by the County House of Culture. He came from Shanghai, while I hailed from Wuhu, a major town of Anhui.

I had always wanted to become a prose writer or novelist. Jin was well-grounded in Chinese painting and wished to become a painter. We had many things in common: we were both high school seniors close in age, both in hot pursuit of a literary or artistic career, and now both cast by the hand of fate out to a poor, unheard-of place, our dreams dashed by the tidal waves of the Cultural Revolution. We soon became close friends who could pour our hearts out to each other. Jin was severely near-sighted and wore thick glasses. Not good at speaking, he always listened quietly to your words, but behind those glasses, it was easy to see the sincerity and goodwill in his eyes.

When the training class ended, we agreed to keep up a regular correspondence. Both of us were then transferred to teach in village schools. He soon wrote me that he felt lonely and invited me to visit him when I had time. Since the rice-planting season was over and classes had not yet resumed, I walked more than twenty kilometers to see him. The rugged mountain paths were soggy and slippery in the continual spring rain. Dusk was approaching when I arrived at his village. A cow herder told me that Jin lived in an adobe hut near the office of the production brigade, but when I got there, I found his door locked. He was obviously still at work. It was getting dark when I saw him coming, wearing a broad bamboo hat and a coir raincoat, his legs smeared with wet clay. He grabbed my hand and gave it a hearty shake.

Jin had spent the whole day plowing. Since two of their oxen had frozen to death in the wintry cold, the villagers had to rely mainly on manpower. Jin had been working in place of an ox, pulling the plow forward, his feet sunk in the freezing cold water of the farm fields, and thick ropes wound around one shoulder. An elderly peasant had navigated the plow behind him, frequently bursting into work songs. They had to trudge back and forth many times to work a plot of land.

Jin looked exhausted and hungry. I heated water on the kitchen fire for him to wash his feet, and started cooking rice for our supper. I asked if there was anything to go with the rice. "I knew you were coming," he said with a grin, "so I prepared a dish of salted pork stewed with beans." He heated it over a small kerosene stove. The kitchen fire gave our faces a reddish glow, and the cold, damp room warmed up as it filled with the aroma of meat.

After supper, we heard the wind and rain rising outside, and thunder claps that heralded an early spring. Lying down and wrapped in bedding, we talked about our families and native towns in the faint light of a flickering oil lamp. We were probably doomed to stay in these poor mountain villages for life, we told each other with heavy sighs.

The weather cleared up that morning, and sunlight flooded into Jin's small hut. After a quick breakfast, we decided to go to the county seat for a brief tour. We also hoped to get some information there about job opportunities. We were on our way out when two peasants rushed up to us and said that an old man in the neighboring village had just passed away. His family wanted to hang a portrait of the deceased in their mourning hall but since he had never had a photo taken in his life, they wanted Jin to draw a sketch of him. We hurried with the peasants to the old man's home, where the family were wailing and crying. They stood aside to let us enter.

Jin asked them to prop up the old man's body in a sitting position and put a roll of bedding behind it to prevent it from falling over backwards. Then he started to do a quick sketch. Since the old man's eyes were closed, Jin asked the family which of his sons looked most like the father. One of them answered that he resembled the old man most. Jin then asked that son to sit beside the body so that he could model the old man's eyes on his. When the sketch was completed, everyone marveled at its strong likeness. The entire family expressed their gratitude to Jin, praising him for bringing the spirit of the old man to life. They insisted on our having lunch with them. Before our departure, they presented us with twenty boiled eggs. Jin politely declined at first, but they insisted, saying that local custom demanded it.

The following autumn, Jin came to visit me on a breezy, cool day during the national holidays. He spent part of the night drawing a sketch of me under an oil lamp. Then we took a walk along the Yijiang River. Beneath a starry sky with a crescent moon, we listened to the roaring water and watched the fishing boats' flickering lights. Next morning, we took a ferry and visited Xihe Township just across the river in a different county. We walked on the flagstone street and soon reached a busy rural market on the bank of the river. At a crossroad, Jin soon became absorbed in sketching the folk dwellings with white walls and black tiles typical of the area. Security men patrolling the streets soon came over; they suspected that we might be spies. They asked us to go with them to a police station, where several of them took turns interrogating us. We explained to them again and again that we were here just for life drawing. It was not until Jin produced a pictorial magazine containing some of his works that they became convinced and politely saw us off.

Jin made many sketches in the small township: children with bared bottoms, an old man taking a nap under the eaves of his house, a peasant woman nursing her baby by the roadside, a barber at work beside his stand. All of them reflected people's everyday lives and had a strong local flavor. Jin set great store by these sketches and took good care of them.

In 1973, my first story was included in Beside the Yijiang River, a selection of stories produced by a major publisher in Anhui. Jin's traditional-style Chinese painting Poor Old Peasant Narrates Village History was displayed at a provincial art exhibition as well as at a Shanghai exhibition of art works by *zhiqing* from the city. We encouraged each other with our initial achievements.

In 1975, both Jin and I bade farewell to the countryside after many years of anxiety and expectation. Because I was my family's only child, I got the preferential treatment of being given a job in my hometown, Wuhu. I worked in a small community-run chemical factory that made products for daily use. Jin was sent to work in a local fertilizer factory in the Nanling county seat. We turned twenty-eight that year. Each of us earned a monthly apprentice pay of only 18 yuan, but that was more than enough.

The following year, Jin came to Wuhu on business. He found me in the small factory in the shadows of an old alley. I was operating a circular saw that cut timber into sections. Wearing a leather apron and mask, I was working right in front of the machine, which whirled with great speed. He lamented, "You're doing a dangerous job. A highly capable man taking a small job!" I switched off the electric supply and had a chat with him. Seeing some old copies of textbooks on mathematics, physics and chemistry on my workbench, he asked whether I was preparing for college entrance exams. I nodded and said that a great historic change was in sight and we had better be prepared for it.

College entrance exams were resumed that winter as expected. I sat for the exams and was admitted by a normal college – my last chance to get a higher education. Jin wrote me saying that the leaders of his factory persuaded him not to take the exams. They said he was a little too old and asked him to stay with them. As a probationary member of the Party, he had to obey their decision. After that, I got more news from him: he had become a section chief and gotten married. His wife, surnamed Mei, had also come from Shanghai as a *zhiqing*. She had worked in the same commune where I had been. In my memory, she was a girl of few words, simple and honest, and different from the usual type of Shanghai girls who behaved like spoiled children. I thought they were a good match. Later, he told me that he had been elected a delegate to the Provincial People's Congress. I knew he had won that honor by merit and was glad for him.

In the early 1980s both of us were transferred to new jobs and moved to new places. We lost contact for some time. Later I learnt that Jin had a teenage son who had been living in Shanghai with his grandmother. It was common for *zhiqing* who were unable to return to their home towns to send their children there and leave them in the care of relatives. Most *zhiqing* did this in the hope of giving their children a better education. In the case of *zhiqing* themselves, the government would have to help with job opportunities and living quarters once it permitted them to return, but their children had no such problems. Official policy stipulated that their children were allowed to stay in their home towns as regular residents while they themselves were not. This policy caused many problems for Jin and his family. Only once every year could Jin and Mei see their son when they traveled to Shanghai during the traditional Spring Festival holidays. The couple always felt guilty about not being able to look after their son when he was still so young. Jin told me it was his plan to retire early so that he could go back to Shanghai to take care of his son and help him prepare for college entrance exams.

Jin left his factory in 1996 when it was on the verge of bankruptcy. He and his wife were allowed to move back to their home town of Shanghai for the first time in thirty years but without an official change in residence. They lived with their son in a dark, cramped room in an old house. A former schoolmate helped him find a job with a small advertising company. His wife managed the household while looking after their son. He sent me a family photo after their reunion. Photographed in the setting sun against the gray wall of the old house down in the alley, Jin looked much older than his actual age. He had not yet turned fifty. In any case, the family had a shelter now, and they were together. They wanted to start a new life, with the couple's hopes resting on their son's future.

In the autumn of 1998, Jin wrote me a letter which contained only a dozen lines. He told me the sad news that his son had jumped to his death from the balcony of his aunt's apartment on the ninth floor. He had just turned eighteen. The letter did not explain why his son had committed suicide. Stunned, I could not hold back my tears.

Fate was too cruel to Jin and his wife. I didn't know how to console them. Since Jin had no telephone at home, I immediately called Liu Zhiyi, a professor at a Shanghai college and an old schoolmate, asking him to see the couple on my behalf and convey my deep condolences. Prof. Liu went to see them the following day with a basket full of magnolias. They were deep in grief, he reported. Mei in particular could not stop shedding tears. She could hardly drink or eat.

Prof. Liu reported to me how the tragedy had happened.

Jin's son had lived with his grandmother since early childhood. Without parental love and care, he had become an unsociable introvert, an indifferent student, and a timid individual often bullied by his schoolmates. He would come home from school but say nothing to his grandmother. He became gradually more depressed as the years went by. With the approach of college entrance exams, the pressure on him increased daily. That weekend, he went with his parents to visit his aunt. While his parents were in the kitchen helping to prepare the dinner, he went to the balcony alone and jumped.

Prof. Liu told me that "*zhiqing* children" had posed a problem in Shanghai all these years. Close to a million young students had left the city for the countryside during the Cultural Revolution. With the rise of the nationwide "return-to-city wind" (*fancheng feng*) in 1979, the majority of them came back, but there were still 200,000 *zhiqing* remaining in the countryside, where they had found jobs and settled down. Official policy permitted their children to return to Shanghai and stay with relatives, but this created a number of problems for the host families, most notably one of space, making their usually small quarters even more cramped. The boarding children often found it difficult to live with their relatives. Their parents away, many in remote border regions, they lacked parental love and care. Such children generally grew up eccentric and unsociable. In Shanghai, they were viewed as a special group among their peers. The phenomenon of "*zhiqing* children" attracted the attention of the local authorities. The Shanghai Municipal Committee of the Chinese Young Communist League made social surveys and held forums on the subject, but whether the local authorities did anything to solve the problem remains unclear.

I went to see Jin in 1999 when I was in Shanghai for a meeting. He still lived on the second floor of an old house in an alley. Beside the staircase I saw a woman cooking porridge on a coal stove. Her profile reminded me of the young Mei I had known when we worked in the countryside. She did not recognize me but told me that Jin was upstairs. I climbed up and found Jin bare-chested in trousers cleaning a refrigerator. The room was dark and had a low ceiling. It was hot and stuffy for lack of air conditioning. Jin seemed pleasantly surprised to see me. While he hurried to pour a cold drink for me, I looked around and saw the small space was crowded with old furniture and household appliances. On a small bookcase stood a portrait of his son, gazing from the frame with frank, honest eyes. This led to an embarrassing silence. I made a few random comments to divert our attention.

The other end of the room served as a parlor, above which a tiny loft had been constructed. Jin told me that was where his younger brother, his wife and their child lived. The brother had also been a *zhiqing* in Anhui. He had returned to Shanghai the previous year and would have to stay in the loft until they could find a place. In the past few years, about 100,000 Shanghai *zhiqing* had left their work units as de facto retirees (*nei tui*) and come back to take care of their children. Some of the returned *zhiqing* tried to find new jobs or start their own businesses.

With Mei's permission, I brought Jin to my hotel. We felt

more comfortable there with air conditioning and more space, and we stayed up all night talking. Outside the window was the magnificent Oriental Pearl Tower, one of the tallest skyscrapers in the world. With all its lights turned on, it created an illusion of daylight. Nocturnal Shanghai was like a wealthy lady in dazzling jewelry. Behind the silhouettes of tall buildings lived multitudes of folks like Jin in crowded houses and shanties. Still worried by problems related to living space and their daily meals, they were the abandoned "orphans" of Shanghai. Their splendid dreams of youth had been shattered in remote villages, grasslands and barren wilderness. They had returned to their native town after some thirty years, when they were long past their prime. Their departure had given this biggest metropolis in the East a sudden spell of quietness. Now, upon their return, the city greeted them with a stern, detached look.

Jin told me he was afraid to go back to the countryside in Anhui. Folks there all knew he had a handsome son and would ask about him, but Jin lacked the courage to tell them the truth.

What he hoped for most was to get his full pension and live a secure life when he reached the formal retirement age of sixty. Since the block of old houses where he currently lived would be demolished the following year, the government permitted him and Mei to apply to buy a cheap apartment and finally regain their official status of permanent residents of Shanghai as returned *zhiqing*.

Jin would never emerge from the shadows of his life as a *zhiqing*. He was only one of the hundreds of thousands of people in the mega city who shared this fate.

Days When I Awaited Employment

by Xiao Fuxi

Like almost all other *zhiqing*, I went through a period of unemployment after returning from the countryside. It was a bleak time for me. The Chinese phrase *suan tian ku la* (sour, sweet, bitter, hot) is probably the best way to describe my experiences and feelings in those days.

Beijing did not welcome me as enthusiastically as it had sent me off to the Great Northern Wilderness several years earlier. In fact, it treated me coldly, all but obliterating me from its memory. Everything that should have looked familiar – Stonemason Alley, Qianmen Gatehouse, Gongxing Department Store, the public toilet, the date tree in our courtyard, the black lacquered door, the window frames covered with rough sorghum papers, the leaking water pipe – now looked unreal and illusory as if they had dimmed into surreal emptiness during my absence.

I was surprised to see the female shop assistant at the small food store next to our front gate. She had been a young girl my own age before I left Beijing--not a beauty, but pleasant enough to see and speak to. Her once pink cheeks had lost their luster. Now pregnant, she looked much older as she waddled around like a penguin with a big belly. The sight of her was the first mild shock I received following my return. She was a mirror in which I could see my own reflection. Having wasted the best years of my life, I could see I had aged as rapidly as she had.

The second event that surprised me was the visit of a beautiful policewoman. One day I came home to find her sitting on one of our worn-out chairs. She made me nervous, not because she was young and beautiful but because I was afraid of the police, especially when they visited my home. When I was on home leave a few years before, some policemen knocked on our door at night. They had come to check whether everyone had a residency certificate, and they sternly urged those of us with temporary residency permits to leave Beijing as soon as possible.

Now, here was a smiling, cordial policewoman much younger than I was. When I walked in, she took a piece of paper and several banknotes from her small handbag and said, smiling, to me, "At the start of the Cultural Revolution several years ago, your father handed in several silver dollars.[8] Now, to implement official policy, the money is returned to you." She asked me to sign my name on the piece of paper, and with that, the smiling policewoman left our home.

The whole thing seemed unreal, like some kind of comedy. So now the government was "implementing" some kind of "official policies" that brought me money? Did they have any "official policies" that could be "implemented" with regard to us returned *zhiqing*? The more I thought about it, the more upset I became. Even capitalists who had been censured and whose homes had been searched at the start of the Cultural Revolution had benefited from the implementation of official policies. Some of their belongings were now returned to them, and their once-withdrawn salaries paid back to them. But how about us? Who cared about us? It was only then that I came to understand, more or less, that in recent historical upheavals, we *zhiqing* were a truly pitiful bunch. When we were needed, we were like a flag that flew high as the wind blew hard. When no longer needed, the flag was rolled up and cast aside like an abandoned cleaning rag.

I knew I shouldn't complain. My unemployment was not long and my siblings never stopped supporting me. Neverthe-

8. A kind of currency used under the old regime – Ed.

less, it was an extremely unpleasant period for me, not only for financial reasons, but because I had become an object of disdain and humiliation, and as such, I had to learn to be humble and forbearing.

I then realized that finding a job in Beijing was harder than finding a spouse. In looking for a spouse, you can keep lowering your requirements. But in looking for a job, you have no options. You have to accept any job assigned to you, without any chance to speak about your own requirements.

I started to serve as a substitute teacher at No.3 Elementary School, my Alma Mater, and then worked at a neighborhood factory, making cardboard boxes, transporting goods, copying documents, and whatnot. In short, I did anything I was bidden to do, like an obedient donkey turning a millstone.

The most difficult job they gave me was to deliver goods on a tricycle with a freight platform. I was terrible at operating the tricycle. It would lean to one side as I started to pedal it, and soon I was on the sidewalk. I was stupidly slow in mastering the skill, which should have been quite simple. But I dared not openly admit it, fearing that I might be ridiculed or even rejected. Instead of pedaling, I would push the tricycle along, cursing my own stupidity.

I remember once having to deliver a load of clothing to Dashilar, a famous shopping street southwest of Tiananmen Square. Though the load was very heavy, pushing the tricycle in Stonemason Alley was not too difficult, but navigating along the busy Qianmen Street was a different matter--there was so much traffic and the tricycle so hard to control, especially when crossing the street. Since a hand-pushed tricycle could only move forward slowly, drivers of vehicles behind me tried to hurry me up by sounding horns or shouting at me. I panicked and became drenched in sweat. Many passersby looked at me with curiosity, which embarrassed me all the more.

Whichever job I undertook – working as a substitute teacher or as a deliveryman – I was never paid a cent. But I had to leave a good impression on the elderly housewives now managing the neighborhood committee. They were sarcastically called "detectives with bound feet" since governments at the grassroots level used them as informants. A good impression would mean a better job, as the power to allocate jobs to returned *zhiqing* lay in their hands. In the earlier years of the Cultural Revolution, they had controlled the destinies of "ox ghosts and snake monsters" (as "class enemies" were called). Now, they controlled ours. The Cultural Revolution had emancipated those old housewives. Their power had risen to unprecedented heights along with their status.

During the interval, another event took place which stunned me and made me realize that life was bleaker than I had imagined. This concerned a young girl I got to know named Xuefang (Snow Fragrance). She was just over twenty and as pretty as her name. We became acquainted because her elder sister and I had studied in the same elementary school. Having worked on a paramilitary farm in Yunnan, she had come back on sick leave. I knew that most of the *zhiqing* who had returned on sick leave were using sickness as a pretext, so I assumed that Xuefang might not really be sick.

At the time, there were few returned *zhiqing* like us in the neighborhood. We rarely met people we knew on the streets. Our courtyard and the entire neighborhood looked deserted. Like me, Xuefang spent her days in solitude, living an aimless and bored existence.

Since she lived only a few doors away across the street, we used to exchange greetings when we met. Sometimes she would go to the neighborhood committee to help with their work, and when we met there, we would trade remarks. Later, she began to visit me frequently, and sometimes invited me to her home. We soon became friends. Talented in many ways, she was good at water color painting and Uighur dancing. She often showed me her paintings and, when she was in a good mood, would jump agilely like a fawn onto her platform bed to perform a dance for me. I really didn't know she was sick.

Once she astounded me by telling me about her experience in Yunnan. She had served as a member of a Mao Zedong Thought propaganda troupe at the regimental headquarters of a paramilitary farm. I knew she must have been an outstanding performer, but what I didn't anticipate was that she had become a target of sexual assault by the regimental commander. Initially, she just thought her leader had a fondness for young talented people. But one night when she was asleep during a performance tour away from the farm, the regimental commander jumped on her like a wild beast, trying to rape her. She fought him off and ran into the wild fields shrouded by darkness....

When she told me her story, I couldn't help thinking of the great number of female *zhiqing* who had been raped by officials of the 16th regiment under the Heilongjiang Production and Construction Corps. The corps ran many paramilitary farms in the Great Northern Wilderness. I had worked as a *zhiqing* on one of them. The officials who committed those crimes were severely punished, and a few of them were executed.

It pained me deeply to think of what Xuefang had been

through, but I still failed to grasp the gravity of the shock the experience had given her. She could no longer walk out of the shadows but had developed a serious mental illness. One day, while her mother was out shopping, she swallowed a bottle of insecticide. She lay dead on the very bed on which she had performed the Uighur dance for me. I was dumbfounded by the news. A young, blooming life had ceased to exist.

Xuefang was such a beautiful, talented girl, she would have had a bright future had she lived. If she had persevered a few years longer until the Gang of Four was toppled, she might not have been so depressed. With her great talent, entering a college or finding a good job would not have been difficult for her. Instead, she was swallowed by the shadows of one nightmarish episode.

Her death was a great shock to me. It provoked me to reflect anew on the whole Sent-down movement to which I had enthusiastically dedicated my youth. I no longer took things at face value. I became more cautious but also more appreciative of my life. I knew I would never follow in Xuefang's footsteps whatever the hardships I encountered. I would not regret the past, but treasure the present and the future.

My friends and I had been bold, public-spirited young team members when we were on our way to the Great Northern Wilderness, but now I dared not offend the people at the neighborhood committee who could cause me difficulties. The old mettle and valor had been replaced by patience and forbearance.

On January 10, 1974, I received a telegram from a former schoolmate still working on the farm in the Great Northern Wilderness. He told me that all *zhiqing* in that area who had attended high schools in Beijing would be enlisted as teachers to work in the capital. He advised me to go back to the farm to complete all the necessary procedures. I immediately packed up my things and left Beijing the following day. I was particularly thrilled that I could get a job without seeking favors from those "detectives with bound feet" who used to scrutinize me.

Once on the train, however, I had a strange feeling I could not have explained. Well aware that this might be my last visit to the farm at the northern borders, I didn't know whether I was joyful at the prospect of returning permanently to my Beijing home or sad because of my sentimental ties to the Great Northern Wilderness, where I had spent the best years of my life, from 21 to 27. The confusion has remained with me to the present day.

Love of Birds Changed His Life

by Xiao Fuxing

自力更生
艰苦奋斗

It is painful to negate one's innermost self.

Thirty-two years ago, Baoguang was a student in a junior middle school in Beijing when the Cultural Revolution broke out. An average student academically, he was very good at raising birds, which was his only hobby. He had nimble hands and a subtle mind, and he could make beautiful bird cages out of bamboo strips or iron wires. He trained his birds to fly in and out of their cages in response to his whistling, and his birds were there to keep him company when he did his homework. His house echoed with their chirping every day. When a neighbor's cat ate one of his birds, the neighbor apologized profusely, but Baoguang responded with screams and insisted on being paid for the lost bird. The story circulated among his neighbors and fellow students for quite a long time.

One day, a group of Red Guards came into Baoguang's courtyard. They threw his bird cages on the ground and trampled them, killing all his birds.

Baoguang didn't cry or make a scene. He convinced himself that raising birds must be a hobby of the bourgeoisie, something typical of their leisurely and carefree lifestyle, and an obsession with such a hobby could lead to a loss of drive and ambition. Though negating his former self was painful, he did this out of a true conversion of heart. He began to study Chairman Mao's works seriously and continued to do so when he went to the Inner Mongolian grasslands as a *zhiqing*. Because of his good performance in political studies, he was considered a model student in learning Chairman Mao's works. The more he studied, the greater his enthusiasm became. He regretted that he had had no opportunity to sacrifice his life for the revolution like some well-known martyrs, or to perform like the Chinese Red Army men who climbed snowy mountains and passed through uninhabited grasslands. But now, he was able to join the same kind of struggle by raising aloft the red banner and striving to liberate two thirds of humankind – the oppressed peoples and nations the world over.

Truly, there is always a dominating ideology in each epoch, which remolds people's minds and penetrates into all aspects of their material and spiritual life, not excluding their hobbies.

After working for ten years in Inner Mongolia, Baoguang returned to Beijing. Already past the prime of his life, he had few accomplishments to his credit. The harvests he and his companions had reaped from crop fields in Inner Mongolia were not much more than the seeds they had sown.

Like many people of his age, he faced the problem of unemployment. No one cared that he had been a model in learning Chairman Mao's works. Physically exhausted and mentally crushed, he felt like a wounded soldier returning home after defeat in a war. Walking along Beijing's busy streets, he tried to hide his face with a worn-out cap. The city that he had known so well now seemed alien to him. Somehow, he managed to find a job in a factory, where he had to start from scratch and compete with much younger people.   T w o more decades passed, and he was approaching fifty. During the interval, he had married and had a son. No longer harboring any ambitions, he just wanted to do his job at the workshop and give his son a good education. What he had lost, he hoped, could be retrieved by his son. After all, Baoguang was working in a state-owned enterprise. Though his income was low, once he reached retirement age, he would enjoy security for the rest of his life.

One year later, he and his wife lost their jobs. Their "iron rice bowls" disappeared into thin air. The couple no longer had any "work units" to take care of their basic needs. His son was about to enter middle school, and his father was lying on a sickbed, adding even more to their expenses. Their family of four was suddenly in financial straits, like a small boat adrift.

With great effort, however, Baoguang's wife managed to find a job cleaning offices, earning just enough to support the family. Baoguang also tried to find employment, but to no avail. There were too many people like him. Who would employ someone approaching fifty? He felt that youth was like a bird that had flown away, never to return.

One day he passed by a bird market he had known well but had been too busy to visit while at work. Attracted by the chirping of the birds, he peeked inside. He wandered among the various merchants' stands with nothing particular in mind, but the fidgety little creatures reminded him of his boyhood, which now seemed so remote. He felt as if he were approaching old age without ever having had the chance to enjoy life. Squeezing his way through the crowded aisles, he caught sight of a merchant selling a pair of kingfishers at the unbelievably high price of 1,000 yuan. When he saw a customer actually pay this sum, it struck him that the times had changed again. This fanned the smothered flames in his heart, prompting him to take action.

He immediately went home and asked his wife to give him part of their savings, explaining only that he needed it to buy some birds. Infuriated, she said they did not have enough money to feed the family, much less raise birds. Eventually, though, she relented and gave him some money. He started by buying a pair of inexpensive jade birds. Very soon, he sensed that he was much better at raising birds than he had been at the workshop.

Three months later, the two jade birds bred four offspring, two of which survived. He nurtured them with great care, and when they matured, he sold them for several hundred yuan. With his expanded business and his growing reputation as an experienced bird breeder, his income rose steadily.

People began placing orders for his birds at the incubation stage. Among the rare birds he raised were a pair of lovebirds which Chinese bird lovers called "white peony parrots". They could fetch more than 13,000 yuan on the bird market, but he held them back for even higher prices.

His wife no longer complained. She began to see him in a new light. She had never anticipated such great potential in him. Raising his head high, he started bossing around everyone in the household. The family had three bedrooms. To make more space for his birds, he ordered his son to vacate his bedroom and share a room with his grandfather. The son's old room became a bird house in which rows and rows of bird cages were arranged on several platforms, with dozens of birds chirping in a perpetual symphony.

Deprived of his own space, Baoguang's son had to do his homework on top of a sewing machine on their balcony. The chirping birds kept him company, just as they had his dad in his boyhood. For a period of time, Baoguang's wife and son felt some inconvenience in adapting to the new environment. But with a sizable family income, and the singing birds to entertain them, they did no grumbling at all.

It would occur to Baoguang every now and then that if he had not lost his job, he would never have taken up bird breeding as his occupation and had this chance to bring his special talents into full play. He had found a new lease on life only after he had been driven to a dead end.

For years after his return from Inner Mongolia, Baoguang had relied on the "iron rice bowl," taking a job that guaranteed him a secure income but little else. Only now did he realize that this old concept was wrong. Nothing in the world was going to save him and bring him happiness. He would have to rely on his own efforts. It was late in life – approaching fifty – for him to be realizing these simple truths, but he was filled with gratitude toward his dear birds. It was they who had helped him fly again with wings that had once been broken.

.... 自力更生
艰苦奋斗 ....

V. Confessions And Reflections

An Eternal Regret

by Liang Xiaosheng

In 1971, the third year after I was sent down to work in the Great Northern Wilderness of what used to be called Manchuria, there were already more than 200 *zhiqing* on the paramilitary farm to which I was assigned. I was the leader of a squad in our company, which was responsible for running part of the farm.

Though we were generally referred to as "educated youths (*zhiqing*)," a term we ourselves accepted, we did not in fact have much education. The youngest members in my squad were then seventeen and had only been through middle school.

That year, the ideological catchphrase "cutting off the tail of capitalism" was all the rage. In keeping with this concept, our regimental headquarters laid down rules prohibiting the raising of hens and other domestic fowl and animals. The rules primarily targeted farm employees--mostly demobilized soldiers and immigrants from other provinces who had arrived before us and established families there.

Raising hens was not permitted since they could lay eggs and so belonged to the "means of production". The same logic applied to sows, since they could give birth to piglets. Once they were raised by farm employees, "original accumulation of capital" would take place. Even raising boars was not allowed because, when fattened, they could be used for "hoarding and profiteering," particularly in those years when pork was a scarcity.

We were all warned that violation of these rules would cause the "tails of capitalism" to grow. If one did not cut off such a tail of one's own accord, others would help one to do so. "Cut it off forcefully, painfully and thoroughly until the blood shows" was a current slogan.

We had a farm employee working as a member of my squad in the mountains at one point. Our assignment was to open up land and set up a new production base. One day in May I suddenly heard the chirping of chicks coming from a carton box placed in the furthest corner of a *kang*.

"What's that sound in the box?" I asked the farm employee, whose name was Yang.

He smiled and said that it was the chirping of birds.

"It sounds like young chickens," I said.

"How can there be farm animals so deep in the mountains?" He responded with a straight face. "I found a bird's nest in the woods. Probably the parent birds had died. The young birds were starving. The Buddha inspired me to bring back the whole brood in their nest. I'll set them free when they grow up."

He seemed serious, and other members of my squad bore witness to his story. I didn't bother to climb up onto the *kang* to look into the box.

Not long afterward, I saw Yang feeding his "birds," all now fluffy and bigger than a closed fist.

"What are they?" I asked Yang.

"Tell me what you think," he said with a smile.

"They are chickens, not wild birds," I said.

"If we feed and keep them as birds, aren't they birds?"

The other squad members joined in. Some insisted that they were birds, while others pleaded for Yang to keep the chicks, knowing that I could not be so easily fooled. They said that raising a few chickens in the mountains shouldn't be a big deal and that I should not take the matter too seriously. Still others said raising chicks could serve as some sort of entertainment in our spare time. After all, we were leading an isolated and monotonous life. I dropped my objections.

People could hardly believe that the chicks—or, in Yang's words, his "little birds"—had been incubated by hand at nighttime under his bedding. The whole process took about two weeks.

The leftovers from our meals were sufficient to feed the chicks, and they grew very fast. Under Yang's meticulous care, all of them were approaching maturity in early autumn.

In the meantime, the regiment leadership remained undecided on whether or not to establish a new production base, and members of our squad continued to stay on the mountain.

On October 1, the National Day, Yang killed the two biggest roasters and the whole squad enjoyed delicious chicken soup.

Before the Chinese New Year, the regiment leadership informed us of their decision to abandon the plan to build a new production base and instructed us to come down from the mountain. We had been expecting this for a long time, but now we had to worry about what to do with the chickens. In the end, we decided to kill and eat them all.

Yang raised his knife to kill the four hens, only to put it down several times. He could not bear to kill them and said imploringly to me, "They have started laying eggs, Squad Leader."

"So what?' I responded.

"It would be a shame to kill them."

"What else can we do?"

"Let me take them back to my home in secret," he implored me. "My family lives at the end of the village and people will not discover them. Even if they are discovered, I'll bear all the consequences. I have so many children to feed."

I could hardly say no, but I never anticipated that one squad member eager to be admitted to the Communist Youth League would report the matter to the leadership. As a result, a criticism session was held in our company, and an official circular publicized the criticism to the whole regiment.

I was the one who had to draft a speech of criticism and read it at the session on behalf of our squad. The leadership ordered me to do this, and then they dismissed me as Squad Leader.

Yang was an honest man who treated all *zhiqing* exceedingly well. He was enraged by this betrayal and considered his public criticism a huge disgrace. One night, he hanged himself in a tree behind the *zhiqing* dormitory.

We were instructed to handle matters related to his death. It was only then that I visited his home for the first time. And what a home! What a family! There was only a worn mat on the *kang* bed, Yang's three children were all in rags, and his widow looked fragile and haggard. The sight of the poor family was excruciatingly depressing. His death brought us not only sadness, but a persistent sense of guilt. We dug a very deep pit in which to bury him, and we wept inconsolably as we lowered him into it.

From that time on, every Sunday night, we laid a bundle of firewood at Yang's door.

I later became a teacher at the village primary school where Yang's three children went, and I treated them with special care. I bought satchels and exercise books for them. But they were afraid of me and kept aloof.

Then their mother fell sick. All members of my squad traveled more than twenty kilometers to the hospital to see her and offered to donate blood. During that period, I stayed in her hut to cook meals for the children. I would tell them stories and help them with their homework, but they were still afraid of me and kept their distance. This was true even when they were listening to my stories with wide-open eyes.

I was later transferred to the propaganda section at the regimental headquarters. On the day I left our company, many people came to bid me farewell. They stood in a circle surrounding the horse-drawn cart that was to transport me. I discovered Yang's widow standing in the back of the crowd, but I couldn't tell if she was looking at me. When the cart driver shouted "Giddap!" Yang's widow pushed her three children forward and had them call in unison, "Good-bye, Teacher!" The tears streamed down my cheeks.

In those years, I hardly knew how to protect myself, let alone use my position to protect someone like Yang. The thought helps me stanch the bleeding of my emotional wound to some extent, but I can never undo what I allowed to happen in that sad year.

More than thirty years have passed since then, and my regret is like an unhealed vaccination scab. Like the new flesh beneath the scab I sense a new concept emerging: Love for other human beings stands out above everything. This should be the most basic, essential principle for our society, and when it is trampled upon, one should not be a slave to the current epoch. But what a price we have paid for learning such a simple principle!

Participating in
"Class Struggle"

by Zhang Mengjie

The term "class struggle" appeared in Chinese media more frequently than any other during the 1960s and 1970s. "Never Forget Class Struggle" banners could be seen in almost all public places. Waging class struggle was viewed as an essential means to thwart the restoration of capitalism in China.

In truth, however, "class struggle" remained a vague idea to me while I was still in school. All I knew about it came from mass media, books, and the teachers' political lessons. In my mind, class enemies were stereotyped figures. All of them were cruel, treacherous and shamelessly debauched. I had the opportunity to witness "class struggle" and participate in it firsthand when I went to work as a *zhiqing* in a commune-run wood farm in the Ta-pa Mountains in China's West in September 1964.

The commune Party secretary came to our farm in the early morning of the third day after our arrival and told us that, instead of work, we were going to attend a struggle meeting that day. We new arrivals were temporarily staying in a house evacuated by some peasants, with us boys living in the central row of rooms and the girls in the wing-rooms. The rooms enclosed three sides of a courtyard that could hold an assembly of as many as 200 people. A rostrum was set up just in front of the central rooms. The struggle meeting seemed to have been arranged especially for us *zhiqing*, and we were all very excited.

Peasants from around the farm arrived in small groups after breakfast -- men and women, young and old. They all wore garments made of hand-woven cloth dyed an ugly black or blue, and each of the elderly people, irrespective of sex, wore a white head turban. Their rustic wear posed a sharp contrast to the urban dress of us *zhiqing*. Sitting on the ground, the men began to hand-roll tobacco leaves for their pipes. Some of the women started stitching soles of cloth shoes, while others bared their breasts to nurse their babies. Very soon, heavy smoke hung in the air along with a babble of voices.

The target of the struggle session was an ex-landlord, about 40, named He. He was dressed in the same coarse cloth as the other villagers but with a "landlord" label pinned to the upper left side of his breast. A skinny man with grizzled hair and beard, he looked timid and servile, entirely unlike the landlord image in my mind's eye. He stood before the rostrum facing the crowd, his head bowed and body bent forward. His wife and children sat in the front row like accomplices in a public trial.

The commune Party secretary opened the meeting and read the indictment in the local dialect. The villagers helped us to grasp the main points of his speech. The principal charge against He was that he had intentionally let his ox loose to intrude in commune fields and damage the crops. Hé stammered, "I am guilty. I caused damage to collective properties. I shouldn't have been so negligent as to allow my ox to snap the rope and trot off." He was interrupted by someone in the crowd who shouted, "None of your whitewashing! You did this intentionally."

The Party secretary then said in a raised voice, "Commune members and *zhiqing* comrades, our enemy is tricky. Class struggle is acute and complicated. We must always heighten our vigilance and guard against sabotage by the enemy."

Provoked by his words, several *zhiqing* rushed toward Hé and started beating him. He let out a shriek and shielded his head with both hands. Some in the crowd shouted, "Well done! Well done!" Encouraged by this response, I charged forward and said to the landlord: "Show us your records for regime change (*biantian zhang*)!"

In political class, our teachers had explained to us that ex-landlords and rich peasants used to conceal records of who had confiscated their lands and properties so that they could easily retrieve them when the KMT government came back.

He looked at me with bleary eyes, his nose bleeding. He seemed not to have understood me. Enraged by his slow re-action, I slapped him in the face and kicked him, causing him to fall on the ground. His wife ran up and knelt down before me, crying and begging me to stop. I had a thrilling sense of triumph, but when I turned around, I spotted hatred in the eyes of He's children.

After the struggle session, the commune Party secretary praised us for our firm stand and courage in fighting class enemies He also warned us to heighten our vigilance and guard against retaliation by the enemy.

We were eating breakfast the next morning when a small teenage girl entered our courtyard with a bag of vegetables on her back. We had had no vegetables to eat in the days following our arrival, so the commune leadership had called on local peasants to share some of their vegetables with us, which they did every day, bringing them as gifts. We imme-diately accepted the young girl's vegetables with thanks, but after putting down her load, she seemed reluctant to leave. "*Zhiqing* elder brothers," she stammered after some hesita-tion, "I beg you not to beat my dad any more. He cannot even get out of his bed this morning."

Suddenly awakened to the fact that this was He's daughter, we looked at one another, not knowing what to do. Then someone shouted: "That landlord son-of-a-bitch wants to bribe us!" We all started throwing the vegetables at the girl, shouting: "Who wants your vegetables? Think you can bribe us, huh?"

She was momentarily stunned. Then she let out a cry and ran off. A few of the female *zhiqing* grumbled, "Don't overdo it!" "Bullying a young girl won't make you a hero!"

I couldn't sleep that night, haunted as I was by scenes of the struggle session and the image of the plaintive girl, eyes brimming with tears.

I was born into a family with a scholarly background and had been taught since early childhood to be polite and helpful to others. I had never taken part in a fistfight, nor had I beaten anyone. My teachers always saw me as an outstanding student, both morally and academically. I was surprised at my own actions at the struggle session and couldn't help wondering why I had acted like that. Actually, the answer was simple: My father had been branded a "counterrevolutionary" and was then undergoing labor reform. I wanted to show that I had made a clean break with the reactionary classes.

When we got to know each other better, I was told by the peasants that He was one of the smarter people in the village. Previously, he had not been rich at all. The areas around the village had a great number of tung candlenut trees, the source of tung oil. Local peasants had little use for the oil besides lighting, or painting their pails, so the price was fairly low. He managed to learn that tung oil could fetch a much higher price outside this region due to its scarcity and high demand. He soon became a wealthy man transporting tung oil and selling it in Chengdu. His good fortune started a year before the founding of the new republic when a landlord in a nearby village went bankrupt because of his obsession with opium smoking. He took the opportunity to buy a few acres of farmland from him and hired some farmhands to till them. According to the land reform law, He was later classified as a landlord while the bankrupt landlord became a poor peasant. Local folks used to laugh at He for being outsmarted by himself, saying that he had picked up the hat of the bankrupt landlord and put it on his own head.

Getting to know all this made me feel uneasy about my mistreatment of He. Not long afterwards, the Cultural Revolution broke out. During the campaign to "make a clean sweep of all monsters and devils," my father became a target of attack by the Red Guards. He had graduated from the Central University in KMT days and was a professor under the new regime. He was beaten to death with copper-buckled leather belts. Heaven seemed to have punished me for my wrongdoings.

In subsequent years, I was summoned to attend many more struggle sessions sponsored by the commune authorities, and each time a few dozen former landlords and rich peasants were herded to the meeting by armed militiamen. They were all in rags and wore stunned expressions on their faces. To me, the most unforgettable sight was an elderly woman around the age of eighty wearing the usual white cloth label of class identity on her breast. She had to stagger along to the meeting aided by her two sons, to be denounced and insulted. Later at college, when I had a chance to read William Shirer's *The Rise and Fall of the Third Reich*, I realized that this practice, which was similar to what the Nazis had done to the Jews, might have been borrowed from Hitler's Germany.

Like many of my companions, I had a certain feeling of novelty when first attending struggle sessions, but soon found them boring and meaningless. Afterwards, when parents of some *zhiqing* came under attack at struggle sessions, we began to develop sympathy toward their rural counterparts. Our loss of interest in "class struggle" resulted in our total avoidance of such meetings.

In the summer of 1986, I traveled with my son to the Tapa Mountains, hoping to revisit the peasants around the wood farm who had initially shaken off poverty thanks to China's opening up and reform. I again met He the ex-landlord. His political status had been changed and he was no longer regarded as a member of the hostile classes. After ending the Cultural Revolution, the Party Center had abolished the communes and given former landlords and rich peasants new status as working people, with all the rights enjoyed by other Chinese citizens and no labels to wear. He appeared to have forgotten that I had hit him. He warmly invited me to his home, where he told me that he had picked up his old line of business -- transporting and selling poultry products to the cities. He had become one of the first wealthy men in the neighborhood. I was glad for his success.

Coming back from the wood farm, I have often prayed that the preposterous farce of "class struggle" will never appear again in our land, which has suffered so many disasters and tribulations owing to this one mistaken theory.

Dialogue Between Two *Zhiqing* Brothers

by Feng Tong

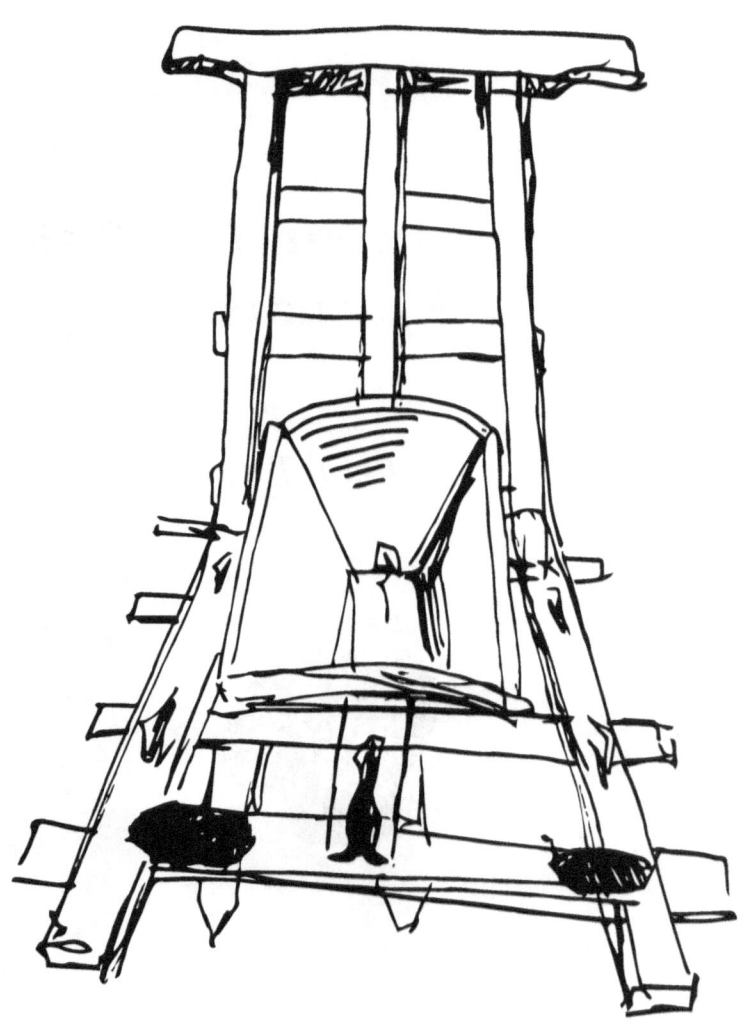

Three of the four children in my family, all of us middle school students, were sent down to the countryside during the Cultural Revolution. One of my younger brothers, Tang, went to work in 1968 in Tuquan County, Jilin Province of northeastern China. The following year, my younger sister and I joined the Production and Construction Corps of Inner Mongolia.

When colleges resumed enrolling students in 1977, Tang and I took entrance exams and both of us were admitted. Tang majored in world history, specializing in French history, which enabled him to examine the rustication movement from a broad perspective. I studied engineering, focusing on hydrodynamics.

Tang completed his research at the University of Provence, France, and departed for China in the autumn of 1998. During a change of planes at Amsterdam, I met him at the airport and had a conversation with him, which lasted several hours. The following are excerpts from our dialogue about the rustication movement.

Tong: Why did you select France, and the University of Provence in particular, as the place for your academic research?

Tang: Provence was the place where the Crusaders assembled before embarking on their eastward expeditions. The University of Provence is the center of studies of those events. There are many historical sites related to the Crusaders in southern France. At the Council of Clermont, an ancient town in south-central France, Pope Urban II called on all Christians to fight for the liberation of Jerusalem. Some of the crusaders started their sea journeys from the south coast of France in all subsequent eastward expeditions.

Tong: What is the reason for your special interest in the subject of the Crusades?

Tang: After the end of the Cold War, the world order fell into a new pattern. A theory represented by the American social scientist Samuel P. Huntington argues that the clash between civilizations has replaced ideological conflicts to become the driving force in remaking the world order. His theory has exerted considerable influence on US diplomatic strategists.

Tong: I see your point. In his book *The Clash of Civilizations and the Remaking of World Order*, Huntington points out that conflicts between Christian and Islamic civilizations go back to the time of the Crusaders. Many statesmen and intellectuals in the Islamic world still regard the Gulf War as the modern version of the Crusaders' eastward expeditions.

Tang: The study of the Crusaders is not a purely academic matter. The Department of World Politics of Peking University has a responsibility to provide a theoretical basis for the formulation of China's diplomatic strategy. This was one of the reasons they sent me there.

Tong: Aside from the official task assigned you, did you have any personal projects?

Tang: Yes, I did. As you know, it occurred to me several years ago to do a historical study of the rustication movement, especially from the perspective of world history. In recent years, an increasing number of people in China have done research on the rustication movement with varied results, but none of them have examined the movement from the perspective of world history.

Tong: Rustication was a movement that took place in China. Why is it necessary to study it from the perspective of world history?

Tang: The reasons are threefold. First, China's rustication movement was not without parallel in the international communist movement. In the fifties and sixties, the Soviet Union recruited great numbers of young people in its campaigns to open up virgin lands. Like your Production and Construction Corps of Inner Mongolia, these campaigns all ended in failure. Second, the rustication movement was not merely an activity for material production. Its spiritual and intellectual side should by no means be ignored. From the very start its objective was to oppose and prevent revisionism, to realize communism, and to build up an ideal state. One can find similar movements urging young people to set up ideal states, not only in the history of the communist movement, but throughout the history of world civilization. Third, history is such a queer thing that the more recent a historical event, the more difficult it is to see it clearly. In studying a recent historical event, historians are inclined to seek a parallel in remote history and put them side by side for comparative study. Adopting such an approach will enable us to see and explain things more clearly. But we must find the closest parallel in history and be very cautious in making a presentation.

Tong: By adopting such an approach, did you find a historical parallel for your study?

Tang: Yes, I found a historical parallel in the Children's Crusade. I would rather call it the Juvenile Crusade, which may be more precise in view of the age range of the crusaders.

Tong: When embarking on an expedition, most of the Juvenile Crusaders were fifteen or sixteen, about the same age as our younger sister when she went to Inner Mongolia. Very few Chinese know about this historical event.

Tang: Even in the West, few people are aware of it. This is because the Juvenile Crusaders were a phenomenon that existed for a very brief period, and there were only two detachments of them. In 1212, one took boats from Marseilles, and the other started from Germany by crossing the Alps.

Tong: Why did they recruit these young people?

Tang: Since all three previous eastward expeditions had failed to recover the Holy City, a new theory emerged that attributed the failures to the sins the adult Crusaders had committed, claiming that only sinless children could liberate Jerusalem.

Tong: It seems that compared with the three previous crusades, the Juvenile Crusade had stronger implications of a holy war.

Tang: That was true. And the end result was more miserable.

Tong: What are the similarities between the rustication movement and the Juvenile Crusade?

Tang: There are at least five similarities between the two. First, both were launched by an all-powerful institution under a dictatorial system; second, both targeted juveniles; third, their goals were alike -- to set up an ideal state (religious or ideological); fourth, both were started in a disorderly manner and later abandoned with a perfunctory denouement: fifth, a doleful outcome awaited both of them.

Tong: These five points also apply to the Production and Construction Corps of Inner Mongolia, which only existed for six years. After *zhiqing* returned to the cities, many of them soon faced the problem of unemployment. Life was difficult for the majority of them. Forming a new disadvantaged group, they did not enjoy the benefits of China's economic boom. These similarities provide enough food for thought, indicating historical retrogression in both cases.

Tang: The Juvenile Crusade took place in the Dark Ages of medieval Europe of the 13th century, while the rustication movement occurred in the 1960s and 1970s, which was also a period of historical retrogression. People wanted to accelerate the progress of history, but the result was to retard it.

Tong: How do you historians evaluate the historical contributions made by a specific generation of people?

Tang: Historians always consider the two aspects of civilization – the material and the spiritual – in discussing people's contributions.

Tong: We can find very few contributions to material civilization made by the *zhiqing* during the rustication movement.

Tang: I agree. The goal of the movement was not the development of production. It aimed at the spiritual and ideological side – to oppose and prevent revisionism. Despite the failure to achieve this aim, a big contribution was made in the sphere of spiritual civilization.

Tong: Don't you mean the emergence of great writers and scholars from among the *zhiqing*?

Tang: Absolutely not. In fact, that would be impossible. The spiritual shackles on us, characterized by "foolish loyalty" and "blind faith", are of such a kind that a lifelong effort is needed for *zhiqing* scholars to remove them. Not to mention the fact that the best years in the lives of our generation were not put to good use.

Tong: Then, what do you mean by "a big contribution"?

Tang: What I mean is that our generation, along with the previous generation, eventually succeeded in stopping the revolutionary tide that had rolled on since the 1911 revolution. Our many hardships and ordeals helped us to achieve this. A rare opportunity appeared, which was the first in the last hundred years, to bring Chinese society and the Chinese people's consciousness back to reason. This was a great contribution, a collective contribution made by millions of *zhiqing*, including those who sacrificed their young lives.

Tong: Could you elaborate a bit on the revolutionary tide since 1911?

Tang: Since the 1911 revolution led by Sun Yat-sen, one revolution followed on the heels of another, culminating in the Cultural Revolution which claimed to have reached out to people's souls, requiring everyone to fight self while fighting revisionism. The Cultural Revolution advocated fighting against imperialism (with the US as the main target), revisionism (with the Soviet Union as the archenemy), and the reactionaries of various countries. It was similar to the Empress Dowager's declaration of war in 1900 against the eleven powers. The Cultural Revolution put China in grave danger by placing the country in an unprecedented state of isolation. Except for the eight years of the War of Resistance against Japan, revolutions persisted throughout all six and a half decades from the 1911 Revolution to the conclusion of the Cultural Revolution in 1976. Each revolution was carried out on a scale larger than the previous one, with aims set ever higher. China's political life was like a huge stone ball rolling down a slope at accelerating speed. No one knew where it was going or when it would stop.

Tong: Your analogy is very vivid.

Tang: A political movement must mobilize the masses and make use of them as the driving force. The continuation of the Chinese revolution needed a new generation of people like us to provide the slope for the stone ball. But instead, we removed the slope and leveled the ground. The huge stone ball was stopped by force of friction. The Chinese revolution came to a halt when the rustication movement was met with resistance. This outcome was never anticipated by the initiator of the movement.

Tong: The ground was not only flat but covered with grass. A single blade of grass may be fragile, but millions of grass blades produced friction that could not be ignored. *Zhiqing* were not that docile. Many of them began to think and rebel. On the whole, *zhiqing* adopted a passive stance by slowing down work.

Tang: Of course, when the rolling stone ball came to the flat ground covered with grass, it stopped. Otherwise, the Chinese revolution would have kept rolling, like the situation in North Korea.

Tong: What was the "rare opportunity" you spoke of a moment ago?

Tang: I mentioned two key words in my presentation: reason and opportunity. By reason, I mean rational political thinking. We must return to the realities of China, abandon ideological straight-jackets, proceed from practice, and seek the way to maintain good governance and long-term stability. Chinese traditional thinking suffers from worship of authority and lack of rational thinking. Our problem is one of "starting to resort to reason" rather than "returning to reason". Much work needs to be done in the sphere of enlightenment. The difficulties involved shouldn't be underestimated. That is why I spoke of a "rare" opportunity for China to resort to reason: it is only a possibility, not an inevitability.

Tong: Every generation has its own limitations. It was good enough for our generation to help provide such an opportunity. We've done our best.

Tang: Yes. This is something worth writing into history. At the turn of the century, we served as a nexus between the preceding and the following generations. Ours is a generation that can inform the younger generation about our experience in the Cultural Revolution and the rustication movement, including your experience in Inner Mongolia, and share our reflections with them. I presume that all *zhiqing* would expect their children to grow up with an ability to think independently and never follow our path of "foolish loyalty" and "blind faith". It is our common wish that our children will lead a new, much richer life, in both the material and spiritual senses. Our life experience as *zhiqing* represents an invaluable intellectual heritage. It will exert a profound influence on the development of Chinese society. This was our great historical contribution.

Tong: You're absolutely right. My son has often said to me: "I won't be as foolish as you when you were young, Dad."

Tang: We place our hopes on the next generation and on the future.

My Wish for Redemption

by Ren Guoqing

The paramilitary farm where I was assigned to work in 1970 was still in the initial stage of development. Operating as a regiment under the umbrella organization known as the Production and Construction Corps of Inner Mongolia, the farm staff had to do everything from scratch. A large swathe of uncultivated land on the edge of Kubuqi Desert had to be opened up before the freezing season in order to make farm work possible the following spring, and the construction of adobe houses for the rank-and-file had to be completed within six months. Feeling the pressure, regimental and company leaders launched successive campaigns for adobe making, digging irrigation canals, and leveling the newly reclaimed lands. Everyone was required to work hard. However, in almost every company, there were a few unruly *zhiqing* who used to break discipline, slack off in their duties or get into fistfights. The story I am about to tell occurred in the late autumn of that year.

One evening, when everything was quiet outside, an orderly came and asked me to go with him to our company office, where the instructor was waiting for me. The instructor said that he had looked at my application form for membership in the Chinese Communist Youth League (CCYL), praised my desire for political progress, and told me that I had to face a severe test. The regimental Party committee had just launched two "educational campaigns" targeting those unruly youngsters, who were to be disciplined by two separate groups of *zhiqing*, one male and the other female. The objective was to subdue them by any means necessary, however violent. Liu Shengli, he said, was the first one to be "educated". He told me not to be shy, saying that with the backing of the Party organizations at both regimental and company levels, I would be given a free hand in beating him up. Even if Liu were beaten to death, he assured me, we could conclude the matter by throwing his body into the Yellow River, and the instructor himself would bear all the consequences. He then gave me a new shovel handle from the company's storeroom and signaled me to leave for our dining hall, an adobe house where the "education session" was to take place.

The adobe house was lit by several smoky kerosene lamps which cast human shadows on the walls. I was the last to join a dozen or so *zhiqing*, including leaders of the first and second squads and our platoon leader. All of them had applied for membership either in the Chinese Communist Party (CCP) or the CCYL. They were all carrying shovel handles and seemed ready to kill.

The platoon leader pushed the door slightly open and signaled Liu Shengli to come in escorted by two *zhiqing*. Tall, thin and slightly hunchbacked, Liu had a fair face, arched eyebrows and bright eyes. He looked like a gentle and quiet boy except for a rebellious air that hovered around his mouth. He was about my age, 17 or 18.

The platoon leader closed the door and put a wooden stick against the door to keep intruders out. Turning around, he said to us, "I have gathered you here to render 'special aid' to Liu Shengli. Who will speak first?"

The first squad leader responded, "Liu Shengli is a member of my squad, so let me speak first." He then raised his voice and declared, "Liu Shengli, let me enumerate five crimes you have committed. First, you oppose our Great Leader Chairman Mao. Do you own up to this?"

Liu answered, "I have nothing but admiration for Chairman Mao. How could I oppose him?"

The first squad leader retorted: "But you said Chairman

Mao worshiped Lu Xun[9]. What sort of a dolt was Lu Xun? How could Chairman Mao worship him? This shows that you are against Chairman Mao."

Brooking no self-defense by Liu, the first squad leader continued to denounce him by saying, "Second, you sabotaged construction on our farm."

Liu answered back, "Our farm is so huge. How could I sabotage its construction?"

The first squad leader replied with a grin, "I have iron-clad proof of that. You can't deny it. All the adobe blocks we make weigh 19 kilos apiece. I have just weighed the adobes you made. They are only 15 kilos apiece."

In our company, Liu was a notorious slacker. To lighten the weight of clay and hence his labor in making and transporting adobes, he used a planer to reduce the upper edges of the standardized wooden molds, which had been delivered to us by the regimental headquarters. The adobes he manufactured looked no different from what we made, except that they were thinner. Knowing that sheer denial wouldn't work, Liu argued, "The adobes I made were slightly thinner. That didn't amount to sabotaging construction on the farm. How could I carry that terrible label on my head?"

Grinding his teeth, the first squad leader snapped back, "Excellent. You're man enough to own up to it. Third, you spread backward ideas to dampen the revolutionary zeal of our people."

Liu again answered back, "I can't understand what you mean. Which of my words are you referring to?"

"You once said, if one didn't join the CCP or the CYCL, he or she could save two yuan (for membership fees) each year. Were

9. Lu Xun, called by Mao "the saint of modern China," was a leading figure in modern Chinese literature.

these words backward remarks? They were simply an anti-Party statement." While making the accusation, the first squad leader pointed one end of his shovel handle at Liu's nose.

Liu thrust his head forward to confront the handle, saying, "Dear friends, I know what you're after. You intend to beat me up. If you want to be a show-off, just say so. I will give you a chance. But listen carefully. I won't be a real man if you can elicit a groan from me. But don't forget to leave some breath in me. Well, come on." After saying this, he doubled himself up and lay sidewise on the ground, clasping his hands around his head and using his forearms to cover his temples. He squeezed his legs together to shield his private parts.

All of us were stunned by the sight as Liu said, "Dear friends, what are you waiting for? Don't feel embarrassed. Come on." His words enraged me. I threw my shovel handle aside, unfastened my buckled belt and doubled it by grasping the two ends in my hand. I thrashed Liu fiercely and repeatedly with the belt, from the left side and then from the right.

Beating someone up was a thrilling experience. I was timid by nature and never got into fistfights. Not until then did I realize that it could be such a pleasure to beat a person--not an ordinary pleasure but an ecstatic rapture that made me quiver. Anyone without such an experience would never know how exhilarating it could be. I whipped Liu with the belt, applying each lashing with ever greater force until I felt totally exhausted. Liu was indeed a tough nut to crack. He didn't utter a single groan.

Until then, I wasn't aware that I had such bestial tendencies inside me. Maybe I was harboring a secret sadism in my soul. I bore no personal grudge against Liu. In actual fact, we were friends on no bad terms. He was ideologically backward, and behaved like a rogue at times. But did this justify my assault on him? Could it be explained away by my "sense of righteousness" or "class hatred"?

When the platoon leader saw that I had stopped my whipping, he cast a contemptuous glance at me and said, "What are you doing? Scratching where he itches? Step aside and see what a lesson I'll teach him."

He picked up a shovel handle and struck fiercely at Liu's back. The handle broke in two. He used the upper half of the handle to deal another forceful blow at Liu. It again broke in two. He cast away the short stump in his hand and picked up another half-handle from the ground. He gave Liu a third blow and again the half-handle broke into two stumps.

The third blow was unusually powerful. Liu uttered a terrible cry that makes me shiver even now and begged for mercy.

At this juncture, leaders of the first and third squads and all those who had applied for membership in the CCP or CYCL vied with one another in beating Liu savagely. It was indeed a contest in cruelty. The logic was that the more brutal you were, the more revolutionary you would become. None of us present wanted to be considered irresolute in the campaign to "educate" those "backward elements".

When all the shovel handles were broken into short stumps that scattered around Liu's body, a couple of female *zhiqing* working in the dining hall brought along their rolling-pins, which were made of wood much harder than the shovel handles. The beating continued until these rolling-pins also broke into short pieces.

At first, Liu uttered squeals as he begged for mercy, but these soon became faint murmurs. Finally, when the rolling-pins fell on him like raindrops, there wasn't any response from him except the thumping sound of the blows against his body.

A stream of blood flowed from under him, followed by another, and then a third. A female *zhiqing* came in with a bowl of cold water. The platoon leader poured the water over Liu's head, but he did not respond. Then a second bowl of cold water was brought in and poured over him. With a jerk of his body, Liu became conscious for a while and asked, "Where am I?" Then he fell into a swoon again.

The clinical record left by the doctor who came to rescue him read: blood pressure: 40/20; heartbeat: 23/min.; body temp.: 42°C; skin injury and hypodermic gore covering 95% of the body; fractures of the left forearm, fingers and ribs; mangled scalp.

That very night, Liu was given cardiotonic injections and tetanus jabs.

Soon after, similar campaigns were launched on a regimental scale. For several weeks on end, shrill cries for help in male and female voices could be heard from our dining hall and the company office. The names of the *zhiqing* victims I can remember include Yu Yongsheng, a boy from Qingdao, Shandong Province, and Kang Yinghua, a girl from Tianjin Municipality.

Zhiqing of the female punishment group had their own ways of dealing with the "backward elements". They resorted to pinching, biting and pulling off hairs from the scalps of their victims. Kang Yinghua came out of the "educational session" with only a few scattered strands of hair left on her head, just enough to identify her as a woman.

An orphan since childhood, Yu Yongsheng was eccentric and unsociable. After coming to the farm, he used to rise late and often missed morning exercise. Because of his sloppiness in life and work, he was sent to an "educational session" held by the female group. To him, this meant adding insult to injury, since to lose face in front of women was the most terrible thing for a young lad. Members of the female group brought in broad wooden knives originally used as props in dramatic performances. Flailing at him, they struck Yu fiercely in the head, which he tried to protect with his hands. Very soon, his head, face and hands were covered with blood.

Similar episodes took place in all ten companies of our regiment. At the start of the "educational campaigns", the political commissar made rounds among various companies. In his speech at every rally, he focused on mobilizing supporters by spreading the idea that "Beatings are an expression of affection, and abuses are manifestations of love. Dispensing with either would invite woes and troubles." He assured us that the "educational campaigns were the most reliable methods to maintain the fighting capacity of our ranks."

After going through the ordeal of the "educational session", Kang Yinghua returned to Tianjin on home leave and never came back. She had been a fellow pupil sitting next to me at elementary school. Since our two families were close neighbors, I later learned that she had developed a mental illness after returning home. Once she ran out of her home at midnight, naked, crying: "Mom, I didn't slack in work, but they beat me up...." Later, because she wasn't allowed by government policy to stay in the city for long, she married a peasant in the Tianjin suburbs in order not to go back to our farm.

Not long after the "educational sessions" took place, the platoon leader was admitted into the CCP, while the first and third squad leaders were accepted as CCYL members. One year later, the platoon leader was sent to study at Nankai University in Tianjin.

In 2002, at the age of about 52, Yu Yongsheng died of alcoholism on a Tianjin street. Liu Shengli, an alcoholic like Yu, was once imprisoned for habitual gambling. In 2005, he died of illness at the age of 52. I don't know if their alcoholism, gambling and untimely deaths had anything to do with the beatings they suffered at the farm.

During the past several decades, I often looked for an opportunity to offer my apology to Liu Shengli. But each time I returned to Tianjin, I missed seeing him. One time when I was sure that he was at home, I decided to go see him, but a former *zhiqing* at our farm urged me not to. "You'd better not mention the affair to him," he said. "After that event, each time he heard someone mention it, he would wet his pants."

I heard that Liu was once sentenced to imprisonment on a gambling charge after returning to Tianjin. Now, I can only say to him through this article that I feel deeply sorry for having almost killed him. At the time, I could hardly explain why I did it. In retrospect, it was clear that I had my own axe to grind: I wanted to demonstrate that I had drawn a line of demarcation between myself and the "bad elements" and their misdeeds. I was motivated by a desire for self-advancement, including membership in the CCYL. These selfish aims were concealed in political wrappings such as "sense of justice" and "devotion to a lofty cause".

I will not ask for Liu's forgiveness, because the damage I caused him was irreparable. It must have done him life-long harm. It is easy to say "I am sorry" and hope that it somehow lessens my sense of guilt. If there is any way for redemption, I will do whatever is needed.

Historical Background Essay

China's Sent-down Youth (Zhiqing):
Two Perspectives

by Wang Youfen

Between 1962 and 1979 a total of 17.7 million middle school graduates from Chinese cities, mostly aged 15 to 17 and referred to as "educated youth" or *zhiqing* in Chinese, were relocated by the government to work as peasants mainly in remote places in the Chinese countryside. This "Sent-down" program involved a population shift from city to village whose scale and nature are unique in world history. The Chinese phrases "youth spent with no regret" (*qing chun wu hui*) and "years being idled away" (*cuo tuo sui yue*) capture two competing perspectives on the *zhiqing* experience.

The policy of sending *zhiqing* down to work in the countryside actually started in the mid-1950s when it served to provide rural areas with needed record keepers and technicians. In subsequent years, especially when the economy was stressed, it was used to relieve unemployment and food shortages in the cities. During the Cultural Revolution, however, large-scale Sent-down campaigns were launched in the name of revolution, to fulfill a clearly ideological mission.

Historical Background of Mao's Instructions

In the first two years of the Cultural Revolution, which was launched in May 1966 under Mao Zedong's direction, the Red Guards attracted much of the limelight on China's political stage. By the summer of 1968, when the Cultural Revolution had entered its third year, the most radical phase of Red Guard activity was ending as the young rebels were induced in most places in China to staff so-called Revolutionary Committees alongside old Party veterans and military representatives. However, a portion of the Red Guards chose to go their own way, carrying on factional strife, and even large-scale armed confrontations. This displeased Mao. On July 27, 1968, in a meeting with five major leaders of the Red Guards in Beijing, he issued a stern warning to them. In the months that followed, he made statements on three separate occasions stressing the need for young students and intellectuals to receive re-education from workers, peasants and soldiers. In his famous instruction made on December 22, 1968, he called on young students to go to the countryside to be re-educated by poor and lower-middle-class peasants, describing it as a necessity for them. From these statements, one may discern some of his considerations, both immediate and long-term.

By that time, Mao had guided young students in the completion of a series of tasks that ranged from "eliminating the Four Olds" (i.e., old ideas, old culture, old customs and old habits) to "toppling the capitalist-roaders." Now that all schools had closed and few factories needed recruits, young people who stayed in the cities could become troublemakers, he felt. It would be much better to send them to the countryside in the care of peasants.

Mao had consistent contempt for book knowledge and regular education. In a speech he made in 1964, he spoke disparagingly of prestigious schools like Peking University and praised his own so-called "University of Greenwood Rebels," referring to the rural communist guerrilla bases of the Revolution's early days. He believed that hardships in rural life could temper and toughen urban children to become worthy successors of the revolution.

Mao was also enthusiastic about eliminating the three great differences that Stalin had identified as impeding the realization of communist society – the differences between industry and agriculture, between cities and the countryside, and between physical and mental labor. His decision to launch the Sent-down movement can be understood as a logical outcome of these various ideas.

Mao's call to go to the countryside soon developed into a vast political movement. Propaganda and political agitation went into high gear to support it. Factories and military units dispatched work teams to schools, where they did an effective job of "persuading" parents to allow their children to submit applications to become *zhiqing*. With schools closed and recruitment at factories and colleges suspended, leaving for the countryside was often the only option available for urban teenagers. In 1969 alone, 2.67 million *zhiqing* flocked to the rural areas "out of their own volition." In subsequent years, approximately 12 million more joined their ranks.

Disillusionment and Resistance

Widely scattered throughout the country, *zhiqing* fell into two major categories, depending on whether they worked in villages or on state or paramilitary farms. Areas where *zhiqing* were most concentrated included the Great Northern Wilderness in Northeast China, the Inner Mongolian grasslands, the mountainous province of Yunnan in Southwest China, the loess plateau of Shaanxi in the Northwest, and the Xinjiang Uighur Autonomous Region in the Northwest where many big farms were run by the army.

A great number of *zhiqing* came from big cities such as Beijing, Tianjin and Shanghai, as well as provincial capitals like Shenyang and Chengdu. These naive teenagers soon discovered that conditions in the countryside were far different from what they had been told at mobilization meetings or what they had imagined. The natural environment and life in the countryside were generally harsh, and a sizable portion of *zhiqing* were still unable to support themselves after working for several years. According to 1977 official statistics, such failing *zhiqing* comprised a slight majority in more than one-third of China's provinces and municipalities. Their inability to earn a living was a heavy blow to their self-esteem and their confidence in the future.

The *zhiqing* also discovered that many of the peasants they came into contact with were not advanced in political thinking, nor were local leaders and officials always honest. Cases of corruption, theft, and misappropriation of food and other materials allocated for *zhiqing* were also known. Much more serious were reports of the raping of female *zhiqing* by certain local officials, village leaders, and local scoundrels.

From the early seventies, the State started sending a number of *zhiqing* every year to colleges and professional schools. Nominally, candidates were selected by merit on the recommendation of peasants or farm workers, but decision-making lay in the hands of Party organizations at various levels. *Zhiqing* with powerful family backgrounds or social connections could often gain their wishes by backdoor interventions. Such abuses of power, together with hardships verging on starvation in some places, aroused strong discontent among rank-and-file *zhiqing*.

Zhiqing in different localities lodged complaints and made demands in various forms. Some went to Party and government organizations to air their grievances. Others wrote open letters to Deng Xiaoping and other leaders reporting on their dire circumstances and asking for help. Many *zhiqing* just went home on sick leave or on other legitimate grounds. Some driven by desperation took great risks to cross international borders to find new lives. Thousands of them joined communist guerrilla groups fighting in the subtropical rain-forests of Burma. And thousands more *zhiqing* escaped from rural areas in coastal Guangdong province to become a large share of Hong Kong's 100,000 illegal immigrants between 1970 and 1974.

From late 1978 to early 1979, *zhiqing* staying in Shanghai on sick or other leave held several demonstrations, involving the participation of some 10,000 people. During the same period, similar demonstrations appeared in Xishuangbana and other regions in Yunnan province in Southwest China on an even bigger scale, with strikes spreading to many state farms where *zhiqing* constituted the majority of the labor force. These protests caused a chain reaction among *zhiqing* throughout the country, with demonstrations, petitions and strikes going on almost every day. "We want to go home!" and "Do away with the Sent-down institution!" were their common slogans.

At the end of 1978, Zhao Fan, a veteran of the Communist-led anti-Japanese armed forces in the late 1930's, was instructed by the State Council to fly to Yunnan to handle the situation. He was then a deputy head of *zhiqing* affairs under the State Council and concurrently a vice-minister of agriculture and forestry. A noted writer named Deng Xian, in his novel Dream of China's Sent-down Youth, incorporated Zhao Fan's findings in his description of the *zhiqing* situation in Yunnan. Writing as a novelist, Deng uses pseudonyms to conceal the identities of key figures in the story, including Zhao's. But the story he tells is mostly based on facts.

According to Deng, the farm at Ganlanba in Xishuangbana prefecture was the first place Zhao Fan and his team chose to visit. It was where the demonstrations and strikes had first broken out, sparked by the untimely deaths of a female *zhiqing* and her newly delivered baby at a village clinic due to negligent care. There at the farm, Zhao observed the low, shabby sheds that were used as living quarters for the teenagers. There were many holes in the thatched roofs. Beneath the beds, and in the corners of walls made of thin bamboo strips and earth, wild mushrooms were growing.

According to government policy, funds had been allocated to the local governments for building five square meters of living space per *zhiqing* plus a monthly supply of one ounce of vegetable oil and one fifth of a kilo of pork. But all these supplies existed only on paper. Their actual menu remained unvaried except on national holidays: a bowlful of rice plus boiled salty water with a few shreds of chopped spring onion or other vegetables -- "glassy soup" the *zhiqing* called it.

At another farm in southern Yunnan, Zhao met many young couples, most of them unmarried, living together in crowded rooms in row after row of thatched sheds. He saw some young mothers with small children and was told that unmarried couples with children made up more than half of the *zhiqing* population at the farm. There were no roads, no electric lighting, no entertainment, no cultural life. People had to walk a dozen miles to see a film, and those were shown only twice a year.

At Mengla Farm in southern Xishuangbana prefecture in Yunnan province, Zhao's team discovered a group of boys whose bodies were covered with bruises owing to the barbarous treatment they had suffered at the hands of administrators. Investigations revealed that the young people were beaten, tortured or imprisoned at the slightest provocation, and that all of them, without exception, were malnourished or anemic and had stomach troubles and rheumatoid arthritis. No females were free of gynecological diseases. Mortality rates had been climbing year by year, with suicide topping the death list.

Finally, as spelled out in "Solidarity Brings Us Home" by Ye Feng, Zhao went to see a large *zhiqing* strike at Mengding farm in Lincang Prefecture in southwestern Yunnan. He was rushed there by the State Council because the protest had escalated into a hunger and thirst strike. At a mass rally there, Zhao openly expressed his sympathy as well as his belief that the *zhiqings'* wishes to return to their urban homes were legitimate and could be realized.

After consulting with the Yunnan provincial authorities, Zhao sent an urgent report to the State Council on his findings and proposed drastic policy changes. The central authorities eventually approved the measures proposed in Zhao's report, which would greatly reduce restrictions on the return of *zhiqing* in Yunnan to their home towns, helping almost all those who wished to go home. Although the situation of *zhiqing* in other provinces and regions was not as bad as that in Yunnan, the authorities became aware that the same kinds of problems existed more or less everywhere, and so the measures adopted in Yunnan were approved for application to other areas.

In the months that followed, leaders at the State Council gradually reached a consensus: the official policy of sending *zhiqing* to the countryside was determined to have been a mistake. Deng Xiaoping was rumored to have made a wisecrack to the effect that "We have spent 30 billion yuan to buy discontent from three quarters: from *zhiqing*, from their families, and from the peasants". What he meant by mentioning the peasants was made clear by his earlier statement that *zhiqing* were grabbing food from the rice bowls of peasants. Though the quoted remark was not officially confirmed, several written accounts in the official media recorded similar observations made by Deng and other national leaders.

By 1980, the Sent-down movement had ended. The vast majority of *zhiqing* had returned to the cities. In the history of the PRC, this was perhaps the most successful attempt by the masses of Chinese people to resist—and eventually bury--an unpopular policy. This success may also have been influenced by certain foreign policy factors. At the end of 1978, China and the United States announced their decision to establish diplomatic relations. Deng Xiaoping would soon visit the United States at the invitation of President Carter. The Chinese authorities didn't want a violent crackdown on *zhiqing* to upset their global strategic plans. Moreover, a war was brewing with Vietnam, which Deng thought was helping the Soviet Union to encircle China. There was likely some fear that turmoil anywhere near the border region would play into the hands of the Vietnamese.

The Legacy of the Sent-down Movement

No one can deny that life experience at the grassroots helped *zhiqing* to gain a better understanding of the countryside and its people. It helped strengthen their will and ability to overcome hardships. It also enhanced their political awareness to serve the people. But this was only one side of the coin.

On the other side, many elements in the Sent-down program were inherently destructive. Since *zhiqing* were deprived of the opportunity to continue their education and learn skills when they were still young, many inevitably struggled at the bottom of society after their return to the cities. They formed a new group of disadvantaged people, who remained silent and ignored. Some had difficulty earning a living. Because most *zhiqing* lost their window of educational opportunity, their generation has very few noted scholars, scientists, writers, artists, social activists, entrepreneurs or diplomats in its ranks, and the development of cultural, scientific and technology fields of learning were all severely disrupted.

The cost to society was incalculable in other ways as well. For example, "speak-bitterness" meetings, where former poor peasants were invited to pour out their grievances of the old days, only served to arouse hatred against ex-landlords and rich peasants. Sessions with the recurring subject of "fighting selfishness and repudiating revisionism" (*dou si pi xiu*) produced nothing but two undesirable results. One, they tended to oblige young people to debase and chastise themselves, thus damaging their self-esteem and self-confidence. Two, by encouraging people to think that the pursuit of a good life or love or anything beautiful was revisionist, these sessions actually promoted stoicism. In addition, the *zhiqing* movement suffered all too frequently from abuses such as bribery and other backdoor corruption, lying, document forgery, and tampering with medical and other records, all driven by a desperate desire to find a way to return home.

According to statistics published by the Office of *Zhiqing* Affairs under the State Council, unusual deaths among *zhiqing* amounted to 15,899 during the five years between 1974 and 1979, accounting for 61.9 per cent of the total number of deaths of *zhiqing*. During the same period, cases of persecution of *zhiqing* numbered 41,272, most of which involved rape. How many sad stories are hidden behind these cold statistics! There were a few officials in Yunnan's paramilitary farm system who raped more girls than they could remember--more than 100 in one case. Premier Zhou Enlai was enraged to learn of these extreme cases. He denounced the perpetrators as "fascists." Hundreds of them were punished, several with death.

In recent years, commemorative exhibitions about the Sent-down movement have been held in Beijing and other cities. Some of them have painted a rosy picture of the lives and legacy of *zhiqing*. This author once viewed a Web post which noted that the number of top Party and state leaders who were former *zhiqing* was evidence of the success of the movement. Indeed, in the Politburo of the Chinese Communist Party, elected at the 19th Central Committee session in October 2017, 10 out of its 25 members were ex-*zhiqing*, including three Standing Committee members -- Xi Jinping (PRC President), Li Keqiang (Premier) and Zhao Leji (head of the Party's powerful anti-corruption body). But others point out that certain *zhiqing* were able to benefit from powerful family connections and use their rural experience to advance their political careers.

People should not forget the great effort—and actual accomplishments—made by *zhiqing* in trying to change the face of rural China. Many former *zhiqing* have fond feelings for the land and the people they came to know so well. They treasure the friendships they forged and are proud of the good things they did. These positive feelings, however, should not be confused with troubling signs of a resurgence in China of the ideology of the Cultural Revolution.

Notes on the Authors

and Editors

Wang Youfen, chief editor and translator of the stories in this book and the author of the historical background essay, "China's Sent-down Youth: Two Perspectives," spent the last several years of his life, before his passing on March 2, 2018 at age 90, preparing the manuscript, including the selection, translation and initial editing of the 42 stories. He selected them from thousands previously published in Chinese in books, journals and on the Internet beginning in the 1990s. This book is a capstone of his 68 years-long professional career in publishing in China, driven by his tireless ambition to foster understanding of his country and its history to English readers, and truth, fairness and justice to his fellow Chinese citizens. His own life's story parallels the arc of China's revolutionary history and illuminates its legacy.

Wang Youfen was born on July 5th, 1927 in Wuhan, the capital of Hubei Province in China. His father was the CFO of the Wuhan Dahua Cotton Mill, a well-known Chinese enterprise. His mother was an educated woman from a wealthy family. She gave birth to ten children, only seven of whom survived to adulthood. Youfen was the fourth child among his brothers and sisters.

In 1938, the Japanese army besieged Wuhan. Among the thousands of refugees, the Wangs left Wuhan by boat and sometimes on foot along the Yangtze River to Sichuan Province. They first reached Chongqing, then Mianyang, and finally settled down in a southern suburb of Chengdu, Sichuan's capital. During the long and arduous journey, Youfen's father contracted cholera and died in an air-shelter near Chongqing. With the death of its only bread winner, the Wang family quickly plunged into poverty. Youfen's early memories included selling his mother's dowry pieces in front of

Qingyanggong, a Taoist Temple in Chengdu.

After Japan surrendered in 1945, Youfen was accepted to Nanking University as a major in Agricultural Economics with a full scholarship. In his freshman year, he suffered from a detached retina of his left eye, which forced him to take a year off from his studies. Fortunately, he met a US trained doctor who repaired his retina, and partially restored his eyesight. He then returned to the University in 1947. Since his early days, Youfen had developed a passion for the English language, and he chose to enter the Agricultural Economics department of Nanking University because it had the highest percentage in China of students going abroad for graduate degrees. He was an excellent student and was elected the president of the student body. As a young student, he was disgusted by the corrupt and repressive nature of the Nationalist government and was soon approached and influenced by the underground Communists. In 1948, he was one of the organizers of a student movement in which the students took to the streets of Nanjing, the capital of the Nationalist government. They called for an immediate cessation of the war with the Communists. He was arrested in December of 1948 along with several other student leaders. In January 1949, after a series of military defeats, Chiang Kai-shek stepped down from his presidency of the Nationalist government. As a friendly gesture to the Chinese Communists, the acting Nationalist president, Li Zongren, released hundreds of political prisoners, including Youfen.

After his release, Youfen went to Wuhan with friends and worked underground for the Communist Party. He worked in the Department of Urban Affairs under the Party's Central Bureau and later in the Office of Policy Research under the newly formed Wuhan People's Government. In 1950, the year after the founding of the Peoples Republic of China on October 1, 1949, Youfen received brief and intensive English and journalist training and was assigned to the Special Feature Story Department of the International Press Bureau in Beijing as an assistant editor, one of a handful of English language journalists of the new nation. In 1952-1953, Youfen was the head secretary of the newly formed Foreign Languages Press. He joined the Communist Party during that time. From 1953 to 1957, he worked at People's China magazine as a secretary, a reporter and an editor.

During the Hundred Flowers Movement of 1957, when the PRC government encouraged citizens to express opinions of the regime, Youfen criticized the Communist Party. He was then accused of being a Rightist and was demoted. His party membership was put under probation for more than a year. From 1958 to 1960, Youfen worked as a reporter and an editor in the newly created weekly English language news magazine, *Beijing Review*. During most of the 1960s, Youfen was the head of the English Publications Department of the Foreign Languages Press.

During the height of the Cultural Revolution in 1968, Youfen was accused of being a Capitalist Roader and a spy of Chiang Kai-shek's government. He was publicly humiliated, detained in a makeshift prison and forced to do physical labor for more than six months. In 1969, Youfen and his family were expelled from Beijing, and sent to a small village called Liuwei in Henan province. There the Wangs were to be "reeducated by the peasants". For the next two and a half years, Youfen and his family lived in a mud house among the peasants. They learned how to farm and raise chickens and how to keep their house warm in winter, which required Youfen and his ten-year-old son, Peter, to transport a half ton of coal by pulling a cart by hand from a town 30 miles away from their village.

In 1972, Youfen was called back from the Henan village. He resumed his post as the head of the English Publications Department, and later the deputy chief editor of the Foreign Languages Press. He was transferred back to the *Beijing Review* in 1980, where he was first the deputy chief editor, and then promoted to be acting chief editor. In 1984, Youfen came to the US as a member of the delegation covering Party Secretary Zhao Ziyang's historic visit. During that trip, he interviewed Henry Kissinger and Zbigniew Brzezinski. In 1986, he came back to the US again to set up the *Beijing Review*'s US bureau and successfully launched the Review's North American Edition.

In the same year, he met and became friends with Dr. Jerre Freeman, a Memphis- based ophthalmologist. Dr. Freeman performed cataract removal and lens implant surgery on Youfen. The surgery remarkably improved Youfen's eyesight and changed his appearance as well as his personality. For the first time since childhood, he got rid of his thick eyeglasses. He became more confident and energetic. In 1988, he became the Publisher and Editor-in-Chief of *Beijing Review*.

In the summer of 1989, under his leadership, *Beijing Review* published two issues that supported the pro-democratic student movement. After the bloody crackdown of that movement in Tiananmen Square, Youfen was persecuted, stripped of all his positions and his party membership, and put on probation for the second time in his life. In 1990, he was forced into an early retirement.

Ironically, Youfen saw his early retirement as a liberation. Finally, he had a chance to do what he wanted to do, rather than what he was told to do.

In 1992, when the US presidential campaign was at its height, Bill Clinton was entirely unknown in China. In October of that year, Youfen quickly assembled a team of translators, and in less than two months translated Jim Moore's Clinton biography, *Clinton, A Young Man in a Hurry*. In December 1992, a month before Clinton's inauguration, the first biography of the 42nd American president was published in Chinese in China. A year later, Youfen translated and had published another book, *Eclipse: The Last Days of the CIA*, by Mark Perry.

In 2003, Youfen was asked to participate in the preparation of a twelve-book series on *The Culture & Civilization of China*, a huge project undertaken as a collaboration between Yale University Press and the Foreign Languages Press of China. The chief editor, James Peck, invited Youfen to assume responsibility for the translation of the fourth book in the series, *Chinese Calligraphy*. But when the initial manuscripts were submitted, the Yale editors were disappointed. The three main Chinese authors, though well-known in China, had never written for international readers. Peck was ready to drop the book until Youfen volunteered to discuss matters with the authors. After dozens of group meetings and countless hours of discussions, Youfen persuaded the three proud professors to rewrite their essays and guided them paragraph by paragraph. After four years of hard work, *Chinese Calligraphy* was published in 2008 in both Chinese and English. To honor his contribution, Yale University insisted that Youfen's name, as editor and translator, be printed first on the front cover, followed by the essay authors. In 2008 the book received extraordinary recognition from the Association of American Publishers, winning two awards, one for the best book published in 2008 by all U.S. professional and scholarly publishers in all categories of the Humanities (the Prose Award for Excellence), and another award for the best book of the year published in the Art and Art History category. Also, from 2010 to 2012, Youfen translated major portions of another celebrated book series, The History of Chinese Civilization, jointly published by Beijing University and Cambridge University Press.

At age 84, in 2011, Youfen and several like-minded friends established a private publishing house, New Knowledge Cross-Culture Media Company, in which he took on the roles of publisher and editor-in-chief. The aim of this venture was not to make a profit, but to translate western books that could help promote social progress in China. In an increasingly controlled publishing environment, the new joint venture managed to translate and publish 10 books, including three books by the well-known American author Pete Earley. One of Earley's books, *Crazy*, was based on the author's own experience with the challenges of a mentally troubled son. Its publication in Chinese coincided with a mental hygiene conference in China. Many issues the book dealt with in rich detail and with passion, such as the handling of mental illness in the criminal justice system and related legislation, were heatedly debated in the conference. The book instantly became a must-read manual for scholars and legislators who participated in the conference, and subsequently influenced the drafting of new mental health legislation that was passed that year in China.

In 2016, Youfen celebrated his 90th birthday with a traditional Chinese observance. In that year, a pair of documentary producers became interested in the topic of the Sent-down Youth, the *zhiqing*, nearly eighteen million middle and high school graduates from Chinese cities who were sent to live and work in the countryside, some for over a decade, during the period 1962 to 1979. The producers took Youfen along on their research trip because of his reputation as a journalist. When they realized the intrinsic difficulties of the project, however, they abandoned it. But Youfen decided to go ahead on his own. He planned to select some 40 personal memoirs written by *zhiqing* and translate them into English. He bought and borrowed hundreds of memoirs, many out of print for decades, and he carefully selected, edited and rewrote one story after another. Through a close friend, he found a well-known book agent to represent the project, recruited an experienced writer/translator to edit the text, and later brought into the project a leading historian of the *zhiqing* historical experience to write a foreword for the book. After two years of hard work, he was 95% done with the project. The day before his death on March 2, 2018, he was planning to meet Zhang Kangkang, a famous writer who was also a *zhiqing* some 50 years before.

Along with his work as a journalist, translator and editor, Youfen quietly supported many charities related to education. He and his family supported seven college students from underprivileged families and one middle school student. He also helped two physically disabled girls. One of them, Chen Jiahe, he continuously helped for over 13 years. Jiahe suffered from a severe form of Rheumatoid Arthritis, and Youfen raised funds for her knee replacement operations. Later, Youfen persuaded Jiahe's university to waive her tuition, and to lower her rent for her entire college years. In 2017, Youfen used his influence and reputation to find her a job in the county government. Six months before his death, Youfen supported a Brittle Bone Disease patient Zhou Huifang. In 2018, the girl underwent her third operation.

Youfen had a passion for life. He was curious about everything, especially all things new. Among his friends of similar age, he was the first one to type Chinese characters on a computer, the first to send an email and the first to surf the Internet. He always had the newest and coolest gadgets: iPad, Kindle and a laptop computer. At the age of 90, he acted like a young man: chatting on WeChat, buying things from Taobao or Amazon, paying his grocery bills over Alipay and managing his bank account via his cell phone apps. He had traveled many places inside and outside of China, and the short list of his next destinations he discussed at his 90th birthday party included Russia, Eastern Europe, Taiwan and Liuwei, the small village he was exiled to during the Cultural Revolution. Youfen never stopped planning for the future and never stopped striving to communicate to readers across the world the insights he had obtained through deep study, a love of truth and human potential, and a very big heart.

Michel Bonnin, author of the foreword, is Professor Emeritus of the School of Advanced Studies in the Social Sciences, Paris, France, and the founding director of *China Perspectives* magazine. He is the author of the celebrated book on the *zhiqing* program, *The Lost Generation: The Rustication of China's Educated Youth (1962-1980)*, published in four editions: French (2004), Chinese: Hong Kong and Beijing, and English (Hong Kong: 2013).

Robin Radin, editor, assisted Youfen Wang with the selection and editing of the translated stories and the editing of his historical background essay. Following Mr. Wang's death at age 90 on March 2, 2018, Mr. Radin carried forward the preparation of this manuscript for publication. Mr. Radin taught Japanese and Chinese history at the University of Miami in the early 1970s and previously studied Japanese history at the University of California, Berkeley and Kyoto University, among other universities. Since receiving a law degree from Harvard Law School in 1979, Mr. Radin has continued his professional involvement with Asia as an international lawyer and businessman. He lives in Sarasota, Florida.

www.ingramcontent.com/pod-product-compliance
Lightning Source LLC
Chambersburg PA
CBHW030348130626
46549CB00004B/1414